e last d

D1612744

"BEYOND THE HILLS"

BEYOND THE HILLS

AN ULSTER HEADMASTER REMEMBERS

By

W. HAUGHTON CROWE

1971
PRINTED AND PUBLISHED BY
DUNDALGAN PRESS (W. TEMPEST) LIMITED
DUNDALK

" I will lift up mine eyes unto the hills, from whence cometh my help."—*Ps.* 121.

DEDICATION

For all those fortunate enough to have lived
amid the hills of Down
and especially
for
Gladys

New Education for Old
Man, Mind, and Matter
In Banbridge Town
Verses from Rostrevor
Verses from Mourne
The Ring of Mourne
More Verses from Mourne

First published
by
Dundalgan Press (W. Tempest) Ltd.
Dundalk, Ireland

PREFACE

WHY an autobiography? This I cannot answer except to say that one reaches a stage in life when the past assumes more importance than the present or the future and, if one has the writing urge, one feels compelled to commit to paper, at least some of the happenings of a lifetime. Before long it may be that a computer, fed with certain details, will be able to spell out the whole of a man's life and character. The time has not yet come, thank God, when this can be done; so in the meantime, I hope, the great adventure of life—of anyone's life—may continue to be of interest to one's fellow men.

What makes us what we are? The problem has exercised the minds of philosophers and poets, thinkers and theologians, and men-of-letters throughout all ages and generations. There are those who contend that Will is an illusion; that our unconscious minds, our glands, and the chemistry of our cells are the controlling factors; that before we make a decision the matter has been decided for us by forces of which we are scarcely aware. On the other hand, the theologian asserts that we must listen for " the still small voice," and then direct our lives accordingly.

These philosophical problems may never be resolved; but of this I am certain, that however we may talk of personal freedom, its expression must be within the matrix of our common life; only a child—or an existentialist—would think otherwise. We are all dependent on our fellow men: each man may be an island, but he is an island surrounded by the connecting sea of our common existence. Looking back on my own life, I realize that whatever I may have accomplished, for what is vaguely termed The Good, could not have been done without the interest, the generosity and, if I may say so, the love of those with whom I came in contact. Maybe I have been lucky—I don't know—but I have certainly found these qualities around me in no small measure. My whole life has been buttressed by the help and love of others; and, if I have not mentioned specific people in the succeeding pages, it is to save embarrassment; and also because I have already done this to some extent in *In Banbridge Town*.

I hope the reader will be interested, not only in my own personal story, but also in the contemporary educational and social history involved: Ulster folk have too often been represented as a people imbued with bigotry and hatred; maybe this is true of the few, but it is certainly not true of the many. Looking back through my own life and contacts, I cannot think of many of my contemporaries who either held, or practised, such attitudes. If this book does no more than dispel, qualify, or modify such ideas it will have served its purpose.

ACKNOWLEDGMENTS

The Author wishes to express his indebtedness to the following:

Messrs. Bord Failte Eireann for photographs of Glangevlin and Dowra in Co. Cavan, and Glencar in Co. Sligo;

Mr. John Hewitt and his publishers for permission to publish some lines from his poem, " Rite ";

The Principal of the Royal Belfast Academical Institution for permission to reproduce pictures of " Inst." and Queen's College published in a *History of the Royal Belfast Academical Institution*, by John Jamieson, M.A. (Messrs. Mullan & Son);

Mr. F. N. Hoggett, M.Sc. and Mr. Philip Kelsey, M.A. for photographs of Leeds Grammar School reproduced from Mr. Kelsey's History of the School;

Messrs. M. B. Yeats and Macmillan & Co. for permission to use lines of W. B. Yeats from his poem, " The Stolen Child ";

The Secretary of University College, London, for permission to use the photograph of the College;

Mr. A. J. Armstrong of Blacklion, Co. Cavan for the postcard photograph of Lough Macnean.

Mrs. Lesley Gregg, the Rostrevor Artist, for her unusual and beautiful drawing of a corner of our final home "Beyond the Hills".

CONTENTS

LIST OF ILLUSTRATIONS

CHAPTER I

CHERRY VALLEY

I WAS born in Youghal in the County of Cork on the 4th of June in the year 1902. That I was born in Youghal on this date was not a particularly important event, either for me or for the world in general. It was not important for me because I understand we left the interesting town of Youghal when I was six months old, and indeed I don't think I returned to it again until I was about three hundred and sixty months old. Based on the logic that to be born in a stable doesn't make one a horse, I make the assertion that Youghal had little or no influence on me. As to the importance of the event for the world in general, this is for posterity to judge; I would, however, hazard a guess that the judgment will not come down heavily in my favour.

And yet ... and yet ... I think I would rather be able to say that I had been born in Youghal than in Ballymena or in Belfast. Who wouldn't? Maybe this is a form of snobbishness, but the fact remains that we all like to think we have, hidden in the secret corners of our chromosomes, some traces of genuine wild Irish blood of a type that one does not usually associate with either Ballymena or Belfast. How often have I heard people loudly protest that they were not real Northerners, that this or that parent hailed from the wilds of Connemara, from the fairy-haunted hills of Kerry, from the golden vales of Tipperary, or from "Dublin's fair city." Even my own mother, who was born within a stone's throw of where Bernard Shaw lived—and probably was more or less unaware of his existence—was always flattered when her Dublin accent was recognized. Few of us like to boast we have a strong northern accent; and most of us are disagreeably surprised when our voices are mechanically produced for the first time.

Like it or not, however, the northern accent is inescapably there, as I realized the first time I broadcast; for, with the imitative mind of a child, most of us absorb the accents and characteristics, not of our parents, but of our general environment. I was no exception; in spite of my southern birth and my Dublin and western ancestry, I acquired many of the traits of the district in which I grew up, and in which I was educated.

And what a strange and strangely beautiful district it was in those days. Though we did not go to live in " The Park " until I was about three, I distinctly remember earlier incidents. They tell me I could not possibly have remembered them, that I thought I *did* merely because someone had described the incidents to me, and so on. What rubbish ! I swear by all the powers of the air that my recollections of these happenings are as clear in my mind as if they had taken place only yesterday. Yes, I can recall being taken up to the Belmont Road to see the first, brilliantly illuminated electric tram; I can remember the horse trams; and what a shock it must have been for my parents when one day I disappeared; I had a coin which I was fully resolved to spend on the purchase of a wheel-barrow at Miss Bothwell's shop at Knock Road corner. Fortunately, some kindly gentleman found me wandering about; he promptly placed me on his shoulder; thus transported I was soon safe and sound once again in my mother's arms.

We moved to The Park when I was about three. It was a suburban road, but a suburban road with a difference; it was unique not only in its situation, but also in the characters of its residents. It was bounded north and south by two crystal-clear streams, both of which contained unlimited quantities of " spricks," some eels and occasional trout; each of these two streams was a boy's paradise. To the south the green, whin-covered drumlins of the County Down billowed upwards into a range of hills which, to our childish imaginations, seemed like a border, beyond which was a land undoubtedly flowing with milk and honey. This was in the days before the motor car, when even to " go up the hills " on foot was quite an adventure. In later years as we ventured further and further on our bicycles, we found that the hills went further and further until eventually they merged with Slieve Croob and finally with the Mournes.

Eastwards a long wide valley swept away to Strangford Lough, marked at its end by Scrabo Tower perched on its high

mound of Triassic sandstone. At the end of The Park was
" The Valley." The Valley was lined with trees of many kinds,
in particular with wild cherries. At the appropriate season the
wild cherries lay around in profusion; we ate them and in this
way maybe we made up naturally for a shortage of vitamins
at a time when the word " vitamin " had not even been coined.
More than anything, however, I remember this valley when,
for the first time, the full glory and beauty of spring began to
penetrate my being: the cherry blossom, the light filtering
through the silky green tracery of beech lanes, and the vivid
green of the sward running up from the far side of " The
River " to the Station Hill; all these are memories so deeply
enshrined that they have affected my thoughts and way of going
throughout my life. God help the children of the future who
may grow up so urbanized that only urbanity will be known
to them !

Up the hills a little was " The Glen." It was a glen in
miniature and it had everything that a glen should have: high
tree-covered banks, a stream, a waterfall, and in parts deep,
almost impenetrable, vegetation. It ran down past a small
white-washed school to a farm. Above it the hills rolled down
to our back gardens; so that it was possible to reach it either by
road, or by making our way through the fields. In our very
early days it was peopled by fairies; and indeed I am sure there
were fairies in it, but they have gone to ground now for there
are houses all around. Later it became peopled by red Indians
and cannibals who shot arrows at us from unexpected places.
In the early stages of the first world war we made dug-outs in
it from which to foray across the fields to imaginary German
lines. Later, when adolescence began to emerge into adulthood,
it was to The Glen we took our girls to explore its beauties,
and to explore the secret places of our hearts.

In those days we dared each other to climb the highest trees;
to drop from the highest branches; and to jump across The
River at its deepest and widest places. How we survived I don't
know. Sometimes we even chased each other across the roof-
top of one of the highest and largest houses. But we survived,
without, as far as I can remember, even a broken limb, until

our jungle-like tendencies began to give way to the sophistication of more organized games.

What about facilities for games at this time ? Why there
were wide open spaces all around us; and there were innumer-
able flat fields that could be used either illegitimately or
legitimately. Besides, local clubs did not look with disfavour
on young bloods who wished to kick about on their fields at
off-times. Even the local golf club was not unduly fussy about
reasonably well behaved young boys trying their hands at the
royal and ancient game, without becoming involved in
expense which few could afford. The result of all this was
that any of us, who wished to do so, could learn the rudiments of most of the major games and sports, even before
we went to schools where these could be learned in a more
efficient way. In this sense, and in others, we had the best of
both worlds, rural and urban. Most of us learned to swim, too,
at an early age. All you had to do was to induce your parents
to buy a cheap season ticket to enable you to attend the public
baths—a short tram ride away. Having learned to swim,
there were ponds, dams, streams, and the sea, all of which could
be reached, if not on foot, at least on one's bicycle.

But to come back to more general activities, and to those
joys and pleasures most of which have long ceased to exist.
People lived among us, and we lived among people; the policeman on his beat, the lamplighter, the night watchman in his hut,
the hurdy-gurdy man whose parrot told our fortunes and whose
tunes I still love to hear, the baker who could sometimes be
induced to give us sweet buns; all these were our friends and
rarely seemed to be cross even when we were most mischievous.
Then there was the milkman who would give us rides in his
cart or van. I can still smell the inharmonious mixture of milk
and metal, harness and horse sweat, man and manure, as we
clopped, clopped, clopped along the hard metalled road.
Ah, there are so many memories flooding in on me now that
I scarcely know which to put down next. There was the man
with the dancing bear, a sight that no child would ever see
now—at least not on a public road. How we gazed at the sad,
almost human, eyes of these fearsome brutes that seemed to
have lost all their fearsomeness and dignity. The bear-man

used to camp out in the quarry in the Gilnahirk hills. Maybe his condition of life was not much better than that of his chained bears ; one thinks with horror now, not only of the bears' sufferings, but also of those of the man.

Sometimes I would be sent up to the cobblers to have the family shoes mended. Up the hills I would go, past the farm where I would see a horse going round and round in circles pulling the lever that worked the threshing mechanism inside. Then, if I had time, and there always seemed to be time to spare in those days, I would go up to Gilnahirk Village, where, literally " under the spreading chestnut tree," I could watch the blacksmith's " broad and sinewy hands," as he hammered the white-hot iron sparkling like a meteoric shower on a November night. With luck he would let me work the great bellows which caused the dull fire suddenly to erupt into spouts of hissing flame. Fascinated I would watch, as he placed the hot shoe in position on the singeing hoof of the patient horse; even as I write this I can recall the acrid smell of burning hoof in my nostrils.

And so down to " The Cobbler's Lane "; at the end of it I would find the cobbler in his white cottage; there he would be, this leather-aproned ancient, bent double on his stool, working at his last; and glancing over the top of his glasses at the view to be seen from the tiny cottage windows. As I listened to his homespun philosophy I, too, would glance at the splendid view down the valley to Scrabo, up to the great city, and across to the wooded Stormont hills with Stormont Castle in the foreground.

Whatever one may say about the city of Belfast, few would argue about the beauty of its situation. From up there at the cobbler's, had I been older, I might have said: " Babylon, the great is fallen, is fallen." Not indeed that there was, or is, anything Babylonian about Belfast; remembering this scene, however—the wooded Holywood hills, the precipitous Cave Hill marking the beginning of the Antrim plateau, the blue lough on which, as likely as not, one might see the sheer prow of a great ship thrusting her way up to the long harbour at the mouth of the Lagan; remembering all this one is the more horrified that this otherwise happy, lively community of people should have brought upon themselves—or should have had thrust on them—such misfortunes.

One or two other incidents from those very early days still stand out in my memory with unusual intensity. There was the day when my mother, in a rather scared voice, said to me: " Willie, you must come in to meet your Uncle Henry."

Somewhat reluctantly I was brought into—what was then called—the drawing-room, there to behold a jovial, hard-bitten little man with a goatee beard. I was to learn that this was my grand-uncle, Captain Henry Haughton, home from the seven seas. That he had been enjoying his time ashore liberally and well was probably all too evident to my mother, but not so to me, as I had not yet learned to distinguish between natural joviality and that inspired by slight over-indulgence in alcohol.

" Sure, 'tis a grand boy that," said my uncle. " He's a keen eye in his head; one o' these days he'll be settin' sail to discover the North Pole." It was years later that I discovered the meaning of what he said.

" Now," said he, " would you like to come for a ride in a car ? "

" I would," said I.

" Right," said he, " heave ho ! me hearty ! " and then, after a short conference with my mother, I found myself being bundled up into the " well " of an " outside car."

" Gee up ! " said the jarvey, cracking his whip, and soon we were trundling down the hill of The Park, and along The Valley, with me sitting proudly up there hoping that all the world could see me.

Arrived at " The Hack "—short for Ballyhackamore—the jarvey pulled his horse up in front of what I now know to have been Lamb's public-house.

" Sit quiet there now," said my uncle, " and we'll be back in no time."

After what seemed to me an interminable time the two of them came out looking more jovial that ever; but instead of setting course for home on an easterly bearing, they proceeded in a westward direction toward the city, and were soon lost in a maze of parks in the Bloomfield area. In one of these they said: " Now show us the house." By some miracle I realized that they were lost in the wrong district, and by some even greater miracle I was able to help them to find their way home.

So began and ended my acquaintance with my Uncle Henry. What became of him in the end I don't know; but I rather suspect it was always hoped that in some of his travels he might have discovered hidden treasure, or that at least, being a bachelor, he might have saved a "neat wee pile" to pass on to the members of the family. I don't think these dreams were realized. Whether he reposes at the sea's bottom or in some other unknown grave, is a moot point, but whichever way it is, I feel sure that his spirit is in some sailor's Valhalla; if it's not it ought to be, for at least he gave one small boy the thrill of a lifetime, at a time when a small boy's thrills were few and far between.

It was usual in those days in middle-class suburban areas for every family to have a maid; and we were no exception to the rule. Many of these were Catholic girls from the west of Ireland; and many became good family friends, notwithstanding conditions far from conducive to friendship. Maybe these conditions were much better than at home: otherwise who would have sat alone every evening in front of a range; who would have put up with one evening out in the week with nowhere to go save into the fields with a boy if one had one; who would have sat in front of a cold range from the first day of May irrespective of the weather; who would have acted as nursemaid, washer-up, cleaner, cook, laundress and general family slave for the magnificent sum of twelve pounds per annum?

Under such conditions it was natural that there should be many not exactly dedicated to the job. Sometimes my mother was fortunate, sometimes unfortunate. One was taken away by detectives because of something that had happened at a previous place of employment; another, slightly deranged I think, threatened the postman because he did not bring her an expected letter from Australia; yet another would entertain her boy friends in the parlour when my parents were out for the evening—in fact on one occasion I can remember falling asleep on the hearth-rug and wakening up to find a strange man in the room. All of these were discharged in due course.

However there was one—a " superior " girl who lived not very
far away—she was a good maid, but, what might have been
considered in those days, a "bad" girl. Indeed she was the
first to give me direct knowledge of the facts of life by describing
her experiences with a local grocer's assistant. Some hint of
this must have filtered through to my parents, because in due
course she also disappeared; and my mother, after those unhappy
ventures, decided " to do the work herself "—at least for a time.
This last girl came back to visit us after many years; she
had just returned from France and Germany whither she had
gone with her employer as a lady's companion.

    I don't know why my memories should suddenly leap from
unsatisfactory maids to unsatisfactory horses, but that's how it
is: memories of early days come surging out of the unconscious
with strange irrelevancy and with chronological inexactitude.
One morning, reading one of my father's letters from the West,
my mother said " Papa's bought a horse." This announcement
was no less sensational than if she had said that the moon had
dropped out of the sky. Having been born on a farm, my
father always liked horses, but dedication to his work, his
church, and his family had, to some extent, prevented him
from pursuing any latent sporting instincts, or interests.
Anyhow, the black, glossy, graceful creature was soon to be
installed at a nearby riding school; and thereafter of a Saturday
afternoon an admiring family audience watched Papa set off
along The Park on a spirited young horse not yet fully
broken in. Then one Saturday afternoon we heard that Mr.
X, a vet., was coming to tea. Mr. X proved to be the
brother of a girl, a family friend who often came to us at
week-ends, while she was a boarder at the Methodist College.
The bronzed young man in knickerbockers and leggings
fascinated me. Would I could remember the pre-tea conversation in the parlour ! I can recall vaguely talk about bellies,
withers, spavins, and various other parts of the equine anatomy;
and I had a vague feeling that my father was becoming slightly
depressed; and that his hopes of a profit on the sale of the horse
were gradually disappearing beneath his financial horizon.

    But even if the horsey conversation did not interest me
greatly, I gazed with shining eyes at my temporary hero as he

told stories of his escapades at camp with the Campbell College Officers Training Corps; the kinds of prank and adventure that I, in following years, was to recount to other small boys who looked at me, I hope, with eyes shining with admiration. It was only when I reached adulthood that my father told me that his adventures with the horse proved to be too adventurous; that his spirited mount had proved to be too-spirited for suburbia and for middle-aged bones; and that he had decided on a sale in the hope that at some future time he might repeat the experiment with an animal whose temperament was more in tune with his own. But this was not to be; no doubt the clouds of civil war piling up on the political horizon, and later the throes of the Great War put paid to many of his cherished dreams; so that, in the end, he had no recourse but to keep on working until arthritis and old age put an end to his working life.

Reference to horses reminds me of holidays at my grandfather's farm in County Cavan. Experiences there gave me an interest in four-legged animals and in farming; an interest which came back to me in full flush years later when I acquired a farm of my own. The things I may describe now do not necessarily apply to a first visit, but are, in fact, a series of incidents and impressions spread over the years.

"Going to Aunt Annie's; going to Aunt Annie's!" I awakened in the darkness of the morning to hear my father hissing this into my ear. Before long we were dressed, breakfasted, and in the cab on our way to the Great Northern Railway station in Belfast. There was the fussing for tickets, the fussing for a porter, the search for a carriage in which we might remain undisturbed, the guard's long whistle, and we were off as the dawn mists were still rising from the fields. Two changes no less! and, while we waited at Clones station, a big hot cup of tea and great shiny brown buns with currants in them. Then the second change at Enniskillen where we boarded the narrow-gauge Sligo, Leitrim and Northern Counties train for Blacklion.

Now we were running through some of the loveliest country on earth; by Lough Erne through the bracken-covered, heather-covered hills of Fermanagh, past Upper Lough Macnean and the Hanging Rock to Blacklion, where we were met by my

B

uncle and the jaunting car. I have never forgotten alighting at
this station, seeing the wild hills of Ireland all around, and the
sight and smell of the blue turf-smoke as it rose lazily from the
village chimneys.

Up the hill we would go, higher and higher until we arrived
at gate number one; there were at least seven such gates to go
through until at last we would arrive at the thatched cottage.
" Look back, lad, look back ! " my father would say. " Did
you ever see a view like that ? " And indeed I never had;
for it was a Killarney in miniature with its island-studded lake,
and its little hills and mountains which seemed to leap at you
from all points of the compass. And then: " Look at that old
man up there; he may have a rough hand but he has a heart
of gold." What a tribute from a son to his father ! And as
I was soon to learn, this was no mere piece of sentimentality
but a genuine sentiment echoed by every member of his family,
and by many others in the district in which he was a local
magistrate at a time when to be a local magistrate had a
meaning.

There he was, this old Irishman, with his cutaway coat, his
bowler hat, beard, and the blue of the lake and the sky in his
eyes. " Welcome me boy ! welcome me boy to the Black ! "
he would say. He was supposed not to have been strong in his
youth, and to have been fit only for lighter work, but he
could turn a hay-rake or a wheel, or catch a horse better than
most, and I never knew him to do less than his share of the work
when it came to harvest time. He was " the boss "; was
always referred to when decisions had to be made; and was
usually addressed by everybody, his family included, as " Sir."
Though he never tried to force his religious beliefs on anyone,
I remember him wrestling with his God at his bed-in-the-wall,
rather like an Old Testament prophet. No doubt this helped
to sustain him through a life fraught with trouble and difficulty
from the time my grandmother died at an early age, and he was
left alone to cope with every difficulty.

But I could write a book about Blacklion. I could describe
journeys with my grandfather to the creamery in the early
morning; journeys in the creel on the side of a donkey up to
the turf bog from which one could see Lough Allen and the

great river Shannon. In later years, after I had learned to ride, often I would go on horseback up over the rough carboniferous limestone rocks at the back of the house, past one of those seemingly bottomless limestone holes, Poll-na-Ban, to where I could see Cuilcagh below, whence the Shannon bubbles up out of its cauldron, The Shannon Pot. Or I might ride the horse down to The Cross, tie him up at Pat's, cross a field or two and the railway line, undress and swim over Lough Macnean to a tiny island.

The house, if it were still in existence, would be a museum piece; a low thatched cottage, a jamb wall between the hall and the kitchen, a living-room at one end of the hall, communicating bedrooms at the other with a bed-in-the-wall in the first, the kitchen with its half-door into " the street," the scrubbed old dresser, the great open fire-place with its crane, its pots and pans, the turf fire that had glowed and flickered and flamed for centuries, the muzzle loader, with its powder and shot bags and ramrod, over the mantle, and the ladder to the loft where the man or the maid, or both, had their sleeping apartments.

Sides of bacon and ham hung from the ceiling. With what stirring of boyish appetite I would watch my aunt fry the turf-seasoned rashers, and the fresh eggs with sometimes a mushroom or two brought in by my uncle from the early morning dew-soaked fields. With what pleasure I smelt the bubbling yellow meal, and the rich odour of a " cake " browning in a lidded pan covered with glowing turves. The only beverages were milk, and buttermilk, and tea. Tea ! Tea ! Tea ! There was tea in the morning, tea mid-day, tea after dinner, tea in the afternoon, tea for supper, tea if you came in wet, tea if you came in hungry, tea when visitors arrived, tea at a wake, tea at a wedding. Without tea the world of Gort na Legg, and of Ireland in general, would have collapsed; and the Irish might have been madder than they are. Which reminds me of a story told to me by an Irishwoman living in Manchester. She said that because of the war-time tea shortage people in the west were compelled to drink coffee. One old lady, a near centenarian, died; at the graveside her son was to be heard crying: " 'Twas the coffee that killed her ! 'Twas the coffee that killed her ! "

But the tea meal I liked best was that brought by " the girl " to the fields during haymaking. What associations came to mind ! The sweet brown-topped buns fresh from the pan, the sweet strong tea, the sweet-smelling clovery hay, the sweet music of the hopper's tick, and sometimes sweet wild honey turned up by fork or rake. Such were the sights, and sounds, and smells of those days; though the pattern is still similar in many of the more remote places, I fear it is only a matter of time before the picture may have changed out of all knowledge, so that future generations of young people may never again experience the joys of a holiday spent at grandfather's farm.

An older sister accompanied me when we were very young, but later I went alone; and I am jumping ahead now in time to visits paid much later. One of these must have been in the latter stages of the first world war, after nineteen sixteen when tension, though I was unconscious of it, must have been high. It is perhaps wrong to say that I was unconscious of tension; I think I accepted it in a youthful, light-hearted way; it was a part of life. " The girl " must also have accepted it in a youthful light-hearted way; for it was she who taught me to sing:

" It's all round me hat
I wear the tri-coloured ribbon-o;
It's all round me hat
Until death comes to me.
In the streets of the city
The wee birds are singing,
The foeman is calling
Ould Ireland be free;
So it's up de Valera
You're the pride of the country. . . ."

It's significant that I never knew the words nor the tune of " The Sash " until I was about sixty ! The girl who taught me such wickedness is still, I believe, very much alive and happily married.

When one is young who can be a better companion than a girl cousin, especially when she happens to possess a bicycle, and can provide you with a similar mount ? So one day we set off on our bicycles to

" Where the wandering water gushes
From the hills above Glencar,
In pools among the rushes
That scarce could bathe a star."

But I didn't " seek for slumbering trout " in those days, nor
was I aware of the existence of W. B. Yeats, and the beautiful
poetry with which he invested this beautiful land. What
missed opportunities to study Yeats, and the perusal of the
gentle art ! Why was it that so much of my life passed before
I became deeply interested in either, or both ?

No doubt my Sligo uncle knew " Mr. Alfred," or at least
he must have known some of that family of whom Yeats
wrote :

" At all those death-beds women heard
A visionary white sea-bird
Lamenting that a man should die;
And with that cry I have raised my cry."

For my uncle worked for the firm of Pollexfen; and
later was to use his influence in getting permission for me to
fish the firm's excellent salmon pool at Ballisodare. But it was
with my youngest uncle, whom I loved like the brother I
never had, the uncle whose body now lies in a lonely grave in
Switzerland, that I first cycled to Sligo and then around Lough
Gill where, for the first time, I saw the Yeats-hallowed " Lake
Isle of Innisfree."

We must leave this enchanted country; we must leave the
Shannon Pot, The Hanging Rock, the Marble Arch with its
stalctites and stalagmites. We must leave the winding lakes,
the limestone hills, the caves, and the pot-holes to the fairies
who inhabited them when I first began to go there. Later I
saw no fairies; instead I was the cowboy rounding up the
cattle at night; later still I was the callow blazered youth, no
doubt " mistrustless of his smutted face "; and finally I was the
dashing student who knew more than his dons. But in all
these roles I found a ready sympathy and a welcome from
those who no doubt loved this country and appreciated its
beauty, but whose love and appreciation must always have

been tempered by the gruelling necessity for scratching an existence from its bare hills.

As a postscript to this account of my early visits to Blacklion I would add that my wife and I returned to the village in recent years—not greatly altered, I thought; if anything improved. The old creamery was still there, unused I think, and the little Methodist Church with a memorial tablet to an uncle killed on his way to the Boer War. The blacksmith's forge had gone; the old railway had been replaced by a motor road; but my little wave-lapped lake isle still lay undisturbed. The old house was no longer there; and the mountainy farm, divided up long ago, was in a sad state of neglect. Change and decay all around with, I think, the balance on the side of change rather than decay; for the village had been painted and decorated with tubs of trees and shrubs; it had better shops and better pubs, and it was less wild. The Georgian house, Toame, where my cousin lived was a club-house and its lands a golf course.

In conversation with the local Garda Sergeant, who was interested in such things, I learned that the country round about was an archæologist's paradise with its cashels, cairns, souter-rains, cromlechs, and all those monuments of man's strivings to shake off the fetters of his animal ancestry. It was the sergeant who first told me about the famous "sweat baths" similar to the Swedish *sauna*. Though he proclaimed himself to be Irish to the backbone, he said he had the greatest respect for the R.U.C.; that they were most co-operative, and the best police force in the world. A little more talk like that; a little more mutual respect, and we should be well on the way to a solution of our problems.

Leaving the place when I was a boy, all one had to do was to cross the bridge over the river connecting the upper and lower lakes. Arrived in Belcoo one was in the same country. Now one is still in the same country, but the powers are different. In my early days you could cross without let or hindrance; now you would be required to account for a pound of tea let alone a bottle of the "crathur." Once we seemed to be free, now having gained freedom we appear to be bound more tightly than ever. Ah, me! how strange is the wisdom of our wise leaders!

My arrival back in The Park was a joyful reunion for in those days it was usually a case of " quis separabit " with all of us. Having given an account of myself we would soon be back at the same old games: making huts along " The River " banks, building huts in trees, forays against " The Village " boys, or more likely, being chased by the village boys, lighting fires, roasting spuds, and gathering " cheesers," wandering in and out of each other's houses as freely as the wind that blew down from the Gilnahirk hills, and on wet days working at our various hobbies. I had one friend that I loved above all others; to be asked to his house for tea was sheer joy; he had a steam engine that worked by steam; he had a model boat; he had many of those things for which a boy has a craving as natural as the craving for food; before long he was to be denied the greatest gift of all—life; and for the first time in my life I was to come up against the awful finality of the death of a friend.

The Park was a closed community; and a community composed of a strange conglomeration of people. It was cosmopolitan. Thinking back, I can remember few who could honestly claim to be North of Ireland people—at least not in a previous generation. There were English, Scottish, Welsh, Cornish, Manx, and a sprinkling of southerners. Of my own immediate friends two were Manx-English, one was Scottish, one was a Lancastrian, and one was an Ulsterman. Later there were Swiss, French and Belgians within our circle. There were respectable businessmen and unrespectable boozers, accountants and agents, civil servants and servants both civil and uncivil, playboys and professors, soldiers—mostly amateur—and shorebound sailors, ship-builders and house-builders, tarts and teasers; but few, mark you, were *common*. Good heavens, no !

I remember one man who used to entertain me with stories of his own experiences in the Klondyke gold rush. Others were members of the Legion of Frontiersmen; they were to be seen swaggering up and down complete with spurs, leggings, cowboy hats and all the other trappings of this intrepid band of men. But the most sensational arrival was that of an Oxford graduate in plus-fours and ribboned straw-boiler. Report had it that he was hiding from something somewhere; but he couldn't hide the activities of his attractive and discreetly painted wife, for she made little secret of her preference for young officers rather than for an Oxford graduate, even if he did write verse.

It was amid this motley that I grew up. One does not usually associate variety, colour and romance with respectable suburbia, but I submit that all three were to be found in this unusual urban community on the fringe of rusticity. There are those who say that the first seven years of life are the most important; that most of our future life is controlled by environmental influences during these years; and that we can never escape from ideas with which we have become impregnated at this early stage. Looking at my own life as objectively as possible, I am compelled to say: " I wonder ! "

And so in my next chapter I propose to examine more fully the influences at work in this Edwardian world of gas and gaiters, frumps and frock coats, Eton suits and " Eric or Little by Little," cabs, cads, and canes, trams and trains, hopeful Bands of Hope and valiant Volunteers of Ulster and all the ideas, idealism, and sometimes iodiocy of that strange and stuffy age.

LOWER LOUGH MC.NEAN FROM BELCOO ROAD

CO. CAVAN

" I'd go back to an Irish village
By the shores of Lough Macnean "

NEAR MY GRANDFATHER'S HOUSE, AND NOT UNLIKE IT
Glangevlin, Co. Cavan

WHERE THE OLD RIVER IS NEW
River Shannon, Dowra, Co. Cavan

" WHERE THE WANDERING WATER GUSHES "—Yeats
Glencar, Co. Sligo

CHAPTER II

SCHOOL BEYOND THE CORNER

AT the age of four a small boy was to be seen, complete
with satchel, hand in hand with his sister on his way down
The Park to a school at least two miles away. Often afterwards
a kindly neighbour came near to quoting Elizabeth Shane's
" Wee Hughie ":

> " Sure I saw the fright was in him
> When he left the door."

Whether I was frightened or not on my way to school I don't
rightly remember, but I was certainly frightened when I got
there, for the school-room seemed to be filled with great big
hulks of boys, and I wasn't used to great big hulks of boys.
I think I cried all through that day, with the result that I
eventually ended up with " the angels " overhead.

Came the second day, and I didn't cry any more. Vaguely
I recollect some kind of a roll-call when you were asked to
state your religious denomination. Miraculously I knew that
I was a Methodist; I proudly answered accordingly. But I
sensed that they were not specially interested. In fact I have a
feeling that if you weren't a Presbyterian they were not
particularly interested in your religious welfare. The school
was under the management of the local Presbyterian Church
and its minister. He was a powerful-looking, tall, bearded
man. At first I mistook him for God !

When I went there first there were but two rooms: a large
school-room and a room called " The Gallery." The boys
lived downstairs and the girls upstairs. There was no com-
munication whatever between the sexes. The substitute for a
cloakroom was a dark corner in the hall; so dark in fact that
you could scarcely distinguish your own coat; on wet days the
coats hung together in a sodden mass, thus, instead of drying,

each garment contributed to the wetness of the other. The lavatory was nauseating; I cannot describe it in any other way; rather than enter it I suffered agonies. There was a drinking tap somewhere but, as far as I remember, there were no facilities for washing. Cold water wash basins may have been installed later when two additional bright rooms were added to the building.

The bearded Principal, wearing a cut-away morning jacket, green with age, stood on a small platform behind his desk at the top of the room. In front of the desk a card indicated whether " secular " or " religious " instruction was in progress. At the side there were canes placed not " more for ornament than use," for they were frequently in use. From time to time a commanding voice would call out: " Send that boy up to me, Mr. So-and-so, and I'll give him a palm." The unfortunate youth would usually return blowing his swollen fingers to ease the pain. Occasionally one witnessed a sudden and terrifying outburst, when a boy held by the scruff of the neck would be belaboured all around the room with the dust flying out of his clothes at each whack. This often happened to some stupid boy whose stupidity was more innate than wilful.

Classes were in semi-circles, for the most part standing, though some who were writing or drawing would be seated at desks in the centre. Teaching was often by rote, and in some cases—for example, nature study—the words used had no significance for one never saw them written down. I know now that methods of teaching in this type of school had been greatly influenced by the Lancaster—Bell methods; and let none say that teaching was wholly bad: it was *not* ; and in fact in some respects was quite advanced. Not only arithmetic, but also algebra and geometry—or Euclid as it was then called— were taught very well, and up to reasonably high standards. Though most of the geography was taught out of a little blue book, I remember sand tables being used to illustrate physical features. Later, too, there was some general science illustrated by demonstration experiments: measurement of length, area, volume, and mass, the composition of the air, and a rough evaluation of foodstuffs. Drawing and singing were taught well by enthusiasts. I learned much about singing then, and many songs that I have never forgotten. There was one about " chasing the shadows o'er the lea "; I loved singing this on a Friday afternoon in spring and summer because I knew it would not be long before I would be doing this: " chasing shadows o'er the lea."

The Principal taught history in a depressing way, and without any imagination whatever. The method consisted in the dictation of notes, mostly on matters-of-fact which we were made to memorize. Such colourless teaching meant nothing so that the facts were soon forgotten. You could learn French and Latin at a price, but the teaching would have been dear at any price, for the Principal knew no Latin and less French; his pronunciation was a phonetic menace; I believe he would have pronounced *est* as est !

Discipline was of a rigid military type. We were required to march from one class to the other by the rhythmic tapping of a bell. Physical training was P.T. without frills. Except when raining heavily it was conducted outside. When I say there were no frills, I had forgotten about dumb-bells; and I think if you got into the upper strata you were trained in the use of Indian clubs. Later an enthusiast joined the staff; he introduced a new idea which was supposed to give you everlasting health, and almost everlasting life. I practised it into middle age until I got a slipped disc, and then I thought it wasn't such a good thing after all ! But the new method was a bit more imaginative; it involved games and running about in addition to the awful monotony of arm and leg exercises.

There was a system of cards—not a bad idea either—a red one for " diligence " and a blue one for " honour." When I brought home my first red card I was in the seventh heaven; and when I brought home my first blue I was in the eighth heaven, if there is an eighth heaven. A sufficient number of blue cards gained a prize at the end of the year. Though I started slowly, possibly because I had not reached what educationists describe as " the readiness age," suddenly on one never-to-be-forgotten day, I found that I could read easily. This caused quite a sensation; forthwith I was promoted and from then on I never looked back, save during one short period, of which I shall give an account in the next paragraph.

I can remember four masters in addition to the Principal and Vice-Principal; and there were two " monitors "—pupil teachers serving a kind of apprenticeship before going to Kildare Street College in Dublin. One of the masters was a near-sadist: he beat us when we were good; he beat us when we were bad; he beat us on Fridays; he beat us on Mondays; and he beat many on the days between. Once he called out a big fellow—a police sergeant's son—he caned him for spelling " railroad " with an aye sound in the rail and an ah sound in the road, telling the boy that if he was going to swank it one way he'd swank it the other. When I was in this man's class I became ill and was away from school. To this day I don't know whether I really was ill; but they thought I was, and the doctor thought I was, until finally they found out about the master. This was the only complaint I ever made. Immediate action was taken with the result that the master was repri- manded; and later the Principal was to tell me—at that early age—about the iniquities of his colleague who later departed from the school without anybody being a whit the worse for his departure.

As for the principal, I was afraid of him for another reason: he tended to be over affectionate with small boys. The first indication I had of this was on one dark afternoon when he kept me behind in The Gallery after the other boys had gone home. He took me on his knee, kissed me and called me " his son." Unfortunate man !

How could he have known that I was frightened, revolted and confused. Over and over again the same thing happened: he took every opportunity to keep me behind, while I tried to avoid him in every possible way. Maybe this stimulated me to work harder so that he would have no excuse for " keeping me in." Without indulging in an orgy of self-pity I cannot help reflecting from time to time on that gloomy afternoon with its stale after-school smell, and whatever light there was trying to filter through the red-margined frosted-glass windows. Outside the birds sang happily enough in the many trees surrounding the school, but inside was one very unhappy little boy undergoing an experience worse than if he had been ruthlessly caned.

But I learned to live with this; I learned to laugh and joke about it. I soon found out that other boys were in the same predicament, and that the principal had not one " son " but many. We banded together to save each other. This safety in numbers technique made life more bearable, and as mind and body developed we became less afraid to resist—either by guile, or by physical strength—these unwelcome advances. One thing we never did was to tell our parents; they wouldn't have believed us. But there was a crisis once when I thought of entering for a scholarship requiring Latin and French. When the principal heard this he immediately offered to coach me at his flower-filled home—he was mad on plants and flowers, especially cacti in which he tried to interest me. I did my best to opt out of this, knowing what the result would be. I stayed away from his classes without letting anybody know, and I didn't sit for the scholarship—fortunately, perhaps, because the coaching would have done me more harm than good.

As the reader may imagine my first years at this school were far from being happy years. There was a strange medley of boys at it: some of good address and some bad; some well-dressed and some badly dressed. Although a bare-foot boy or girl was not unusual at the time, I cannot remember unshod boys or girls at the school. Half-heard and half-understood conversations were a worry. There would be veiled references to " the polis "; to what would happen if you were away from school for too long. One would hear regularly of " the white slave " traffic, strange things that went on in the streets from which some of the boys emanated—political murmurings of " The Shape of Things to Come." There would be talk of drunkenness, of drunken fathers, and even of boys who had " gone on the drink " soon after leaving school.

On the way home, once along the tree-arched road where the squirrels leaped from branch to branch, we smoked anything and everything: blotting paper, tea, and nuts. Some were regular smokers of " Woodbines " and always had their packets with them. From time to time we would meet an unfortunate woman; she was mentally deranged; she insisted that she was "the Queen of Sheba" and she described her adventures in this role. I don't think the boys made game of her; in fact I think they were all a little scared. None of us liked to meet her when we were alone.

The first I remember of the now notorious sectarian bitterness—and let me say here and now that I never heard anything of it in my own home or, I think, in The Park—was when some of the boys wrote "To hell with the Pope" on the black tarred fence surrounding a large estate. I didn't know what this meant. Later we were stopped by a kindly gentleman in black—a priest of the Church—who gently tried to explain the offensiveness of what we were about, saying that we would not like it if he wrote up similar remarks about our Church. Though I was only involved by circumstances, I never forgot this lesson.

Why was one sent to this school? For two main reasons: there was practically no choice and, secondly, parents at this time knew little of what went on, and few would have known anything of the theory and practice of education in those days before radio, TV and popular education. The only other alternative was a "dame school." Many thought that a national education was better; there were scholarships open only to National Schools; and for those who wished to enter the teaching profession as a trained professional teacher, the only open sesame was the National School. Not indeed that I had any intention of entering the teaching profession in any category at this time; nothing could have been further from my mind. The dame school to which I referred was good of its kind; and probably its pupils did as well as those from the National School; no doubt, too, they were happier in their environment.

Anyhow my particular school, though not perhaps for the élite, was certainly socially superior. I cannot remember any very poor. Small fees were charged, and I think one had to pay for the heating which was of the most meagre description; one small coal fire being the only source of heat in the main school-room; there was always competition for the seat opposite the fire. The spectrum of boys ranged from those living in upper suburbia to those living in lower-suburbia nearer the city. I can remember the sons of men in big business and in small; there were the sons of artists and artisans, of ministers and musicians, of foreman and firemen, of soldiers and sailors, and of policemen and platers.

Mention of platers reminds me of that terrible day when we heard the news that the unsinkable had been sunk—the ship of which Belfast was so proud; the greatest ship in the world at the time—the *Titanic*. Many of the fathers of my classmates had helped to build her. Just down the road her great hull had been slowly raised until it stood, an impenetrable wall against the vagaries of wind and weather. Came the launching and the excitement among the boys who almost felt they had a part in building her. And then came death to the ship, and to so many in her, including the father of at least one of our number, an engineer who had been one of those selected for the maiden voyage.

This incredible tragedy reminds me of another incident; it was about this time that lightning struck the school. As usual we were arranged around the teacher in a half-circle. I suppose a storm must have been in progress when suddenly a blinding light came right through the window opposite, while at the same time there was a crack that shook the building from end to end. The rest was confusion. I have vague memories of a group surrounding one of the monitors who, it appeared, had been struck slightly, or shocked in some way. When eventually we were allowed to go home we saw the damage: not very serious because of the lightning conductor they said; but the stays of the metal chimneys had been broken; and there was a black scorch down the front above the clock face; it remained for many a day, and for all I know it may still be there.

Was that the summer of 1911 ? I don't remember for dates are a little confused at this time; but I shall never forget 1911. It was the kind of summer that makes one think the summers are not what they used to be. It began early and ended late, with long periods of hot sunshine, the end of each period being punctuated by a thunderstorm. We would go out from the shade of the school and its trees into the luminescent glare of the long road home. Oh, the smell of the hot tar as it spilled

out from boiling cauldrons on to the boiling road ! Oh, the
rush to the drinking fountain at Knock Corner ! Heat and
glare and glaring heat, withered flowers and withered grass,
empty wells and empty cows, farmers' moans and parsons'
prayers. Was the end of the world on the way ? These are some
of my memories of those days. The end of the world was not
on the way; but the end of the world that we knew then, and
were never to know again, was certainly close at hand. Before
I left this school " Der Tag," of which one of our masters
had warned us, had arrived; and we were to see the nations
locked in the most bloody conflict that the world had known.

But that is to anticipate. In the meantime life went happily
on; we played our games, did our home-work on the way
home and at home, marched with the Scouts on Saturdays—
for now we had become real Boy Scouts, not amateurs—and
in a way enjoyed life with a boy's potentiality for enjoying life
in any circumstances. I gradually rose in the school until I was
winning all the " honour cards " and prizes, and eventually
I became head boy of the school. I suppose all this helped to
remove some of my inherent diffidence; and gave me some
measure of self-confidence—something I needed badly later
when once again I had to start at the foot of the ladder among
boys who were as good, and many much better, than I was.
Before this was to happen, however, I had a set-back from
which I did not recover for some time.

What games did we play in those days ? Some dirtied their
hands and scraped their knuckles every day by playing
incessant games of marbles on the cindery playground. There
were the seasonal crazes for spinning tops, hoops and kites.
Rounders was a favourite, and a game called " Relieve-o."
To play this you picked for sides by holding your hands to your
mouth, wetting one hand and then saying: " Wet or dry ? "
to your rival captain. If he chose correctly the option was his.
The side holding a den chased the other side to imprison its
members. You could release the prisoners by running courageously through the den shouting " Relieve-o ! " but if you
weren't big enough, strong enough, and fast enough, you
would be tackled and brought down on the hard cinders.

Later, when we became more sophisticated, and nearer to that time when we must either go out into the world or to "real schools"—the sort of schools we had read about in *The Magnet, The Gem,* and *The Boys' Own Paper,* we began to arrange more organized games. Besides, didn't we live near Campbell College ? Hadn't we seen the boarders going off in their cabs for the holidays ? Hadn't we watched as they played cricket and rugby ? Hadn't we seen the boarders on Sundays going to Church wearing straw-boilers and black jackets ? Occasionally, tough boys who had gone to one of the major schools and had been compelled to beat an ignominious retreat either by the school authorities or by their parents, would return to us with tales of all the tricks they had played—you could work or not as you pleased; you could throw things at the masters; you never saw the "chief," the "boss," or the head; they only bothered about you if you played games— these were the stories we drank in with avidity; we believed them because we wanted to believe them, but we were soon to realize that we might have been better to listen to more serious- minded advisers.

Anyhow, we raised some money with which to buy balls, bats, wickets, pads, and all the necessary paraphernalia; and we either hired or were granted the use of a nearby field on which to play cricket. Before I left we had actually played a match against some local junior club. How we raised the money I don't remember. Some of the staff became interested, and I think may have organized a concert of sorts, or possibly the principal was induced to contribute something from the proceeds of his annual flower show. Association football may have been played, though I cannot recall much about it; maybe I wasn't sufficiently interested. At one stage, however, we did form a soccer club in The Park. This continued until we went to schools where such socially inferior games were looked upon with disfavour. What snobs we all were in those days !

But to come back to more serious-minded advisers and more serious things. One who influenced me greatly was a compara- tive newcomer to The Park. He was the son of a bank manager and a boarder at a well-inown school in the far North. I suppose I lionized him to some extent; and why not ? After all this

straw-hatted, white-flannelled, athletic sixth former was the
type of boy a younger boy would have lionized, especially in
those days, when the boarding school boy was the archetypal
hero epitomized in an endless stream of books and papers since
the time of *Tom Brown's School Days*. And maybe he was a
bette hero than the long-haired, reefer-smoking group member
of our own time.

But my friend was not one to play on all this. He, I think,
was the first to make me realize that literature, mathematics,
science, and learning were ends in themselves, apart even from
the necessity of earning a living. He did not come back from
school with exaggerated stories of midnight feasts, escapes
down dormitory walls, ragging of boys and masters, and all
the other lore of school life. Instead, for the first time I came
in contact with a serious expanding mind, and one who took
his school life seriously. Though he was an athlete—an oars-
man I think—he did not talk much about his prowess in this
direction, but he *did* talk a good deal about scholarship and
scholarships; and he told me how he hoped eventually to sit
for a Trinity Sizarship. After he went back to school, I followed
his fortunes and he followed mine, by correspondence. Finally,
he went up to Trinity College, Dublin as a Sizar; his brilliant
career, however, was soon to be cut short by death on the
battle-fields of Flanders.

Largely due to his inspiration I decided to sit for an entrance
scholarship at the Royal Belfast Academical Institution. It was,
perhaps, a foolish choice because there was only one scholarship
awarded to a large entry consisting of the best from all the
schools in Belfast and district. I was privately coached by the vice-
principal, of the National School, who occupied the school
house just off the grounds. Thither I repaired on many after-
noons while summer suns glowed on the fields and woods
outside. My coach was a good man, a sympathetic man, and
efficient according to his lights and experience. Shall I ever
forget the cup of strong hot tea and the two slices of good
bread and butter with which he regaled me before work
began ?

And the lesson over, home to hours and hours, and more
hours, of hard work at my bedroom-cum-study window,

which I always kept wide open so that I could inhale the sweet scents from the garden, and from the meadowland across that other park which led from the pseudo-named Kensington Road; this park had never been pushed through to ours nor, save for the lonely, uninspiring house, had it ever been built on, so it served as a wonderful playground for all of us; and for me it was a miniature prairie ending in a miniature jungle. At that age I did not work myself to anything approaching a breakdown, but I certainly worked so hard that it was many years afterwards before I began again to recover my academic equilibrium, and to win back some love of learning for its own sake. Maybe one should not jump to conclusions from the experience of one individual, none-the-less I cannot help but express the view that concentrated and anxious study at too early an age is bad for the mind of a growing boy.

No doubt it was with feelings of nervous apprehension that I set out for town on the day of the scholarship examination; one's feelings were, however, subjugated by the excitement of a new experience, and the fact that one had a temporary respite from the daily routine of an ordinary school day. But there was no time for any kind of analysis of one's psychological state; before long we were expectantly seated in the old maths. room at Inst.; all of us with shining faces, well-brushed hair, best suits, and an angelic look on our faces, falsely hoping, I suppose, that our appearance might in some strange way influence the examiner's decision. Soon we were hard at it with freshly sharpened pencils, clean rubbers, and newly-nibbed pens.

But it was all for naught as far as I was concerned. When the results came out I didn't top the bill, though I did hear later that I had been reasonably well placed. Apart from my own merits or demerits, I soon realized that I had been wrongly coached for this particular examination; there had been too much emphasis on facts; and indeed I was to learn later that some of the questions had been taken directly from text-books in use in the school at the time. I think if my coach had found out about these books my chances might have been better.

So began and ended my first excursion in the land of more serious scholarship. At the time it seemed a near disaster, but who is to know whether, if I had succeeded, it would have been

for good or for ill ? Who is to know if disappointment and
seeming disaster are not the very moulds that shape the whole
metal of our being ? The winner of this scholarship literally
threw the results of all his academic effort to the four winds;
he became a sailor on the oceans of the world—maybe for
good purpose, I don't know; but he certainly did not fulfil the
purpose of his mentors, nor of his benefactor.

At the end of it all I suddenly felt that I had finished with
learning. Whether this change of heart was due entirely to
disappointment or to the rising of the sap in my adolescent
body, or both, I shall never know. Anyhow, in the months
and, indeed, in the immediate years that followed I threw
myself with renewed zest into violent physical effort. Never
had the birds sung so sweetly; never had the meadow sweet
smelt so sweet; to hell with books and learning ! I thought.
Oh, the tea from the billy-can, the eggs and bacon fried in the
open air, the roasted spuds, the clear scented air as bare feet
touched the jewelled grass and the dawnlight crept up the sky
in pink searching flames !

And there was a purpose in it all now; and whether there
was a purpose or not, we imagined one; for we saw ourselves
as soldiers; sometimes we *were* when we stood guard at
recruiting offices; learned to shoot with .22 rifles; and went out
on bottle parties, not to drink but to collect the empties. How
we enjoyed that travelling all over the city in motor vans,
singing " Tipperary " against the cacophony of clinking bottles,
and in general feeling that our well-led troop of Scouts was
now making a valuable contribution to our very existence.

Again I am anticipating. But I have not forgotten that fateful
August when Lord Grey made the pronouncement that
" One by one the lights were going out all over Europe."
I have not forgotten the journey home from our annual
pilgrimage to the sea when black headlines in the paper
proclaimed the tearing up of " the scrap of paper "; and the
action that was to shake the idea of neutrality for ever. I remember a letter from my father stating that before long we might
all be plunged in the throes of a great war, and that his and our
finances could be placed in a more precarious state than ever.

But we were all caught up in a fever which now seems incredible. My scholarship coach, one day discussing the general question of what was good and what was bad for one, remarked on the young fellows who had joined the army. " See them now," he said, " marching along, uniformed, smart, sun-browned and beefy. Compare them with the pale-faced clerks, workers on the Island and students.." Ah, yes, there they were being fattened and trained like fighting cocks to be slaughtered and destroyed, almost wantonly, with the poppies on the fields of France and Flanders. I recall one saying with reference to a boy scout who had lost his legs during the bombardment of Scarborough and Hartlepool: " The first to receive the honours of war." Could any statement have been more fraught with pomposity and lack of imagination ?

Those early days of the war were colourful days; there were the bands and the flags, and the cavalry on their magnificent horses; all the pageantry calculated to stimulate the minds and imaginations of young and old, but more particularly of the young. There was the first—and last—march of the Ulster Division through the streets of Belfast on a hot summer day. Like most other children I was taken to see all these young men in the flush of manhood. Sometimes the bands would cease, the restive horses would stand still, and the men would stand easy, while well-meaning civilians threw down oranges and refreshments from vantage points along the way. And then there were the first volunteers from our midst. The one who joined a Scottish regiment, and was on his way to the front before most of us had begun to realize that the war was something more than a great game. How I remember this young man coming up the isle of the church with his kilts fairly swinging, his sergeant's stripes on his sleeves, and his Glengarry by his side. Later he was to become a captain and was to survive every major battle in the war from beginning to end without a serious wound.

As it happened we in Ulster were not unaccustomed to men-at-arms nor " arms and the man." The word *volunteer* had been familiar even before the days of Kitchener's Army. For years before, men—respectable men—had been drilling attired in every-day suits, soldiers' hats and belts and—believe it

or not—with German Mauser rifles. Leaders Sir Edward Carson,
" Galloper " Smith and others had spelled out in no uncertain
terms the awful results of Home Rule: " Ulster would fight and
Ulster would be right." In those days the essential rightness
of the Ulster position was never doubted by any reasonable
citizen. If you were a Home Ruler you were a pariah, an
outcast. You hardly breathed when you passed the house of
a Home Ruler lest you should be contaminated by such an
outrageous philosophy.

What an incredible situation ! Ulster would fight England
for her loyalty to England. I often watched local businessmen
forming fours, shouldering arms, presenting arms, and going
through a performance which, if civil war had broken out,
would have been of little avail against the might of a professional
army. I may say that there was nothing esoteric about all this
training—either it was legal or the authorities turned a blind
eye because they could not, or did not, wish to prevent it.
In later years one senior citizen of The Park told me he had
orders one night to stand guard over a ship at one of the
wharves. All night long he waited terrified that, in the event
of an attempt to search the ship by force, he might be compelled to take action. In the morning he was released from his
guard duty; the authorities came aboard; and opened up the
hatches to find nothing. In the meantime guns had been
coming in at other points around the coast.

So that was the picture when we were very young: marching
men; men-of-war off the Antrim headlands; war and rumours
of war throughout our formative years. Black Friday when
the generals resigned from the Curragh, family councils, and
councils with other families. Should we emigrate to Canada ?
Then came the Great War when some kind of bargain was
struck whereby the Ulster Volunteers would join the forces
provided Home Rule was not imposed during their absence.
Throughout it all, however, there was a certain gentlemanly
restraint: as far as I can remember there was a complete absence
of burnings, bombings, manslaughter, murder and all the other
horrors that one associates with present-day political upheavals.
The only blood spilled was when men spilled their blood to
sign the Covenant in their own vital fluid.

Covenant Day ! I remember it well as a sort of school holiday—a fiesta with bunting, flags and church services at which the aid of the Almighty was invoked for little Ulster. What happened at churches presided over by Home Rulers I don't know. Looking back now I have nothing but the most profound respect for those who had the courage— especially parsons—to stand against the tremendous pressure of the current of popular thought. Maybe they were right; maybe they were more far-seeing and perhaps wiser men than those of their generation. Perhaps, after all, their way might have been the right way. We cannot turn back the pages of history; if we could we might try to write them differently.

As to the effect of all this on one's mode of thought, I really believe it had little influence on me and on those with whom I grew up. As most of the people around us were of Scottish or English descent, they naturally accepted that everything English, or British was right. Our roads and districts were often given English or Scottish names: Kensington, Sydenham, Balmoral, and so forth, all in the good colonial tradition. And yet in some ways there was more Irishness about than there is now—stagey perhaps—but there seemed to be more pride in being Irish. The shamrock was worn on St. Patrick's Day by everyone; now it is almost a badge of one's persuasion or political outlook. Irish emblems of one sort or another were for sale in all the resorts. Irish comedians, Irish singers, and Irish dancers were usually featured at concerts, irrespective of religious or political affiliations. Our school readers contained Irish stories and accounts of Irish life and scenery. Indeed I believe that one such account—" A Journey around Ireland " I think it was called—gave me a love for the land of my birth that has never been eradicated. The fact that many of the articles were written by reverend gentlemen of another persuasion aroused no comment. One of these articles, written by a Jesuit Father, was my first introduction to the chemistry of combustion; it was entitled " The Philosophy of a Candle."

There may have been sectarian bitterness in the purlieus of the city; but little of it percolated into our school life and there was certainly none of it in The Park—at least not until political differences became acute. We were of course given to understand that Roman Catholics interpreted the Scriptures wrongly; we were told about the differences, but we were never taught, either at home or at school, that we ought to hate Roman Catholics. The daughter of one of our neighbours married a Roman Catholic; he lived with the family, and attended the Methodist Church and the Roman Catholic Church on alternate Sundays. The arrangement aroused some comment, but neither party was ostracized.

The ugliness and bitterness of the whole situation became really apparent when Winston Churchill visited Belfast. It must have been about this time that I first became interested in the newspapers; at least the headings and the pictures are as clear in my mind as though the incidents happened only yesterday. With characteristic intrepidity Churchill who, at that time was a Liberal and, *ipso facto* a Home Ruler, tried to speak in the very heart of the anti-Home Rule city. But the Ulster Volunteers had other ideas; and so had the mob who tried to overturn his car. Eventually he spoke at the Celtic football ground. Years afterwards, after the first great war, I was to hear Churchill speak at Queen's University. As great words rolled from his lisping lips one could see his cherubic face wreathed in a sardonic smile as, no doubt, he thought of other days and other manners.

But before I go to other days and other manners I must first give an account of further influences at work on my mind at this time—notably that of the church.

CHAPTER III

SPIRES AND CHOIRS

WHEN we were very young, minor festivities could be created around almost anything. Each day had a special significance: washing day, shopping day, baker's day, the maid's night out, mother's at-home day; all these, apart from the major holidays: Good Friday, Easter Monday, Christmas Day, Hallowe'en and the rest. Good Friday, when we waited with exaggerated anticipation the arrival of the baker with those tasteless cookies marked with a pastry cross on top and known as "hot cross buns." Easter Sunday when we went to church to sing lustily "Up from the grave He arose" with our thoughts not so much on the significance of this miracle as on the druidical festival of universal resurrection when we would roll our whin-stained yellow eggs down the Gilnahirk hills. Christmas Day has been described so much in legend, story, poem and song that I need not enter into any full description here other than to say that ours was Dickensian in all its aspects—not even Mr. Pickwick himself could have enjoyed a more conventional Christmas.

Though Christmas was not entirely conventional. There were the usual ingredients: spiced beef for breakfast—this was one of my mother's specialities—turkey and plum pudding for dinner, fancy hats, fancy faces, toys, tin whistles, and all the rest. The unusual part, which would seem dull to most modern children, was a traditional long walk with my father after church and breakfast. The idea was partly to get us out of the way before the dinner preparations, partly because my father loved walking exercise, and the country; and I think he also liked the small male questioning company of his son. Did I enjoy these walks? I think so, though the company of one of my friends—and this occasionally happened—would have made for a better situation. I have memories of the strange

33

Christmas peace that seemed to pervade the whole countryside;
I have memories of the gentle soft Christmas air bringing a
glow to my cheeks and appetite to my body; I have memories
of munching cattle and manured fields, of freshly ploughed
furrows and idle ploughs, and of a vast city down below to
which Christ had brought that " peace which passeth all
understanding " on this one day at least. No doubt I plied my
father with endless questions which, doubtless, he strove to
answer with interest or evasion as befitted the case. But as the
miles slipped by, and my feet began to falter, I had little thought
in my mind other than toys and turkey.

At Hallowe'en we were always sorry for the English residents
who had to wait for another week before exploding their
crackers and using their nut-crackers. What a night ! We
seemed to have licence to do almost anything within reason.
We were all out in The Park—boys and girls—and there were
parties at which we ate oranges, apples and nuts; nearly
drowned ourselves in trying to get a bite from an apple under
water in a basin; or nearly broke our noses in trying to bite an
apple held from a string. There were ghostly appearances and
ghost stories, and ghostly heads made by lighting a candle
inside a cut-out turnip suspended from a tree. Fire crackers,
thunder flashes, jumping jacks, banging squibs, and roaring
rockets streaked and flashed and banged from the Holywood
Hills to the Hills of Gilnahirk, and from Castlereagh to Cave
Hill. As bonfires blazed, excitement crazed, we dared each
other to hold squibs until the last minute, and sometimes after
the last minute; yet in our area at least, I never knew of anybody
to be injured.

Sunday, the weekly recurring festival: strangely enough I
always associate Sunday with sunny days, for the sun always
seemed to shine on Sunday, even when the rest of the week
had been wet. For all of us, and my father especially, as he was
an almost fanatically devout man, it was *the* day of the week.
We were cleaned physically in the steaming bathroom the night
before; and the following morning there would be—oh, such a
ritual of face washing, hair brushing, suit brushing, teeth
washing, and nail manicuring ! After Sunday breakfast, a
better one than usual, we were off down The Park, along the

cherry blossomed valley, across the railway line, and down
to the church—father in his tall hat and frock coat, mother in
her Sunday finery, and the rest of us in the best of our best
clothes.

I grieve to say that I remember little of the many hundreds
of sermons to which I must have listened. At some stage,
however, I became aware of the organ music, the choir singing
and the hymn-singing. Other impressions are somewhat
flippant: for example, the police sergeant, red and beefy,
looking slightly out of place as he put his helmet underneath
the seat; the doctor's family to our right, one of whom would
invariably remove his shoes and stockings, and put his bare feet
proudly on the hymn book shelf—a gesture which caused me to
giggle. There was the sensational entrance of the Roman
Catholic who visited us on alternate Sundays; I suppose many
people thought that he would—in fact *must*—eventually see
the light. There were the men down in front who swayed
around in half-circles as they sang. There were the hard-
working busy men of affairs, who always looked as if church
was a rather unimportant, though perhaps necessary, interlude
in their busy lives.

Special services were looked forward to with zest. The most
important of these was the Harvest Festival. The huge loaf in
the centre, the sheaves of grain, the red apples, and the autumn
flowers formed a colourful fertility symbol, behind which the
special preacher preached a special sermon, and the choir sang
special music. In those days, when few would have known
what the word " ecumenism " meant, people were much more
ecumenistically minded; it was, in fact, usual for many people
to support, not only their own Harvest Services, but also to go
the rounds of the two other protestant churches in the area.
And, needless to state, there was some rivalry as to which choir
could produce the best singing with the result that, on the
whole, the choral work was very good.

In those days church was the central core of existence in
a suburban area; some people might go as many as four
times on Sunday, remain for a kind of after-service on Sunday
evening, attend a mid-week service and possibly some other
function as well. Nowadays we talk a lot about the pace at

which we live: by this we really mean the pace at which we move from one place to another. We have far more lesiure now. What leisure could there have been in the days when a man worked from eight in the morning, came home at seven in the evening, worked on Saturday mornings at least, and put in so many appearances at church ?

We went out four times on Sunday. Only two of these were obligatory attendances; as we became older, however, we asked to be allowed to attend morning Sunday School and evening service. At first I slept soundly throughout most of the evening service, and hated to be roused to go out into the cool night air. On the whole I don't think our service or Sunday School attendances were a great hardship. We met our friends there; had expressed or unexpressed amorous relationship with the opposite sex; and I think we were extremely fortunate in our preachers, teachers, and in the whole church set-up. Indeed I must place on record my impression that musically, intellectually, and—dare I say it ?—morally, the Church was a great inspiration. By morally I mean such principles as courage in the face of adversity, tolerance toward those of different faiths, colours and persuasions; and, in general, love for one's fellow men. Most of our teachers had little to say about the nuances of dogma and doctrine; a few did try to elaborate the orthodox ideas, but on one pupil at least their cathechismic jumble of words, phrases, and sentences had no effect whatever.

But I think we were lucky. Our teachers were good people, dedicated people, and people whom we respected. Well-to-do educated businessmen, students, teachers, and even doctors gave of their time and talents freely. The so-called " lecture hall," though not an inspiring building, was at least clean, roomy and warm; it had two auxiliary class-rooms, and a comfortable carpeted room upstairs known as the " church parlour." As we advanced in wisdom and years we moved up to a Bible class in this room. But the Bible class became more of a round table discussion group; and I recall many a happy hour in this room while our adolescent deliberations ranged over many unsolved problems of life, death, and eternity. One of our leaders was a medical man of wide interests and intellect; he it was who first gently led us from the Garden of Eden to the broader, deeper conception of a universe developing throughout timeless ages, to the emergence of life, and finally, of man.

The church parlour had wide, spacious windows, looking out on the Manse garden, in which there were tall fir trees. It is winter; snow falls gently down, gradually mantling the trees, the garden and the manse in winter's lovely garment. Inside the coke-stove glows and sparks and spurts, and quitely drops its almost weightless ash softly in the pan below. We talk, and learn, and think; though no doubt we are excited at the prospect of snowballing on the way home, and sleighing down the Gilnahirk Hills if the snow holds until to-morrow night. But in spite of the pleasures in store, there is no impatience, no hurried glances at watches. We are happy. How strange ! To be happy in a Sunday school ! Looking back now I think this Sunday school would have made a better day school than most at the time.

Of this group of dedicated men and women two were trained national teachers—God bless them ! After teaching all week to give their services like this on Sundays; could any sacrifice have been greater ? Two young women were international hockey players at a time when there weren't so many women players of hockey. Their approach was modern and progressive; we loved them with more than filial love. One of them was in love with another who was to influence me greatly; he was a chemistry master who gave up mastering to go East as an oil man. I envied and admired him for more reasons than one when he returned on leave, bronzed and handsome. I was introduced to him by his fiancée who knew I was interested in chemistry as a career. He took an interest in me; and advised me to be careful about going into industry, because I could easily find myself doing little more than the routine work of a laboratory assistant.

Much of our early life was centred around this church hall, and its so-called parlour. Our debates were not confined to Sundays; we had our debating societies, guilds, musical and dramatic events, and rehearsals here; and much of these on our own initiative, especially during the first world war. Indeed

I think the independence and initiative we learned stood most of us in good stead in the years to follow. It was here that I first realized—or that someone else realized—I had a voice; and so I was selected to sing " Thou didst leave Thy throne, and Thy kingly crown " at the annual " Flower Service." There I stood surrounded by the strengthening prop of the adult choir; there I stood in my dark suit, Eton collar and stiff cuffs, feeling some-what angelic as the sweet notes of a boy's soprano voice came out of me almost as though I was controlled by some other agency. I remember as if it were yesterday this strange feeling of the delight and power of the human voice. So began a lifelong interest.

Whatever one's views and beliefs may be, and mine are scarcely orthodox, there is a certain nostalgia about those days. I am not sure that I had, at any time, much liking for the hymns specifically written for children; but I had then, and still have, a great affection for many of the powerful old tunes and hymns, not Gospel types, but those written and composed by great poets and musicians: " Guide me, O Thou great Jehovah " to " Cwm Rhondda," " Eternal Father, strong to save " to " Militia," " The Lord's my Shepherd " to " Crim-ond," " I to the hills will lift mine eyes " to " Dundee "; all these and scores of others will remain in my mind as long as my mind remains. I never had much faith in biblical know-ledge as such, but I have great faith in knowledge of the great language and poetry of the Bible; and in later years some of those who taught us gave us an unforgettable conception of man's striving toward the light—the evolution of his religious thought from the sacrificial bull to the sacrificial man, to the idea of personal sacrifice.

As I said earlier formal sermons made little impression; there were too many of them; and many were far too long. Indeed I remember one man preaching for so long that he passed out in the pulpit, presumably from sheer exhaustion. I can recall very clearly, however, the personalities of the ministers of whom we had a great many in those days of triennial itinerancy. Perhaps, being less subjected to rigorous training, they retained their own personalities to a greater degree. To give them their due few preached hell-fire and brimstone, a doctrine supposed to be beloved in those days. Even if they did, or *when* they did, they were not believed, otherwise most of us would have gone about in fearful anticipation. At least one sermon must have been preached on the subject, because I can remember one of the great musical personalities of the choir leaning over to whisper to me the truism that " after all we make our own hell on earth." This statement influenced me more than the sermon. There were wits and humorists; men who made us smile or even laugh; there were scholars who made us think; and men of such kindly mien and character that you felt you would like to go to them in time of trouble—sometimes you did just this.

Church and State: the two have always been united, even when the Church was such a radical breakaway institution as the Methodist Church of John Wesley. When we were young it was all so much simpler; there was one state, and one country— one's own which was Britain. Others didn't count for very much; they were " foreign," and therefore suspect; the Germans were dangerous, the French atheists, and the Russians anarchists. The religions of far-away countries were wrong in principle and practice; and it was clearly our duty to go out into all the world to carry the light of Christian doctrine and freedom into the outer darkness. Few told us that other civilizations might have their virtues, and that other religions might have some content of truth in their philosophies. Our heroes were military and British: Wellesley, Kitchener, Lord Roberts and Baden-Powell; Stanley, Livingstone and the Protestant martyrs. We were not made to understand that soldiers may be heroes irrespective of the countries for which they die, and men are no less martyrs who suffer for ideas not necessarily Protestant, or even Christian.

Divine Providence kept a special eye on one's own country; and great national occasions were celebrated accordingly. The death of King Edward VII was celebrated with pomp and circumstance, not merely in Westminster Abbey, but in every church throughout the country, and in our own church no less than in others. How well I remember the drapings of black and purple silk in front of pulpit and choir stall, the solemn music, and the deep, sad, plaintive beat of the Dead March !

We enjoyed it almost as though we were accompanying our
sovereign on his last great adventure to the very portals of
heaven. Though his pleasure-loving life must have been
anathema to many Methodists, no one doubted but that he
would go to the right place.

Most churches at this time sponsored some quasi-military
organization; the Boy Scout movement was becoming increas-
ingly popular, so it was decided to form a troop—as it was
then known—at our church. Being well led, ours was a great
success; and I take my hat off to those first leaders who sacrificed
so much of their time and energy in the best years of their lives.
I couldn't have done it, for I remember reaching a stage when
I grew out of the scout idea as rapidly and as suddenly as I grew
out of my clothes. This was inevitable with developing
maturity, but in the meantime we had fun. Vividly I recall
days when we had attack and defence games in the woods of
Holywood. To see those magnificent woods, all destroyed
now, to make room for more and yet more houses, is a heart-
break. In spring they were a blue sea of bluebells. Beneath the
shade of larch, spruce, and ash we used to conceal ourselves
from an enemy as real to us, and as crafty and cunning, as if he
were a foreign spy. When the fight was over there would be
the get-together, the camp fire, the boiling of billy-cans, the
songs around the camp fire, and then the long march home.

Those days are gone; the woods are gone; and I wonder are
the scouts as they used to be. Are there as good leaders now
prepared to make such sacrifices of time and energy ? What
happened during two wars when a scout was supposed to be a
brother to all other scouts ? What happened in Ireland where
one saw, after the " settlement," scouts in khaki and scouts in
green ? Were these brothers, or did the Border divide the
brotherhood ? When we began our imaginations were fired
with dreams of universal brotherhood. How soon those
dreams were to be dispelled when we found that guns and
bullets counted for more than brotherhood.

Even if the universal dreams of Baden-Powell, the founder,
were never to be realized, I think it is fair to say that the scouts
did us good. In what ways ? Well I think we learned to be
leaders, not of the coercive bullying type, but of the persuasive

type. We learned tricks that have stuck to us all our lives—
trivial details perhaps, but useful at times: how to light fires
under difficult conditions, simple first aid, elements of nursing
the sick, and even how to look after ourselves when the
necessity arose. Maybe one could learn these things without
being a scout; but it is surprising the number of men who can
be helpless when faced with such minor problems; and these
are often those who were never in the scouts or in similar
organizations.

On joining the scouts we were told that it was a non-military
organization. When war broke out such idealism melted like
snow around the camp fire; and we were soon to be taught the
military as well as the civil arts. When four of us went for an
unofficial camp at Easter 1916, along the shores of Belfast
Lough we did so hoping we would spot a German submarine
making its way up the Lough, but we didn't. But thoughts of
German submarine-spotting were soon to be dispelled by
domestic events, for one day a young scoutmaster came down
to tell us what was going on in the world. He said he had been
sharpening his bayonet and stroking it into the casement—the
pun is obvious. To say we were filled with a sense of chagrin
and frustration is to put it mildly; for it had never occurred to
us that there were people in Ireland so inimical to Britain that
they were willing to place the war effort in jeopardy to get
their way. Such an idea seems ridiculous now, but in the
context of the times it was not so ridiculous, especially when
one remembers that the rebellion came as a surprise to most
people throughout the length and breadth of Ireland. As many
historians have pointed out, it was subsequent events that
hardened the attitude of the Irish as a whole.

Before leaving the scouts, as senior patrol leader, I was to be
the recipient of colours presented by the father of my boyhood
friend whose life had been cut off at such an early age. It was a
father's tribute to the memory of the son he had loved and lost;
as for me, I was as proud as if I had been selected to carry
the colours of the greatest regiment in the world. The flag
still stands in the church as a memorial to the past and an
inspiration for the future.

D

But school and church and scouts were not the only influences at work in those days. I am not sure when I first became interested in literature. I don't think the National School literary teaching was inspiring. Probably the more advanced readers contained excerpts from *The Vicar of Wakefield, David Copperfield* and others; but from a very early age I read avidly everything that came my way, beginning with fairy tales— Grimm. Hans Andersen—and then graduating through *Robinson Crusoe, The Swiss Family Robinson* and - oh yes - ! one of the most fascinating books was given to me as a prize when I was still at my first school: it was entitled *Tales of Romance and Adventure* and was of the Blackwood's Magazine type. There were stories in it about the Boer War and about people's adventures in every part of the world. One in particular comes to mind. It was about a couple who put up at an inn in some remote Balkan state. During the night they were horrified to find the bed moving downwards through the floor into a dungeon below. The purpose was robbery; how they eventually escaped from the awful predicament I don't know, but I do know that to this day I would not stay in a remote Balkan inn under any circumstances.

Then there were the more sentimental books: *Uncle Tom's Cabin, Eric* or *Little by Little,* but more than anything I remember with what patience my father would read to me night after night. I think he enjoyed the reading as much as I did: we laughed heartily over the adventures of Mr. Pickwick; wept—at least I did—at the misfortunes of Oliver Twist; sailed the seven seas with Peter Simple; and explored Wild Wales with George Borrow. The Dickens books smelt as Dickens books should smell; I was fascinated, too, by the rather fearsome illustrations of Oliver being pushed through the window by Bill Sykes, Old Fagin in his den, and a host of others.

In later years I examined our book shelves more closely. Apart from Dickens, Scott, *Tom Brown's School Days,* Jack London, Captain Marryat and some of the more popular books and authors of the day, there were others that seemed inexpressibly dull: some theological commentaries, Sesame and Lilies, translations of the Koran and Talmud, *The Origin of*

Species. One day I discovered *The Sherlock Holmes Stories* and for a long period afterwards I identified myself with Sir Arthur Conan Doyle's hero.

Maybe it was at about the same time I found a new friend and a new hobby. Not only was the friend new, but his home was new and bigger than most. It had a garage, a billiard room, and—wonder of wonders !—its lights would go on at the touch of a switch. My new friend was a modern in the sense that he knew what was going on in the modern world—mechanically I mean. He was interested in motor bikes and cars, and his parents had the means to allow him to forward his inclinations.

But the *pièce de résistance* as far as I was concerned was the billiard room, in which one did not play billiards; at this time it was more a large play-room. Never a great hobby man in the sense of wanting to make things, I was strangely attracted to chemistry and to scientific things in general. Maybe this had something to do with a sort of titillation of the romantic side of my nature by the romantic figure of Sherlock Holmes. Even, as a very small child, however, before going to school, I remember finding what I now know was probably a volt-meter; it had been left by an electrician who had been working at the electric bells. I was fascinated and, when the instrument was removed from me, inconsolable.

Anyhow my friend had a laboratory in the billard room and here we used to play at work for hours on end. No doubt we made the most appalling stenches; stretched our parents' nerves to breaking point in case we did ourselves some damage; and made the most extraordinary conglomerations in the hope that we might discover some elixir vitæ or philosopher's stone. And yet I think we may have carried out accepted experiments, such as the preparation of some of the common gases.

It could be, however, that I am now remembering things another friend and I did later when I was allowed to have a laboratory of my own in a small room at the top of our three-story house in The Park. Here we performed fairly rigid experiments; and I kept a laboratory note-book; I wish I had it now to see if it contained any real glimmerings of scientific intelligence. How we didn't destroy ourselves I don't know, for we used such powerful corrosives as strong nitric acid.

We didn't destroy ourselves, but my friend destroyed something else. One day when I was downstairs I heard a shout from him:

"Billy! Billy! Come up a minute!"

I ran up the stairs two at a time to find him in an agony of fear and apprehension.

"Look what I've done," said he. "My God, what'll father say!"

He was wearing a brand new suit; had spilled some nitric acid down the front of his trousers; this had gone through like fire through paper, and had produced a gaping hole with a brown smoking stain like the edge of a miniature volcano.

Hastily we removed the damaged trousers, daubed them in a solution of sodium bicarbonate, and hoped against hope that our prayers to high heaven would be answered by some chemical deity who, taking pity on two miserable boys, would perform some miracle of heavenly chemistry, so that the trousers would be restored intact before our very eyes. But no such miraculous intervention took place; what happened when my friend reached home is best left unrecorded.

I said I wasn't much of a hobby man; and I don't think I am likely to become one now; but some flamboyant streak in my nature is often attracted when the hobby may lead to romance or adventure. I don't know if we had even seen an aeroplane when my friend and I decided to make a glider. For months we saved and planned and glued, at wood and lath, canvas and wire, until we thought we had something that looked as if it could be airborne.

Came the day when we decided conditions were good for a test flight—a bad day to choose because on that afternoon, as a reward for some unusual goodness, I had been promised a trip down the Lough on the "Bangor Boat." We drew lots as to who should be first to take to the air. I won! Soon I was strapped in; and we chose the highest roof that would allow for some margin of safety, at the same time giving sufficient height for me to be airborne when I jumped into the wind.

I jumped, but was not airborne. Instead the tail caught on the gutter; I was turned over with a sort of loop-the-loop effect; and fell flat on my face in a den of nettles. My shorts and my light summer clothes were no protection against the powerful sting of the vicious weeds; in addition I was winded, so that I lay helpless and writhing until my friend, and his sister, who was a nurse, arrived to succour me in my misery. They said that, through the unwilled tears, all I could do was to bemoan the possible loss of the journey on the Bangor Boat. But I recovered sufficiently to be able to make the trip in the little paddle steamer and, as I watched the green water churning alongside, and the green receding hills of Down on the one side and Antrim on the other, I decided that after all it was better to be borne on water than on the fickle insubstantial air.

Well, well, well, as a County Down man might say—at least those whose work and worry left them little time to study the niceties of grammar—" Them was the days." Were they indeed ? I remember suffering agonies when I first fell in love. Pre-adolescent love can in fact be the most powerful emotion known to man at any stage of his life. She whom I loved had brown hair and green eyes, and wore a brown coat with a fur collar. When she looked at me shafts of light came down from heaven; and when she didn't it was as though a great black cloud had moved between the earth and the sun. This kind of love had as little of the sex element in it as one's feelings about a lovely rose. For a time I think my love was reciprocated. This girl became my girl. It was understood that we were " keen." I used to wait outside our gate even on the off-chance that she might come down The Park. She was the sister of the friend who died young; and the lifelong friend of one who was ultimately to become my lifelong friend—and who at this time was " keen " on the boy who died.

Sex education may have some advantage; maybe, however, a little ignorance is bliss; to be unduly conscious of sex might make one unduly self-conscious about sex. Perhaps we in The Park were precocious—I don't know—but I submit that I cannot remember any time—that is outside the limits of completely innocent childhood—when we were not fairly familiar with the so-called facts of life. How this knowledge came to us is a mystery only known to those capable of tapping the children's grapevine. Every precaution was taken to prevent the dissemination of any knowledge of original sin even to the extent of telling us the gooseberry-bush story.

Boys at least tended to divide the opposite sex into two categories: those whom we admired, respected, and loved, and those who were " bad uns." Even in The Park there were both types, with a preponderance of the former. The Park was a great place for parties; at first of the bun, lemonade, jelly-and-cream, postman's knock and forfeits description; later there were whist drives, dances and musical evenings. At these parties one met good, bad and indifferent girls; and indeed one was soon to learn that " the weemen is worse than the men." When we really fell in love, however, I think I am right in saying it was not consciously for sex or sexual reasons.

This kind of differentiation may have been peculiar to our day and generation; I think it is less evident now when the mystery of girlhood is barely concealed.

My mother had always been fond of music. She would extemporize at the piano for hours, and she had a rich contralto voice. She played the organ once or twice in church, I believe, and often sang in the choir on special occasions. Unfortunately her musical education came to an abrupt halt with her early marriage, and from then on, between managing on a stinted budget, having children and miscarriages, and rearing her children, she had little opportunity to pursue her musical studies. Once we had a young friend staying with us while she was attending one of the many seminaries for young ladies to be found in the suburban areas of our cities at this time. Part of her " finishing " included music; this involved frequent practising sessions. My father often referred to one of these when my mother tapped on the floor of her room upstairs and called out: " Wrong note, Helen ! " The recognition of a wrong note presents little difficulty for most people, but for my father, whose sense of pitch was far from good, this was little short of miraculous.

However, we frequently worshipped at the shrine of the holy art, especially when our Dublin relations descended on us: Aunt Gertie, Aunt Eva, Aunt Susan and their respective families. There was nothing the darkly handsome Aunt Gertie enjoyed better than for us all to be ranged around while she played the senitmental Victorian ballads so popular in Edwardian drawing-rooms.

With all this interest in music it was natural that I should be given lessons at any cost; even my teacher, however, a kind lady, admitted that I was sent to her at a rather early age. I was a disappointment; for, like many other boys, I didn't practise enough. It is all too easy to excuse oneself for one's defects, nevertheless it might be a profitable exercise in educational study to consider what might have been done. First of all I probably began before reaching the readiness phase. Secondly I think a better approach might have been through singing, in which I was always deeply interested, even when I was a small boy; and thirdly, I was taken away too soon, just when I had reached the readiness phase and was beginning to be able to read simple music. The little I learned, however, was invaluable when I came to understanding vocal scores, and the appreciation of good music.

Apart from the mechanics of learning those rudiments without which further education, or indeed the furtherance of the practical affairs of life, would be virtually impossible, the reader will no doubt perceive that, as far as my true education was concerned, I owed much more to my home environment, and to the Church and its ancillary organizations, than to my elementary schooling. If I had any fault to find with our environmental stimuli in those days it would be that the virtues of games and the open air tended to be over-emphasized. How well I remember my mother, with one of her flashes of worldly intuition, saying to me one time when I wanted to be out playing football instead of practising: " You know, Willie, there'll come a time when you'll be in digs with other fellows, and one of them will say: ' Come on Crowe, give us a tune '; wouldn't it be nice to be able to do this?" Once, too, at a dinner at which I had given a song, a big burly six-footer, golfer, boxer and rugby player, said to me: " I wish I had given less time to games and more to music; for games have only a transient value, but music can be a consolation throughout life." Wasn't it Captain Scott, too, who wrote home to his wife suggesting that it would be best for their son to spend more time on the study of nature and less on games. It might be argued that games can be a profession, or may form an integral part of one's profession; but it might also be argued that in my day there was too much emphasis on learning to be pioneers in far-away places, in a contracting world in which there were soon to be no far-away places in which to pioneer.

But there are points which educationists will argue about until the end of time: what to develop and what should not be developed. For my part I have always been pulled in two conflicting directions: the desire to know, to understand, and to acquire the skills of the mind; on the other hand, even when deep in study, I am rarely unaware of the sap-giving sun, the whispering of the wind, the sibilant sounds of the little streams washing over stones, and the oh so sweet smell of meadows on a summer day. Only a Wordsworthian poet could reconcile the two; and I had to see half a century of life before reconciliation began.

CHAPTER IV

INSTITUTION BOYS

ONE day my father said: " Which of the three schools would you like to go to, lad? " I thought for a moment and then said: " Inst. " In those days the Eton, Harrow, and St. Paul's of Belfast were Campbell College, The Methodist College, and The Royal Belfast Academical Institution, popularly known as " Inst." and referred to by some of the rather invidious title of " The Institution." There were other lesser abodes of learning, e.g., The Belfast Royal Academy, an old school—older than Inst.—but out of the way and in decline at this time—besides, they did not play rugby football. Campbell College might have been an obvious choice because of its convenience. One would have expected my parents to insist on " Methody "; I was a Methodist, my sister was already there, and my cousin from Dublin was a boarder and captain of rugby.

I chose Inst. because most of my friends were about to enter the school. Without denigrating in any way the virtues of the other schools, I think the choice was a good one. Campbell was Presbyterian in foundation and tradition; Methody was obviously very Methodist—more so than in recent years. Inst., by tradition and foundation, was the nearest to integrated education possible in the Belfast of the period: Church of Ireland, Presbyterians, Methodists, a few Roman Catholics, and some Jewish boys mixed in a happy unselfconscious relationship. Besides, the school and all it stood for were deeply entrenched in the life of the city of Belfast; and many of the leaders of that city—theological, legal, medical and business—had been educated there.

Let me give you a very brief picture of the history of this great school. Strangely enough it owed its foundation partly to the failure of another: The Belfast Royal Academy. This was founded in 1785 to give an almost universal education, both school and college; but the grandiose scheme failed for lack of funds, inadequate accommodation for boarders, and lack of facilities for day-boys.

Inst. was founded in 1814 to serve a similar purpose to that envisaged for The Royal Academy. It was to be both boarding school and college. The original magnificent building plan was not carried out in its entirety. Even so, the school designed by Sir John Soane, architect of the Bank of England and many other famous buildings, was an outstanding example of late Georgian architecture; and as far as its frontage is concerned it still remains unchanged. But what a pity they allowed the College of Technology to be built in front, so that almost an entire wing of the school was concealed, and the whole building dominated. When I first went to the school the most of the covered wing was used as warehouses or something of the sort. Every time I walk past now my heart bleeds when when I think what a fine and beautiful square this could have been. A plague on ye, men of the past, with so little foresight !

Anyhow, the intentions of the founders of this boarding school-cum-college were far-sighted. It was proposed to appoint independent headmasters of the departments—Classical and English—and Professors of Natural Philosophy, Logic and Rhetoric, and Moral Philosophy. Among those ultimately appointed was Professor James Thomson, the mathematician and father of Lord Kelvin, who attended the school for a short time. In a footnote to the *History of the Royal Belfast Academical Institution*, by John Jameson, we are informed that Kelvin and his brother James wore at the school prize-giving " white trousers with little black surtouts richly braided, and wide, white linen collars and black ribbon neck-ties."

The subscribers to the school were composed of all religious persuasions, and visitors and staff were to be appointed without consideration of their religious affiliations. Such an attitude was enlightened in a city rent asunder by religious differences. The tradition was continued right up to my time when the staff were of all denominations; and I cannot remember any master being regarded differently because he was not of the persuasion of the majority of the boys.

In the years that followed and right up to the appointment of my former Principal, the school was stiff—if one may use a slang term with reference to such august men—with headmasters. There were headmasters of the boarding schools, of the Writing School, of French, and so forth; and when you add to all these the various professors, all fighting for their own share of the cake, doubtless there must have been a considerable amount of bickering. Later a medical school was added with professors of chemistry, materia medica, pharmacy, and midwifery. One of the most famous of these was Thomas Andrews, Professor of Chemistry, whose work on Critical Constants was to bring him world fame.

Many things had gone, but not its fame, when we went to Inst. Gone were the medical school and the collegiate department; gone were the boarding-houses with their pump in the yard and the unsuccessful "steam kitchen," and gone were the green fields with the uninterrupted view stretching away from the back of the school to Divis mountain. But there was much to remind us of those days—famous names carved on desks and dormitory roofs, medical diagrams still around, "common halls" in the old Common Hall—but different from the days when unfortunate pupils were expected to demonstrate their prowess each week in the presence of a visitor, a manager, and all the masters—and the school buildings much as they were in the original, though with some rooms no longer in use, notably the swimming bath, now dry and empty and indicative of days of less financial stress.

But on arrival we were unaware of, and indifferent to, financial stress, nor did we wear "white trousers with little black surtouts richly braided." As the weather was still warm in September, I rather think we proudly wore "straw boilers" with the school monogram on the ribbon, short trousers and, probably, Eton collars with the waspish yellow and black tie. Curiously, my memory about this first day is somewhat blurred, though I do remember lying on the green lawn at recess with my friend. What we talked about I don't know— maybe about the events of the morning, possibly with the wind-like will of a boy our conversation blew this way and that: dreams for the future and present dreams; but for my friend there was to be no future—not in this life anyhow.

Unlike the Inst. of a hundred years before, a great factory stood as a tall cliff on one side, while on the other were the grey Victorian classic walls and corner domes of that other institution of learning, which, no doubt, with the characteristic unreason of the day, we despised. In front the—as we thought then— permanent trams clanked, and sparked, and rang on their permanent ways. Probably, cabs and horse-drawn drays clamped and trotted along College Square, while the occasional khaki-clad officer with rakish unwired cap, bent on transient love or leave, or both, looked this way and that for a cab, either horse-drawn or propelled by gas from its balloon-like bag on top.

It is curious how the educational pendulum swings backwards and forwards: no examinations, examinations, subject examinations, general examinations, comprehensive, segregated, pass and honours, pass only, ordinary and advanced; yes, backwards and forwards as though educationists could never make up their minds. In my day Inst. was really a comprehensive school, though, with a difference; in general the financially and specially favoured boys were to be found in the non-academic business stream, while those less favoured financially were in the academic stream; and for very good reasons: the business stream was, on the whole, composed of boys whose futures were assured because their fathers were in a good way of business, and they were to follow in father's footsteps. The academics were mainly boys who had to work to carve out careers for themselves in the professions.

The result of all this was that I was soon separated from my two friends who went into the commercial " X " Forms On the first day we were assembled in the old maths block; here we were separated into forms based on the science classes, but thereafter we were taught in sets according to our supposed ability in specific subjects. I was placed in the highest sets in each subject; and, save in French and Latin, of which I had no previous experience, I had no difficulty in keeping up. In fact if anything there was a considerable overlap, especially in mathematics—this, I think, tended to make the work come too easily.

Under the old intermediate system there were four grades; preparatory, junior, middle and senior. Initially there were examinations in all four; in our time, however, the preparatory examination had been dropped, though the name was still applied to this division of the school. We began therefore in Prep. IIIa, our examination objective being the "Junior" to be taken two years later. Masters were usually known by their first names—to us I mean—though a few had nicknames, obvious ones such as Boozy and Beakey. We had Archie for maths., Johnny for English, Karl for science, Hal for French, and the ruthless, austere scholar, Bob, the principal, for Latin. None of these names was disrespectful, for all of the men mentioned were treated with profound respect, and often with affection. As the war was on, the school was, for the first time in its history, enlivened by the presence of three mistresses, though if my memory is accurate, I think they were not appointed until later, when the war's toll was beginning to make incursions into the monastic maleness of our normal existence. One of these was a sensation and she, I think, was not unaware of the sensation and of her considerable physical attractions.

Johnny was a Scot, a fine upstanding Celt, dark-haired, florid, and with a black moustache. He smoked a pipe, wielded a good bat, and he was interested in his pupils in a human way. He loved language and literature, and more than anything he loved the highest form of literary expression: poetry. He would go into rhapsodies over

> "Behold her singing in the field
> Yon solitary highland lass."

Or expressing his thoughts as he read

> "Home they brought her warrior dead
> She nor swooned nor uttered cry.
> All her maidens watching said
> She must weep or she will die."

"Boys, Ah didn't like this poem before but Ah like it noo": this is what he said as some new aspect of the poem struck him. This kind of *ad lib.* teaching carried us along with him. Indeed

I think most of his teaching was unrehearsed and unprepared, for he would sometimes say: " Ah think we'll take up geography to-day," or " Ah think we'll take up history to-day." This was before there were specialists in these subjects; and they were usually taught by the English master; on the whole they were not well taught, not even by Johnny. Geography was unscientific and history unimaginative. But a man cannot serve two masters, or three for that matter; and so Johnny's mastery of English made him an unsuitable master of the other two.

Saturday or Wednesday detentions—for minor offences " lines "—were the usual punishments. Failure to turn up for detention, or to be on detention three times in succession, made your position in the school precarious. Some masters had a favourite line; for example, Archie's was: " If you waken, call me early, call me early mother dear." Occasionally a boy would try to get away with one " call me early," but this was usually disastrous. Other boys were said to keep a stock of lines which they would be willing to sell at so much a hundred. There were others who were supposed to be able to work with two pens at once. Sometimes lines were a co-operative effort, but it was advisable to place a page in your own handwriting on top. Most of what I am saying here was hearsay, and never came within the ambit of my own experience.

Johnny rarely gave lines or put you on detention. If you annoyed him unduly he would say: " Outside ! Outside, me boy; oot an' stan' on the stair head ! " You never resented this, because you felt it was justified; but when you were on the stair head you were afraid that Bob would find you there. Johnny's influence was paramount in the school. No boy ever left without feeling that he owed a lot to Johnny, or to his right-hand man, that other Johnny of quieter demeanour, but of equal erudition and sympathetic insight.

I could write a book on the characters of our masters, but we will content ourselves with only a few of the more outstanding. Second to Johnny, no one was more impressive than Karl. He must have been a great innovator at a time when innovation in science was essential. Even when I went to the school he had

raised the status of his subject to a high level, and this the more
remarkable when one considers the fact that we were still in
the classical era, and the school was under the jurisdiction of a
classical head. Even then there were three or four laboratories,
at least two of which had appended lecture rooms.

Karl was a master of the heuristic method. He pushed it to
such limits that any cigarette—picture knowledge you might
have, had to be suppressed, lest you made some awful blunder,
such as using the name oxygen rather than "active air," before
it had been proved to the hilt that the gas was oxygen. We were
allowed to believe in the phlogiston theory until we proved
that the theory was fallacious. If you were interested Karl
was interested in you; but dare to act the fool, or to be a fool,
and you were sure to have your hair pulled while Karl said
quietly in his characteristic drawling voice: " Boy, boy, you
are a most unholy clown ! " Though his methods were slow;
though one did not accumulate a vast knowledge of facts, as
an old boy, now an eminent professor of pathology, said to me:
" Karl *did* train you to think scientifically." Years afterwards
when our paths pointed in the same direction, I found him to
be friendly and charming. We sat on the same committee
for a time; later when home on vacation I met him in
Royal Avenue: " Come up and spend an evening with us,
Crowe," he said. At the end of a pleasant evening of wining,
dining and talking I happened to mention my wife. " Good
heavens, Crowe ! " he said, " you haven't a wife, have you ? "
Somehow one never thinks of an old boy as being married ! "

" R.M." the Principal, the Head, call him what you will,
would have been a head in any society. He ruled with a rod of
iron, though he never used a rod, nor did he permit others to
do so. He was a dignified, austere scholar, and a gentleman
who never lost his dignity under any circumstances. Close
cropped grey hair, grey trimmed moustache, high collar,
bowler-hatted, and scrupulously suited, he was the epitome
of Victorian military-patterned gentility. His square jaw and
cold grey eyes gave an impression of ruthless determination,
and indeed he was both determined and ruthless. With
withering invective he could reduce the most case-hardened
boy to the consistency of a jelly-fish. Though his subject

was Latin he was able to walk into a French or German class, in the absence of the regular master, and he could teach these subjects with the most surprising facility and expertise.

"Stand up on your feet, sir! Stand up on your feet! You have not prepared your work, sir! You are a fellow of the lowest type, a gutter sparrow!" he would say in his high-pitched, controlled, incisive voice. On one occasion I heard him describe a boy as a "Jerusalem cab-driver," and on another he said to an unfortunate youth who was nervously drumming his fingers on the desk: "Get out of my class, sir. Not if you were the Prince of Wales would I tolerate such be-haviour." But slowly, inevitably, and with miraculous facility, you found yourself beginning to read Ovid, Virgil, and Cicero with facility and interest. You never dared use a key with R.M., though you did with George who was a short-sighted, fiery, Welsh Oxonian, and one whose life was contained within the boundaries of the school, rugby football and the classics.

"R.M." ruled his staff, and probably his Board of Governors, with tempered severity. Later in life I remember one of the staff telling me that on a day when he and a colleague were returning a little late from a down-town lunch, they found R.M. standing in the portals of the school; looking at his watch he said: "Gentlemen, your classes are assembled and waiting." But this mask of severity may have been assumed at a time when the headship of the school was a difficult assignment. The school had to survive and he had to survive. Stern measures were necessary, for in the days of the old heads of the schools composing the one school, there was little discipline; down-town excursions to the old Theatre Royal and other places of entertainment, during school hours, were not uncommon.

Occasionally the mask would be dropped, as on the morning following the winning of the Ulster Schools' Rugby Cup, when a benign smile would lighten the severely smooth face; and one knew that underneath lurked the spirit of the boy he must have been; underneath lurked the joy and pride in his Inst. which he had so carefully built out of the chaos of the past. And there were his parties to which we were later to be bidden either as members of the 1st XV or as prefects. Possibly to the

THE GREATEST—BILLY HALL'S TEAM, 1917-18

sophisticates of these days such parties would have been anathema. We went to them with shy reluctance, but were not sorry we *did* go, for there we found Mrs. Principal and Himself relaxed and happy. A supply of pretty girls had been conjured from somewhere; on entry you were given a flower, and then you went in search of your Rose, Lily, or Pansy, or whatever was your corresponding flower. As it happened, mine had " the softness of swansdown " and " the brightness of sunshine "; and I enjoyed the evening. In later years when I met R.M. I found him to be friendly, interested, and kindly—but more about this in a different context. As to his religious views, or views on religion, one never knew anything about this. I suspect that his ethic and attitude toward life were classical and platonic.

But to come back to my early impressions. There were three school sergeants: " Fatty," " Thinny " and the Gym. sergeant. Of the three Fatty was the most popular. He wore a shiny, peaked, crimson cap with gold braid around it, gold-braided trousers, and a frock coat. Part of his duty was to clang a large bell in the middle of the quadrangle, to indicate changes; and it was not unusual for some small boy to push his cap from behind, so that it fell over his eyes while he was in the clanging process. But he was so good-humoured that the joke fell flat after a time. He kept a tuck-shop in the lunch room which had formerly been one of the dormitories. Thinny was rather a sad-looking man who kept a tuck-shop in the quad. The technique when you were a small boy was to stay around the tuck-shop and flatter one of the seniors until he was constrained to buy you a bar of chocolate.

At " Recess " we repaired first of all to the lunch room, drank tea or milk bought with tickets, and bought as much tuck as we could afford. R.M. presided at the head of the masters' table, no doubt keeping control of the level of conversation. Throughout the room there would be a ceaseless buzz of conversation as we discussed our own affairs and the masters. Then downstairs we would run at a speed that would now give me indigestion, into the quad and across to ball alley, or rugby field, according to predilection A game reminiscent of rugby in the days of Dr. Arnold would be in progress with the whole school following one ball; if you were a junior your chances of even seeing the ball, let alone handling it, were pretty remote, none-the-less you followed on hopefully.

Soon—all too soon—clang ! clang ! clang ! and there would be an almighty rush for the long dark locker passage where, if you hadn't lost your key in the meantime, you would extract hastily from a mass—or mess—of books, papers, blotting pads, ink, and what not, an Ovid maybe, or a Hall and Stevens, or a Shakespeare; but if you were lucky you might stroll nonchalantly toward the laboratory with a whole afternoon of the search for truth in front of you, and also the certain knowledge that you need be untroubled by consciousness of those things left undone.

My first intimation of the domination of rugby football over our lives at this time was the announcement in class one day that I had been selected to play for Mr. B's. XV. This was in the days before the advent of Houses, when there was a league competition based on the English classes. Evidently I acquitted myself fairly well, for in a short time I was selected to play in a highly important fixture: Inst. Prep. *v.* Methody Prep ! During the subsequent match I happened to notice on the touch-line my tall cousin who was at that time captain of the Methody 1st XV. Oh, how anxious I was to do something brilliant ! But disaster was not far away, for I sustained a blow just above the knee; it was so painful that I was a passenger for the rest of the game. I could have wept with both chagrin and pain.

But these were my best footballing years. I was at this time physically stronger and heavier than most of the boys in my form, save one who later became an international. For a time I probably envied him, but not for long, for he was soon to become a victim of some progressive illness which killed him at an early age. A fine decent big fellow, he played and taught his beloved game to the end.

Did we win the match against Methody Prep ? I haven't the faintest idea; but the following year I was on the Medallion, under-fourteen side, and we certainly won the so-called Medallion. Toward the end of that year, as I was turning down the locker passage, a prefect member of the 1st XV stopped me and said: " Be back next year, Crowe ? " Of course I'd be back next year, if for no other reason than that this was virtually an indication that I would be a member of the 1st XV. Maybe I just came in at the tail end of the team, but what a team of which to be at the tail end ! Nothing like it had been known in the annals of the school, and it is a safe bet that nothing like it will be known again. It was captained by a great captain who later played for Ireland. He came to see me recently; we had a chat about far-off happy days: the unbeaten record, the times when we had to turn out against hulks of naval men or army teams who wanted a game at a time when there were few games to be had; the training sessions before the cup matches when we trained like profes- sionals; the strain and sweat; the wit and wetness in the old dank changing room at the end of the locker passage, or the green sweet sward, and the cold winds and colder water " up at Osborne."

The wonderful thing about this side was the confidence of the forwards in the backs, and the backs in the forwards. We forwards knew that if he heeled the ball cleanly, it would pass from " Butter " to Billy, and from Billy to Charlie, Findlay, Bobbie, or Arthur for a score, almost as if it were under remote control. This was in the days before modern spoiling tactics. The scrum was kept wide open through the centre; the outside man would hook the ball between the centre man's legs, and it would go out unimpeded.

There was a semi-final at Coleraine when they gave us a stodgy pudding before the match; most of the boys refused it and wisely, for we saw that our opponents refused it to a man. At one stage of the game everything depended on a penalty. Would it go over ? We prayed to high heaven, as though the deities had stopped in their courses to observe the happenings on a tiny plot of ground in County Antrim. Our prayers were answered, the match was won; later even a plunge into the ice-cold water of the plunge bath at this school could not cool our spirits.

And another semi-final—I think it was the following year when the Cup was again won under a different captain. Anyhow I remember " Bap " telling us how he had scored the try that won the match. The ball had come to him far down the field on the wing: said he: " Be jabers, boys, Ah saw nothin' but the line, an' Ah just ran for it ! " Run for it he did with his head down; no swerve, no dummy, no tricks of any description, thrusting, running, handing off, he forced his way through every defender by sheer power and spirit until at last he lay panting and exhausted over the line with the ball held firmly underneath.

There are those who disagree with the idea of a schools cup. They argue that it leads to too much intensive competition and rivalry between schools; that the inevitable lionizing and publicity is bad for the boys. Maybe they are right; maybe, in this day and age, television and radio tend to blow up these events to an undesirable extent. But I don't know. I at least can say that without my memories of the Schools' Cup matches, I would be poorer in mind and spirit. The old argument that playing hard games strengthens character; makes one more courageous and better prepared for the hard knocks of life, may now be at a discount. Putting all these ideas aside, however, there remains the incontrovertible fact that team games do tend to turn an otherwise lone wolf into a better mixer. I do not lay claim to have been a dedicated rugby footballer, but I believe that my school experience, with all its intensive competition, enabled me to get something into, and out of, my blood, at an early stage; so that, as I matured and to some extent grew away from an undue obsession with games, I gradually translated the past into just one more phase of life's unforgettable experiences.

I played in two finals. For weeks beforehand we trained, and trained, and trained: running, dribbling, passing, tackling, scrumming, and all the rest. Those of us who smoked gave up smoking; those of us who ate sweets gave up sweet-eating; and those of us who drank pop gave up pop-drinking. For the time being we were dedicated ascetics. Our girls, if we had any, saw little of us. We were trained by a West of Ireland man with a delicious brogue, and a taste for religion, singing, and girls. He was afterwards to become Bishop of Gibraltar with a diocese extending from Gibraltar to Naples. He loved football; we liked him, and I think he liked us.

Came St. Patrick's Day when our hearts beat under our shamrock-decorated lapels with something more than national emotion. How we got through the morning I don't know. Soon, however, we were at the Balmoral Show Grounds stripped, and ready for the fray in freshly washed yellow and black jerseys, black pants, and yellow and black stockings. Oh, the crowds and the clamour, the excitement, the ecstasy of a score, and the enjoyment when one was lost to all save the game ! And then the final whistle, and one felt oneself suddenly airborne toward the stand, where R.M. stood with the head of the opposing school, both of them with emotions barely concealed behind their headmasterly profiles. Two short speeches, the loser admitting that the best team had won, and the winner saying that the losers had put up a magnificent fight; the yellow and black-ribboned cup tram-borne amid a horde of yelling Instonians; then the sudden aftermath of exhaustion before the Common Hall celebrations on the morrow.

To end the season we played the winners of the Leinster Schools Cup—Blackrock College—and worthy opponents they were. No thought of politics or religion ever entered our minds, though in both respects most of us must have been at opposite poles; only rugby football counted, and the mere fact that at one stage of the game, in the middle of a loose maul, I heard a Goliath of a Blackrock forward shout: " Put your boots in the buggers ! " had no political rancour in it. It was commonly rumoured on our side that the 'Rock men were given a spoonful of brandy at half-time; maybe this accounted for the incitement and the language in which it was couched. We on our side were expected to insult our palates with a lump of sugar, rather than suck the traditional lemon for which we craved. Our doctor follower had a theory that sugar would increase our energy, while the lemon would have the opposite effect; but as old George, who worked for me in later years used to say:
" Aye, it's all right in theory, Docthor, but . . . ! "

My football career virtually ended with the award of colours for two years, and a black velvet and gold braided tasselled honour cap which I now proudly display to my grandsons.

Though I continued to play the game for many years afterwards I did so largely for the exercise, and for social and friendly reasons. Deep down I don't think I had any strongly-rooted ambition to become a great rugby man, even if I had possessed the necessary dedication and ability. As far as games and sports are concerned, I was never a lover of the crowded arena. Later I was to enjoy more than anything, riding alone, fishing alone, and swimming alone, or at least only in the company of one or other of my friends.

Most of what I have recounted above occurred in the midst of " the alarums and excursions of war," both civil and uncivil; and it must be difficult for any young person now, reading of the sickening and terrible slaughter of 1914-18, to believe that, with death virtually stalking at the door of every household, the little enjoyments, affairs, and excitements of life could go on without any apparent unease. Though " The Farewell to Arms " was not far away many of us at school were, in fact, under arms; and we looked forward with continuing excitement to the time when we would be fully involved.

So we joined the newly-formed Officers' Training Corps; we threw Mills bombs into barrels in front of the school; learned to shoot with .22's behind the school; attended lectures at night; performed tactical exercises against the university O.T.C.; pulled our caps back, and hoped that we might be mistaken for the real thing. But the highlight of the O.T.C. was a flax-pulling camp at Eglinton in County Londonderry. We might have been in Holland, for the camp was in a below sea-level site on reclaimed land behind a dyke. We slept in a great barn at the back of a highly prosperous farm. How well I remember the arrival, and how some of the bright boys of the advance party had already labelled the maze-like entrances and gates with the names of famous war trenches. How well I remember the rubicund sergeant, hot from the cook-house and its problems, yet always good-tempered and jolly. How I recall with some nausea the greasy, foul-tasting margarine high-piled like a yellow wall, and the cuts of meat that never came out of oxen.

The flax cut our hands to pieces and the sun burned our bare backs until the fair-skinned looked like lobsters, and tasted the

agony of severe sunburn. Sometimes we would lie down for
a rest amid the stacks until Beaky would say in his deep, round,
southern voice: " Show a leg there ! " and with a boy's
humorous literalism, a forest of legs would instantaneously
shoot up from between the flax stubble. We slept little on our
palliasses of straw on the bare boards of the barn; and the row
at nights was sometimes so bad that Hal was constrained to
leave his cups to admonish us. One night " Tichie," para-
phrasing a popular song, was singing: " Hal is coming up the
stairs, so beware ! " when, in fact, Hal did come up the stairs
to say that " Tich " would not be included in the Doctor's
party on the morrow. Whether Tich was included or not,
I cannot say, but I do remember that he was later to go to
Greypoint—the American Sandhurst—with a view to becoming an officer in the American army.

The local doctor was, as we say in Northern Ireland, " the
heart o' corn.' He had a nice house, a pretty daughter, and a
tennis court. What more could boys wish for ? We played
tennis, ate home-baked scones and pastries, and drank cup after
cup of tea, until even our youthful expansible stomachs could
hold no more; so that the night hours were disturbed for most
of us by footfalls down the creaking ladder from the loft.

Every evening we had a concert as a sort of rehearsal for our
final war-effort concert in the village hall. The wits and wags
joked, and those of us who could sing sang our rather uninspiring songs and choruses. But the event of the evening was
Sergeant's rendering of

> You may talk about écarté
> Or talk of Bonaparté,
> Or any other party,
> And commong vous portez-vous.
>   We learnt to sing it aisy
> The song of Marsillaisi.
> Tulong, Boulong, The Continong,
> We learnt at Killyloo.

Or

> There was ham and jam,
> And beer by the bucket and imported sham;

Ye never saw such a divil of jam
As there was when we all sat down.
With forks and knives
We worked away like buggers for our lives.
All the boys and the girls
And the fellows and their wives;
And we ate up 'alf the town.

His cheerful, kindly, red face and obvious bonhomie would have won for him the sympathy of any audience, even without the comicality of his songs.

Was it at these concerts, or at school concerts, that one boy, with a gift for mimicry, used to take off the Gym Sergeant, who was a very different type of man from the School Sergeant ? He had no inhibitions about describing his exploits; he was of the " old sweat " type; and made the more awkward boys feel more awkward than they were. When Bob came into his classes he was obsequious to the point of sycophancy. It was his custom, when lecturing us, to sit on a high horizontal bar; when he had finished he would show off by doing a somersault to the floor. On one occasion, when R.M. came in unexpectedly, he jumped from the bar, lost his balance, and was unable to gain control before hitting the wall at the rear with his *rear*. The mimicry—not much of an exaggeration— went something like this: " Now I said to Kitchener, I said, why not 'ave block'ouses ? An' Kitchener 'e said: " Good idea '; so block'ouses we 'ad; an' that's 'ow I 'elped to win the Boer War I did." Once I heard him say to a boy who complained of a minor hurt: " W'en I was in the Boer War I got wounded; but I wouldn't 'ave no doctors messin' abaht me; I let it 'eal up itself I did."

Maybe in those days, when death stalked the land, and when the death of a boy was commoner than now, the fact that a boy was taken to Derry hospital never to come out again alive, shocked us less than now, but the incident and the sorrow for the parents still stands out very clearly. Many years later there was to be an even greater tragedy which I still associate with this camp. This was the tragedy of one who was to take the life of a fellow man. He was, without doubt, the most

SOMEWHERE IN DERRY, 1917

conscientious of N.C.O's; he considered it his duty to report boys for smoking the butt-end of a cigarette behind the barn wall at night; and he would refuse all additions to his rations, because he thought he ought to live hard and work hard for the war effort. The army was in his blood and soon he was to be commissioned. The last time I met him he was a sun-bronzed young officer lately returned from one of those little expeditions to Russia soon after the ending of the 1914-18 war. One can only imagine the Brutus or Hamlet-like soliloquies that must have gone through his mind before doing what I am sure he felt constrained to do, because of some obsessive sense of mistaken duty. He had committed a terrible crime in the eyes of the law, but I feel sure his conscience was crystal clear; as clear, in fact, as the conscience of a man might have been if he had shot Hitler.

Then came one of the most dramatic days in history; it spelled the end of the war, and of the Inst. Officers' Training Corps as such. We were paraded in front of the school for an inspection by a " brass hat " from the War Office, prior to the distribution of .303 rifles. But the red-flashed officer, instead of inspecting us, announced that the instrument of armistice had just been signed by the representatives of the German High Command. Whether it was mutiny or not I don't know, but we broke ranks and went on our several ways; and a new world had begun.

Before going forward into this new world let us go back to Inst. to have one last look at the general picture of the school as it was in our time. I have mentioned the classical, literary and scientific sides; but what about the arts ? Art as such was something of a dead letter. We were taught formal drawing and design, but nothing of colour, nor of picture-making. We were shown none of the great art of the past— not even pictures of great pictures, nor of great works of sculpture, nor were we taught anything of the history of art. This is all the more surprising when one remembers that " Daddy," who taught us, was himself a local noted artist, and an actor of considerable merit and local fame.

The subject was taught at the far end of the commercial department and room. Its importance may be gauged by this fact for it was the only subject to be taught in a room in which at least one other class was conducted. This other class was presided over by the Head of the Commercial Department. He also rejoiced in the nickname of " Daddy." When a boy at the far end of the room was troublesome this Daddy would look down over the top of his spectacles and call out: " Send that boy up to me Mr. X, and I'll put him on detention ! " But both Daddies were popular, Daddy the Head in particular, for he had a son, an erstwhile captain of the first XV who, now an officer on leave, travelled with us to some of the cup matches. At one of these I remember him bemoaning the fact that he had wasted so many years of his life before he knew the taste of beer !

As to that holy art which was often to console me in years to come, " While life's wild tumult surged across my way," it was given scant attention, partly because of a theory in those days that a boy's education in song should cease, for a time at least, when a crack in his voice first heralded the onset of manhood. We were taught singing by an excellent musician, unison songs only, whereas at the national school we learned part songs. However, this man did try to interest us in music in a more academic way; and I well remember his playing " Der Erl König " to show us how difficult of accomplishment was the accompaniment to this great Schubert lieder. Once he came in to another class to talk to me about my voice with a view to asking me to sing at a school concert in the Ulster Hall. I don't think this came about, so that I had to wait until some time later before making my debut in front of the school; and this only after my boy's soprano voice had changed to a baritone.

There were school concerts at which we sang the usual unison songs from the " National Song Book," and there were performances of plays such as " She Stoops to Conquer " and the trial scene, " Bardell v. Pickwick." " Daddy " sang Irish folk songs in an Irish folk song way, his great piece being " I know my love by her way o' walking." This always brought down the house, not altogether because we appreciated it, but because we thought it was funny. But the first real non-academic concert I can remember was a war fund-raising effort in the Common Hall. One of my contemporaries, who was to become a lifelong friend, conducted a creditable school orchestra, and I created something of a sensation with my rendering of " The Deathless Army " and " The Company Sergeant-Major," both of them popular choices at a time when deathless armies, and even company sergeants-majors were highly significant. At the end of the concert a pretty girl whom I knew, and who hadn't taken much notice of me before, asked me to leave her home; and so for the first time I realized that the possession of a baritone voice could be an asset in more ways than one. But more important still, on the following morning that splendid man, the sergeant, made a point of speaking to me on the way into school. He complimented me on my singing, told me how and what I should practise, and ended by telling me that if I continued in the way I was going, one day I would be singing in grand opera ! Though I never did sing in opera—grand or otherwise—his words had a profound effect: I continued to sing, giving great pleasure to myself, and some to others, I hope; I learned a lot of poetry and this led to verse-writing; and I found that the trained voice could be of inestimable value in the profession I was ultimately to enter. All of which goes to show that the right word at the right time can do more good to the youthful mind than a mint of criticism.

Looking back through the years, I can see that Inst. had many virtues and some faults. On the virtues side I think its most outstanding feature was the spirit that permeated the school throughout; loyalty on the part of staff and pupils was its theme note; and those unpleasant vices which so often sully relationships between master and boy, and between boys even in day schools, appeared to be quite absent. Political and religious tolerance was respected and practised by all; though I do remember considerable, but open, arguments between J.B. and a boy who was afterwards to become something of a B.B.C. and literary critic. This same boy was a great sponsor of another fiery-tempered southerner whose uncle had been shot in the rebellion. Sometimes the fiery southerner would come to blows with others of a different outlook; a ring would be formed, and one can recall a picture of the blood-bespattered rebel with collar

awry,—aided and abetted by his sponsor,—shouting imprecations
and inviting his opponent to come on now and he'd knock the
block off him. Save for this one instance I cannot think of any
serious differences, and this one was, as much as anything else,
an excuse for two pugnacious boys to have a bout of fisticuffs.

Educationally the school was sound save that on the literary
side the classics tended to take precedence, and I think most old
boys would admit that they spent more time on classical
home work than on any other; and there was no regulation
of home work; you could be set enormous quantities in some
subjects and none in others. Also there was nothing in the
nature of a tutorial or form-master system. Some boys were
marked for notice almost as soon as they entered, either because
they had scholarships, or a father who was a leader in the
Church, or a well-known professional or business man. For
the rest there was little or no guidance or interest; no one to
whom you could turn for help at a time when you needed it
most: when you were young, and before you had made a name
for yourself either in sport or in some other way. R.M., for
all his greatness, was not very approachable; and, while there
was no corporal punishment the element of fear was not
absent; but whether or not fear can ever be eliminated from
school life is a moot point.

Unfortunately—or fortunately perhaps—I have always
tended to give up certain things just when I have become most
fully involved. I gave up music—or was compelled to give it
up—when I had reached the readiness phase; much to my
Latin master's disgust I gave up Latin just when I was beginning
to come to grips with it; and I gave up Inst. when I had begun
to settle down, and when a year or two more might have made
all the difference. On the other hand who is to say what might
have been best for us? Life is full of cross-roads; take one or the
other or go straight on; which is best ? We don't know ; nor can
we ever tell. The fact that I gave up many things at the flood-
tide of their usefulness enabled me to gain time and experience.
One must remember also that it was quite usual in those days
for boys to join a matriculation class, and go on to the university
at an early age. Besides, the war had unsettled many of us;

we had become men before our time, and we wanted a man's status.

So when a friend said to me in the spring of the year: " What about having a go at the Matric ? " I acquiesced with alacrity. We told our masters what we wished to do; they raised no objections, gave us a few extra classes, and helped us in our reading. And so for days, weeks—months maybe—the two of us got together of an evening and quizzed each other about light, and heat, the working of pumps, the Principle of Archimedes and various other physical phenomena. And all this while I was camping out with another friend. From the time when the first blink of summer sunshine began to warm the landscape, he and I went under canvas in his large tree-lined garden where we might well have been in the heart of a jungle. Here I had the best of both worlds: peace when I wanted to work, and that other peace which has always meant so much to me: trees, flowers, the smell of clean air and of wind from the willows.

And of all things my matric. friend, or his father, possessed a motor-car, which my friend drove. Few boys had the use of a car in those days, so that for me it was a thrill to be driven around " the back road " under the great trees overhanging Knock Hill, along the Braniel Glen, past Cregagh. How we crossed the Lagan river in those days I don't know because there was no King's Bridge. However, we got there and the upshot of it was that, to our surprise, when the results of this supposedly difficult competitive examination came out, we had passed without reservation. Thus the autumn of that year saw three of us in a different quadrangle, not the city-centered dark one of the old days, but a green, sun-splashed one surrounded by the bright terra-cotta of mid-Victorian Gothic. Soon we were to go our separate ways: one to engineering, one to medicine, and myself to pure science.

And so we lay there dreaming our separate dreams while the fates stood by pointing the roads leading this way and that toward our individual destinies.

CHAPTER V

QUEEN'S MEN

A T last I had come home. Here in the university I found the sort of intellectual experience for which I had always craved. Here one was a man, even though only a " freshman." I realized this for the first time when a " man " I knew came across the quadrangle, clapped me on the shoulder, and asked would I or any of the other men with me join the O.T.C. Suddenly I felt I was free to make my own decisions and my own choices. I could light a pipe without taking a hasty look around to see that I was not being observed by someone set in authority. I and my friends could discuss every and any subject, moral, immoral, religious, atheistical, political, or surversive, if we wished, without keeping an ear cocked to make sure we weren't being overheard. There was nobody to say you must or ought to do this or that. Nobody implied that it was a moral duty to play football, to join the O.T.C., or to take part in any activity. You could decide to join in anything, or in nothing, and nobody thought the worse of you. While my school was remarkably free of compulsion in most matters, moral pressure was certainly brought to bear, and you were made to feel out of it if you weren't in it, whatever *it* might be.

On that first day there was the usual coming and going of men and women in and out of the office, and across the green sward to departments, union, library or other places where they could fill in forms, meet the deans, consult with friends, and make decisions. I went to the university to study chemistry because I had shown an interest in the subject. My father thought it would be a good subject; as he said " in the future only men of learning, especially technical learning, would get to the top." For my part I was attracted because of all the scientific subjects, it was the most colourful and romantic; and it was one that seemed to enter so much into the literature

70

of the day. With such an outlook it would have been impossible to have been placed under the guidance of a more stimulating professor. During my first year, as well as chemistry, I decided to study mathematics, physics and zoology. Maybe if I had known what the future held in store for me I might have been wiser to have taken another mathematical subject—maths. physics as it was then called—but I had no faith in myself as a mathematician; and I was greatly attracted toward any subject that had to do with life. Anyhow, as I said before, we cannot foretell the future, nor can we be sure that any decision, other than the one we took at the time, would necessarily have been better for us. Besides, I found that my whole outlook was enormously affected by this one year of zoological study; and I would not have missed this intellectual experience for anything.

The Queen's University of Belfast, in which I was now a student, was at this time a compact and attractive looking quadrangleular, cloistered, college building in what was formerly, and still is to a large extent, a residential part of the city. There were grass tennis courts in front and green lawns all around, while the surrounding houses mainly occupied by leading professional men were, for the most part, either Georgian, Regency, or early Victorian showing Georgian influence. Near by were the Botanic Gardens, The Methodist College, and the classical-looking Assembly's College of the Presbyterian Church; on the whole, one might say, a charming district in which to live and to study.

The three Queen's Colleges, constituent colleges of the Queen's University of Ireland, were founded during one of the most devastating times in Ireland's turbulent history. They were founded in 1846, in the midst of the terrible potato famine, by the Government of Sir Robert Peel, but were not opened to students until 1849. Queen's College, Belfast, was designed by the eminent architect, Sir Charles Lanyon, and is considered by many to be one of the finest examples of Tudor revival in these islands. After the dissolution of the Queen's University of Ireland, the Royal University of Ireland was formed as an examining body, so that from 1882 it was customary for Queen's students to sit for R.U.I. degrees. This state

of affairs persisted until 1908 when Queen's was granted its charter as an independent university.

Red brick university maybe, but one with a difference. Not only is it different in the beauty of its design and surroundings, but also in the loyalty of its students, in its intimacy with the city which gave it birth, and in the power and drive of its social and athletic life. I say this without reserve in spite of criticisms to the contrary. It is all too easy to make the jibe that, because the university is younger, it could not possibly have the social life, nor give the intellectual background supposed to be the special prerogative of the older institutions. I have also heard people state, often those who had never been to a university either old or young, that Queen's was a sort of glorified technical college in which examinations were the only matter of importance. Of course examinations are important; they are important in all universities; and the older colleges are as quick as any others in getting rid of students who do not come up to standard. As to the other criticisms, one has only to examine the facts: when I was at Queen's it could turn out a rugby side often as good as the older universities with a multi-college system, and usually much better than the average provincial university side. The same was true of its hockey and athletic teams.

Queen's was in the van of the universities willing to admit women as potential graduates; this from a very early stage had an immediate stimulating effect on its social life. When I was there you could have attended a well organized ball or dance as often as you wished, or at least as often as you could afford to pay for such frivolities. There were frequent lectures by the great men of the day, and debating in the Union or other societies was as light-hearted, as witty, or as serious as in most university societies.

Being a young college, it could be catholic in its appointments; its dons hailed from universities all over the world, and there was a succession of distinguished Vice-Chancellors, each with a fresh contribution to make. Standards of teaching and of research were very high; and indeed the number of men and women students who afterwards became distinguished and

Queens' College Belfast.

GEORGIAN PILE AND GOTHIC STYLE
Inst., 1842 and Queen's, 1861

great in their particular fields was, I should say, higher than average.

At that time there were only limited residential facilities for men. While there is much to be said for these, I think the advantages can be over-estimated. Though few of us lived together, we still found it possible to talk and argue and discuss all that was important to us and to the world in general. Maybe we didn't have sufficient contact with other faculties, but we did meet from time to time in the Union or at social functions, or even in our own homes and districts. Anyhow it could be argued that students meeting none other than students is not a good thing; it could lead to a burying of the mind in a cloistered graveyard of academic interests.

Unfortunately the student life in the Queen's I entered tended to be ruled by men much older than most of us; men who had come through the terrible events of the first world war; these men were experienced, sophisticated, sometimes cynical, and they tended to take the lead in much that otherwise would have fallen to our lot. While tolerance prevailed at school, I am not sure that this was true of the college in which one would normally have expected more of this particular virtue. Once there was trouble between Roman Catholics— or Republicans if you like—and ex-service men; and on another occasion South African students objected to the presence of coloured men in the Union; this led to a public scandal. Thus the troubles, the intolerances, the differences and the indifferences of the present are merely the sad heritage of the past, and they are not in any sense peculiar to our time.

This was my campus then; this the threshold to my particular renaissance. Here for good or ill was the real beginning of the great adventure of life. What I did here must affect my whole future. I am not so sure that the first seven years determine as much as we are wont to think. Certain environmental habits and traits may have their foundation then, but the habits themselves are not as important as the way they are used; I believe that university years, or the years following school life, may be extremely important, not only in their effect on one's career, but also as regards one's whole outlook on life. First, second, or third class, or merely pass degrees: of course these are of vital concern, but ever more important is our attitude toward life. Are we to become tolerant or intolerant, just or unjust, thoughtful or thoughtless, reasonable or unreasonable ? These are traits and attributes which may be influenced enormously by those who teach, inspire, and direct at a time when intelligence is unfolding to grasp life in its entirety.

My first lecture ! We were nicely seated in the chemistry lecture theatre when there was a ripple which grew into a tidal wave; willy-nilly one was borne forward until the surge reached the lecture bench when the new professor of chemistry was caught up on the crest of the wave, swept out to a hand-cart on which he was joyously wheeled down to Shaftesbury Square, then up the other side and back to the University where, with great good humour, he made a little speech in which he exhorted all of us to work hard; if we did the relationship between him and us would be excellent. As my relationship with this small, dark-haired, dark-moustached, keen-eyed man was to become very close in following years I shall not describe him in any greater detail at this stage.

His laboratory assistant was a tall grey-haired, elderly, retired member of the police force. He had a drooping moustache, spoke with a brogue, and wore steel-rimmed pince-nez which also drooped. He had, I believe, been a detective-sergeant who had been spotted by the professor's predecessor when doing some forensic analytical work. In those days John was responsible for a good deal; in particular he was always present during lectures ; I still have a mental picture of him behind the lecture bench gazing lugubriously at condenser or retort, anxious less some potent mixture might become unduly violent, thereby upsetting the well-planned lecture scheme. From time to time he would glance upwards to make sure no violent upset of a different kind was brewing among some of the more recalcitrant first medicals or engineers at the back of the lecture theatre. It was only in later years I found out that John's domestic life was far from happy; that he had a bed-ridden wife but could, none-the-less, smile at a joke, was regarded as a " dear " by the lady students, enjoyed a bottle of stout, was a philosopher, could give one a tip about the work now and again; and was devotedly loyal to the laboratory, and to those who were set in authority over him. Though he was a kindly man who understood students and their difficulties, he never allowed his kindness to outweigh his loyalty to his masters.

I always found lectures in chemistry interesting, maybe because I was always interested in chemistry. But this was not the only reason; the professor concerned, in spite of a poor delivery, had a remarkable flair for interposing interesting material which he presented in an exciting way with the aid of a series of illustrations, analogies, experiments, and details about the times of the great men of science, such as Sir William Ramsey to whom he had been personal assistant.

Anyhow, he gradually built up in my mind a developing picture of the evolution of matter. Taking up a piece of chalk one day he said: " If we could tap it, there's enough energy in this piece of material to drive all the machinery in the city." Perhaps these were not his exact words, but they illustrate the point: he was forecasting the possible release of the energy of the atom. In those days we thought this was just a Wellsian dream which would not come true in our lifetime. But it did come true under the most terrible and tragic conditions.

Not only did I get a conception of the evolution of matter in the Department of Chemistry, but a picture of organic evolution was a little later to be built up by a man of rather different calibre, the Professor of Zoology. How well I remember this big, grey, Scot, with his powerful voice and martial manner, telling us at the outset that evolution was something more than a vague theory; it was an established idea on which the whole of the science of zoology was built up. Scientists did not differ in this belief though they might differ in the attitudes toward the mechanism of evolution. Here indeed was an explosive impact on minds hitherto nurtured on the strict biblical account. How could these two ideas be reconciled ? Whether all this led to my conversion, or whether the natural development of my expanding mind would, anyhow, have led me toward a new concept of the universe I shall never know. But for the first time I realized that I could be free to hold or discard beliefs according to the dictates of my own mind, and not according to conditioning by minds other than mine. It occurred to me also that a belief or a disbelief honestly, sincerely, and intelligently held, is something of which one need never feel ashamed or frightened. Not only this, but one must be prepared to judge the ideas of others only on their merits, never according to some pre-conceived dogma.

Physics did not make a great impact at this stage, though each of the lectures was a carefully prepared work of art delivered by a lecturer of great ability; he was bland and jovial; but there was not quite the same human touch that one found in the department on the other side of the quadrangle. The professor was above us, beyond us and out of our reach. In the chemical department men smoked pipes; they lounged on the benches; they talked about every subject under the sun. You could laugh and talk; flirt with the girl students; and throw your broken glassware into the waste-box with a resounding tinkle. But in physics, those who smoked, smoked cigarettes. People talked about beautiful experiments and about little else. In fact you were afraid to talk at all in case you upset some delicate instrument. You rarely broke any-thing; when you *did* you felt you had destroyed the whole routine of a carefully catalogued organization. In short, there was a total absence of life and humanity about this cold, robot-inhabited wilderness. At this stage and time the subject seemed to be too mechanical to affect one's way of thinking; you touched the lever at one end and something completely predictable happened at the other; the uncertainty principle, quantum statistics, relativity and all that just weren't in the picture; it was only in later years that such ideas began to make their full impact.

Happiness is such a vague term that I hesitate to use it in a general sense. At any stage of one's life there are periods of happiness and periods of unhappiness. When we talk about this or that time being happy or unhappy, what we really mean is that, looking back, the periodicity of the one seems greater than the periodicity of the other. Though my undergraduate life was punctuated with many happy occasions, I cannot say with honesty that these predominated. Lack of money, shortage of time, and the ever-present imminency of examinations meant that one was unable to participate fully in under-graduate activities. Living at some distance, and having to travel by train, tram, on foot, or all three, made heavy inroads on one's time and energies.

I continued to play rugby football. Before I had time to think about it I had joined the newly-formed Instonians, composed largely of those of us who had played together at school. Here again distance presented a difficulty, for the grounds were situated at the other extreme of the city. It seemed to be my fate to be a member of cup-winning sides; that year we won the junior competition, and the next the senior. Though my own contribution to the game was becoming more and more desultory by this time, I was selected to play in the Bateman Cup competition which was open to the winners of the Ulster, Leinster, and Munster Cups.

And so for the first time for a great many years I found myself in Dublin, the city with which we had so much, and yet so little, association since our earliest years. And what a city it was then ! As one walked down from Amiens Street to the " Pillar " one suddenly saw the devastated shell of what used to be described as the finest street in Europe. As I walked down Sackville Street, now O'Connell Street, I got the impression, in spite of the ruins, of a great street in a great city. " A sad city," thus spake an Anglo-Irish friend to me who had been in Dublin at about the same time. Strangely enough I didn't get this impression, maybe because of the irresponsibility of youth; all that was happening was part of the great adventure. Staying as we were in front of Westland Row station, we could hear firing going on all around us throughout the night; and, at one stage, Sam Brown-belted men demanded drinks in the bar of the hotel, literally at the point of the revolver. We played Lansdowne on the first day: the match went on in spite of the fact that a Lansdowne man had been shot on his own doorstep that morning. Exhausted, bruised, and with one or two of our key men suffering from minor injuries, we were no match for the giants of Cork Constitution on the following day, and so we lost the opportunity of carrying home the prized Bateman Cup to the North.

I cannot remember much about examinations during my first year except that I passed all of them without much difficulty; and from then on my course seemed to be set on calmer seas.

Invigilation fees, coaching and tuition fees, and studentships were soon to ease the financial strain both for me and my parents. There would be only two examinations in second year, in the so-called "subsidiary" subjects. I had chosen to continue with physics and to do geology which in those days could be done in one year—as the additional subject. The rest of the time could now be spent on my first love—chemistry.

And one had now become a part of the department; this was easy when relatively small laboratories were such intimate places. You joined the Tea Club; you joined the Chemical Society; you went to the Christmas Party; and you danced at the departmental dances; and, when money and time allowed, at the dances of other departments and clubs. And in those days dances were quite formal affairs: you wore evening dress or the nearest approach to it; and you filled in your programme beforehand, keeping the maximum number of spaces for the lady of your choice. You wore white gloves out of respect for your partner's hands; and your partner *was* your partner; you held her close to you; you paid her compliments; and you tried to make her smile by the brilliancy of your wit; and all this against the background of reasonably soft and sentimental music. But don't imagine there was no gaiety ! Of course there was ! From time to time the lights would be reduced to a soft red, and the music would become more sentimental; and then suddenly up would go the lights, and so would the balloons, and your partner would lean lightly against you to recover her breath; or, if you were lucky, she might suggest that "we sit the next one out" in some gently lit alcove. Then there would be the long journey home, by taxi if you could afford it, or at least by tram. Whichever way it was there was always the hope of romantic adventure at the garden gate !

One night coming home from a dance in the open back of a tram we two looked at each other, and we knew from that moment, for better or for worse, our lives would be inextricably joined together. From then on it would be two against, or *with,* whichever way you like to put it, the world. There followed the brilliantly hot summer of 1921. Subsidiary subjects over, we explored June-kissed meadows of the County

Down together; and later were to meet on the sun-heated rocks of the North Antrim coast. Whether or not at this stage we dreamed dreams for the future, I don't know, but certain it is that with the curious inexplicable intuition of youth, we knew that however our roads might divide for a little, sooner or later they would unite for ever. And so as we watched the clear blue waves wash up the warm white sands, or break into a million sparkling tears against the hard basaltic rocks, we wondered how many of our dreams would roll in on the flood-tide of fortune, or how many would break in tears against the rocks of life.

And on that hot summer, too, there were four of us who went about together talking about everything under the sun with all the flippancy and ebullience of youth. Two of us were budding chemists, one a lawyer on the threshold, and the other an embryonic professor of pathology. As Sir William Ramsey wrote in a letter to his wife: " Here we are in Paris: a lawyer, a doctor, and a chemist, a fearful compound, like $N\ Cl^3$ liable to explode at any moment." Not being in Paris we didn't have the opportunity to explode, but we swam, played tennis, golf and bowls and talked far into the night under the star-spangled aurora-lit-sky on that never-to-be-forgotten Italian-like summer which once visited the North Antrim coast in the days of our youth.

But this idyllic scene was soon to end. The long haul to the finals was in front; and a city was in turmoil. Throughout the long nights of study the guns rarely ceased—at least not until after curfew time. We went to university in trams wired-in as a protection against hand grenades. Burning buildings, with firemen trying to control the flames, was a sight that most of us witnessed on our way from station to college. Dances would last all night long, and if one were a little late in returning home at night, one might have to make a hasty dive for cover on hearing the sound of the patrolling armoured car. Men were shot in the streets; men were shot in trams; and sometimes trams had to make a rickety dash down a long street under full power. This happened once when my mother decided that she must risk the bad areas to reach York Street station. I accompanied her and, mission accomplished, we had to run the gauntlet of York Street for the second time. " Heads down ! " they said, " for there's firing," and firing there was as we made the dash past the sand-bagged streets, and the steel-helmeted troops crouched over rifles and machine guns.

In spite of it all, however, I enjoyed this last year. Whether one was selected to do " honours," or whether the decision was one's own I cannot say; for my part I decided that if I couldn't manage an honour degree at the end of three years, I would be no more likely to be fit for it at the end of four, and so I buckled down to the task in hand: I had to, for I was no scientific genius; there was nothing for it but sweat and tears. I took good notes; I read the professor's extremely readable *Recent Advances* from cover to cover; and, more important to me than anything, I made my own notes. After long hours in the laboratory I would work until the hours changed from big to small, and sometimes big again. But in many ways those were happy days; you had reached the final rungs of the ladder; and you felt you had mastered the climb.

I was lucky in my teachers and tutors; and I was given every opportunity to teach. I was appointed a Student Demonstrator which meant that I gained experience in the organization and conduct of practical classes, and I had no fees to pay. Maybe this year or the next I was given tutorials—more grist to the mill ! but of greater importance these enabled me to get to know how little I knew, and with this realization of my fundamental ignorance—or ignorance of fundamentals—I came to fill in the gaps and so build my knowledge on better foundations. Five people were responsible in those days for the teaching of chemistry to hundreds of medicals, engineers, and pure science students: a professor, a lecturer, and three assistants on a three-year temporary basis. They went to great pains to help us through the mazes of inorganic, organic, physical and analytical chemistry. They all became good friends, and friends I missed very much when I went to other places.

But it wasn't all work and no play during those years. If you had to live in a city, Belfast was in some respects an ideal city in which to live. Standing in its centre, the hills were all around, with the sea a few miles away. Within the hour, or less, you could be in the bluebell-carpeted woods, or along the Lagan towpath, or down by the sea in places where you could imagine yourself on a desert island. Sometimes we would go in groups on picnics to the sea's edge, the primrose-dotted hills, or the meadow-margined woods. How we made the trip I don't know: possibly on bicycles, or maybe by train or bus; one or two had motor bikes and side-cars, but few of us had access to cars, parental or otherwise. We were not accoutred with stoves and other picnic accessories; there seemed to be no limit to the amount of dry timber lying about in those days. The boys gathered sticks and lit the fires, while the girls made tea or did whatever other chores were necessary. We bathed; danced around the fire; sang and played games. Those who had formed attachments drifted away to the quiet places. Permissive were they? I don't think so—not many would have gone beyond the bounds of the proprieties of the day: furtive petting, perhaps, but there it ended for most, and the joy it gave them was sufficient. Drinking in any form—even beer drinking—was almost unknown in our set at least, and it was quite unnecessary; for our young bodies acted in such harmony that pleasure came easily and without the aid of stimulants or sedatives. In spite of the carnage of 1914-18, in spite of the Civil War, hope was always with us. It seems to me that in this you have the difference between our young generation and the present young generation; does it lie in this lack of hope for the future, and the future of mankind? Is this a fair judgment, or am I merely depicting my own changing state of mind?

The dissemination of culture of one sort or another may be more widespread in these days; but even in such a remote provincial city as Belfast, in the period about which I am writing, social pleasures and pleasures of the mind were more easily attained than they are now. Travel and accommodation were cheap, and so many of the best repertory companies, opera companies, Shakespearian companies, comedy companies, and variety stars, would have a season in the city's theatres from time to time. As one grew older Saturday night rarely passed without at least a visit to " The Gods " at the Opera House. The other day in conversation with an old friend he asked me did I remember the night three of us went to see "Charlie's Aunt," and I laughed so hard that I had the whole of The Gods laughing with me ! My best friend and I never missed a season of the old Ulster Literary Theatre. How many times we saw Sam Waddell's " The Drone " I don't know; but on each occasion we laughed our heads off at the apparent incompetency of the drone-like Daniel who, in the end, turned out to have " a great head on him."

Every year there was an excellent season of Gilbert and Sullivan. When you could afford it you took your girl to one of the productions, or possibly to the latest musical comedy— " The Maid of the Mountains " and later, " Showboat," were our favourites. You bought her a box of chocolates and, if some financial miracle had happened, you took her out to supper at one of the many inexpensive, but clean and roomy, cafés with which the city abounded in those days. I don't say this happened very often—perhaps not more than once a term—but it was a red-letter night to which we looked forward for weeks beforehand, and which gave us pleasure until the next time.

I knew one man who could quote Shakespeare by both the linear and poetic foot. He was a businessman with no academic attainments; he told me he learned it all sitting in " The Gods " at the Belfast Opera House. My own introduction to the theatre from pantomime to Shakespeare and grand opera, is owed to the same source. Ibsen, Shaw, Wilde, and many others: I had scarcely heard of them until I saw their names on the Grand Opera House posters, and was therefore impelled to spend a " bob," or whatever it was, on buying a seat on the hard steps of " The Gods." There were celebrity concerts in the Ulster Hall at which many of the world's great singers were presented; but these were relatively expensive; so that we were unable to attend them until later years brought a little prosperity. It may seem strange to younger people that so much did go on when the city was involved in troubles far worse than any that have occurred in recent years.

I remember the professor on his rounds one day saying how difficult it was for us having to face final examination at a time when the bullet and the bomb were so much a part of daily life.

However, face them we did and, with that strange perversity of human nature, adversity increased our determination. Anyhow only the stout-hearted would have survived final examinations in chemistry such as they were then; possibly they require an equally tough response now. It wasn't so much the theoretical papers: you could do the questions or you could not; having done them, however, you knew that what you had written was reasonably correct. But the practical examinations, lasting for the greater part of a week, were very different. Here one slip, one inaccuracy, one piece of ill-luck, could make a marginal difference sufficient to affect one's whole career. You were meant to go out for food at some stage; in fact there were one or two days when I ate nothing. I could not face such an ordeal now; in youth, however, there is a reserve account of strength which becomes overdrawn in later life.

We were told the results would be posted on the Saturday in the late afternoon. How did I spend that day? I haven't the faintest idea now. I cannot remember being unduly perturbed. What was the use? You had done your best. Nothing very serious had happened to put you down. If you only got a third or a pass, what of it? There was nothing you could do about it anyhow; and if the worst came to the worst, well you would just have to think again about your career. These were the thoughts, the doubts, and the uncertainties that must have gone through my mind, and the minds of some of my contemporaries.

Anyhow, on that rather dull June afternoon I strolled across the quadrangle, looking nonchalant I hope, but no doubt with reluctance, toward the laboratory door. The quad looked deserted and lonely. Suddenly I, too, felt deserted and lonely; I felt like somebody caught naked in the glare of a searchlight; this was the moment of truth; I was on my own. I was like one about to be shot—nothing could save me. I must walk toward that door; I must read my fate on that piece of white paper; fifty yards from the entrance, thirty, twenty, ten; I was there; a few others were gathered around. Congratulations, Crowe, a first!

Was I jubilant—elated? Feelings are difficult to remember. We certainly did not rush off to the nearest pub. to celebrate.

Those of us who felt we had something to celebrate did meet some time later for a meal and a visit to the theatre. My immediate reaction was a very sober one: I must get home to let my parents know; and above all I must send off a telegram to the one person who, I knew, would be most interested. Then there was the inevitable aftermath: a certain feeling of humility: was it worth it all? Was I worth it? It was only the end of the beginning. What difference would it make anyhow? I still had my life to lead; and I doubted if the possession of a fairly high intellectual qualification would, necessarily, make that life any happier or more successful.

Celebration! What better celebration than the one in front of me? My friend and I had been invited to London, Folkstone and Belgium. Now I would be able to go with a joyful heart, a clear conscience, and money in my pocket. In London we were taken to see all the usual sights which, to me then were unusual but which were soon to become as familiar as Castle Junction. And, of course, we were taken to the theatre for my friend's brother-in-law, with whom we stayed, was theatre mad; he was, in fact, brother of the famous and popular West End actress, Hilda Trevelyan. God bless the memory of this pair just lately settled after surviving all the perils of the first world war; she as a nurse and he as a R.F.C. pilot. With what interest and generosity they brought us to theatre, concert, and music hall, up the river and, in fact, to everything in which they thought two young men would be, or ought to be, interested.

From the gaiety of Ostend to the post-war desolation of Ypres. There we stayed in a wooden shack hotel. It was like living in the Wild West. Each night the local and foreign searchers after the gold of reconstruction would come in to drink beer, wine, or absinthe. We drank the first two; you couldn't do anything else, for the water was undrinkable; in the heat we often longed for a glass of cool clear water. Ypres was much as the war had left it; the Cloth Hall and the other famous buildings had been blown out of existence or were mere shells. All around were the famous trenches, salients, and all the rest, so pock-marked that in places the land looked like the moon's face. Gas masks and accoutrements of one sort or another still lay in trenches, some of which were to be preserved for future sightseers and tourists. On the day we arrived a fête was in progress to raise funds for the remnants of a local family, some members of which had been decimated by an unexploded shell which had gone off while they were at work.

We were taken to Vimy Ridge to see the great volcanic-like craters where General Plummer's men had blown up the mines that had taken months to construct under the German lines. But what interested me more than anything was the extraordinary persistence and courage with which the Belgians had set about restoring their devastated country. I remember talking to one lonely Flemish-speaking peasant up in the bare, barren, at this time, almost uninhabited region of " Hill 60 "; there he was working away with the most primitive implements in an effort to restore his one plot of earth.

Our host was an ex-officer who seemed to be held by some strange attraction to the place where he had witnessed so much fear and horror. He and his brother between them ran a garage; they drove tourists to the battle-fields, and bereft parents to see their sons' graves. He was engaged to my friend's sister, none-the-less I cannot help reflecting now on his extraordinary decency and generosity. He took us by car to most places, and he had contacts everywhere; in Belgian chateaux, in Bruges, Brussels, and Ostend. In Brussels we went to the Trier Nationale where the terrible tragedy of the shooting of Nurse Cavell had been enacted. There appeared to be heated arguments with the Belgians from time to time about the part of our respective countries in the war; and I can remember one Belgian explaining with vehemence that Nurse Cavell wasn't the only one; that there was a number of Belgian women suffered the same fate. In those days even heroism was a matter for international jealousy and rivalry.

Soon, but not too soon, I think, for we had our girls to see, we were once again streaming up in the misty hours between the sweet hills of Down on the one side, and " The Blue Hills of Antrim " on the other—the peaceful gateway to a city still far from peaceful, as I was soon to discover. It was customary in those days before the advent of universal motoring for a Belfast family to migrate to the coast, maybe for a month.

two months or three. My future finacée's family on this particular summer had made their usual migration to the little County Down village of Groomsport, famous as the landing place of Schomberg on his way to join William III of Orange at the fateful—and for Schomberg fatal—Boyne. But Groomsport deserves a place in the annals for other reasons, which I shall explain later. Anyhow, I was to lose no time in making my way to this pleasant little seaport; for the purpose I borrowed my future brother-in-law's motor cycle which he, with characteristic generosity, was only to pleased to lend.

With the time-ignoring recklessness of all young lovers since time began, I stayed until my fair one bade me haste on my way; and so, with throttle full open, I roared through Bangor and soon was lost in the autumn mist-filled heights of the Holywood hills. The darkness of night came down and the inevitable happened, the bike stopped. Hearing a patrol in the distance, and having no wish to spend a night in gaol with the drunks, I decided to go to ground. I stepped through a nearby gateway to find myself in a large garden in which I could smell the sweet scent of dew-damp hay. Then I spied two large earthenware drain pipes; I crawled into one of these and, pulling some damp hay over my feet, I strove to sleep. But how could I sleep with the sound of the patrol coming nearer, and the drain pipe acting as a funnel along which the gentle cool autumn wind was more like an Arctic gale ? The patrol came up the hill, seemed to pause and then, with a bang from the exhaust that brought my heart to my mouth, he was soon off down the other side of the hill.

I welcomed the gentle dawn as I would have welcomed a shy maiden coming over the hills to keep me company. As soon as I thought it was light enough I said " Hang the curfew ! " I can wait no longer ! " After some preliminary fiddling with the carburettor, the bike started easily enough; and I was on my way once more; this time to be stopped by a foot patrol near Holywood. As he was blocking my way with a rifle held in an ominous position, I thought it would be advisable to stop.

" Curfew not over yet," he said.

" Is it not ? " said I innocently.

" It is not ! " said he, " and what the hell . . . ? "

Then coming a bit closer, he peered at me and said:

" Why it's Billy Crowe, sure I was at school with you."

" Och, of course," I replied, " you're so-and-so."

" And there we stood talkin' of days that are gone " until curfew was over; and once more I was soon snarling along the last lap of the long road home.

Considering the troubled times, it was not unnatural to find the family in a state of alarm; my father in particular gave me a somewhat cold reception, but the chilly reception was soon dispelled by a warm bath and a hot cup of tea. Before long, too, I was between clean sheets undergoing the restoration of that deep sleep which is youth's great ally in all situations.

Times were difficult for men of business who had to travel from north to south. Once I remember my father calling me in to show me where I would find his papers in case anything should happen to him on one of his journeys. And indeed things did happen, though without serious consequences; for example, he was ordered out of a certain town; he refused to go until he had completed his business. Another time his train was stopped in the night; he and all the other passengers were compelled to get out, and forced to march at gun point to the nearest town, which was some miles away. In the meantime the train was sent off driverless at full speed; it passed through the next station and finally crashed into the embankment.

If you asked me why I decided—or why it was decided— that I should continue with academic work for another year, I should find it difficult to reply. Save for people who knew precisely where they were going, it was the normal thing to do—at least for those with a good primary degree. And a good primary was an open sesame to the necessary finance, because of the various scholarships, tutorials, and demonstratorships which could be had for the asking—or which one might be asked to have—once the first major hurdle had been surmounted. Not that all these made one wealthy, or indeed made one any more than an impecunious student, but they served to relax the parental burden.

So the autumn of 1922 saw me back again in the alma mater, this time to do research. This was a good year; it was the type of existence that suited me; it was bohemian. You could work when, how, and where you liked. You were under no pressure or strain. There were no exams. to be faced at the end; only the writing of a thesis, and writing for me was never a great labour: I liked it; I liked to see words flowing out from my pen even when those works were the mere prose and jargon of scientific writing. When I was doing research, too, I found I learned quickly and unconsciously, in contrast to my normal way of slow conscious learning.

The work we did was good in inception, but probably not very good in execution. We studied the effect of ultra-violet light on the speed and nature of certain organic reactions. But there were far too many variable and uncontrollable factors—at least uncontrollable with the comparatively unrefined apparatus at our disposal in those days. Without going into details the point I wish to make here is that, though not considering myself to be a mathematician, and being relatively ignorant of higher mathematics, I found myself applying and using maths. in this work, because it was necessary to do so. There is a moral for educationists here: even though the method may be slower, the way to knowledge is by action. As my own former science master used to say: "You don't know anything until you have done it." As far as book knowledge is concerned, too, I found myself reading, reading, reading all around the subject, because of the interest and excitement of working with some definite end in view. This, I think, is the chief advantage of doing any piece of research, even for a short time. I might add also that I gained a great deal from the association with my two excellent colleagues, one of whom was to become a fellow headmaster, and the other an industrial chemist. Not being sufficiently familiar with the dangers of ultra-violet radiation I—and I think to a lesser extent—my colleagues suffered a good deal from artificial sun-burn; but worse than this was an inflamed optic nerve; for a time I suffered from the terror of temporary blindness which I thought might be permanent. Anyhow it taught me the unforgettable lesson that undue exposure to ultra-violet radiation is a bad thing, whether

SOMEWHERE IN BELGIUM, 1922

UNIVERSITY COLLEGE, LONDON

the rays are created naturally by the sun or artificially by a mercury-vapour arc lamp.

At the end of that academic year two of us became further graduands at the same ceremony, an education diploma for her and a master's degree for me; and that summer we plighted our unbroken troth on the gentle rock-bound, green-margined, coast of County Down. Temporary separation was to come soon; but in the meantime we wandered over our Elysian fields; drew water from the village pump; went down to the village for the milk and the messages; cleaned the already clean cottage; dived and swam; and in the early morning collected mushrooms from the mushroom-mottled, dew-soaked fields. And at nights with hands clasped, we would dream dreams as we watched the starry hulls of the cross-channel steamers ploughing their nightly furrows across the moonlit Waters-o'-Moyle.

It was not long before the two of us were to be out there on the waters on our way to our different appointments: she to the cloistered isolation of a seminary for " Gentlemen's Daughters " in Tunbridge Wells, and me to the far from cloistered isolation of London's University College in Gower Street. Oxford or London was the choice, I chose London then; given the same choice now it would probably be Oxford. But I suppose I fell for the lure of the bright lights, and the fact that some of my friends were to go to King's, the other London college with a good school of organic chemistry. University College was founded in opposition to Oxford and Cambridge as a radical college to which entrance was not confined merely to members of the Established Church. Thus it was a cosmopolitan community of students and teachers of many nationalities and religions. Later King's was founded in opposition to University College; it had its own chapel and went through a period when it accepted only members of the Established Church. The main building of University College was impressive; it was quadrangular classic with its domed and Corinthian-columned façade facing Gower Street in the heart of London's faded Bohemian quarter. In those days the trot of a horse along the street was not unfamiliar; the hurdy-gurdy man's tinkling music-maker was a daily sound; and the muffin-man's bell and rolls were a regular feature—as regular, probably, as when the poet Browning was a student in this same college.

To those who have found themselves alone in London, the loneliness of London is a common denominator. But the long corridored department with its separate rooms and isolated research men had a coldness about it completely foreign to one fresh from the happy camaraderie of Queen's. Here there was no one to talk to, and there was no one to whom one could turn for help. My professor was scarcely a confessor; he was lean and sallow, and he went about the place, on his rare appearances, like a wraith surrounded by the mist of his own making, from his great crooked pipe. He was the embodiment of Sherlock Holmes with his long narrow high-domed head, and lank, grey, back-drawn hair. He wore a Norfolk jacket and knickerbockers; and his voice proceeded from the depths, expressionless and without emotion. He was a mountaineer of distinction, and had been on Himalayan expeditions. Mountains had been named in his honour, and he believed in the " Grey Man of Ben Nevis " who had followed him—at least so he asserted—maybe it was a case of " Der Doppelgänger " ! His holidays were spent on the Isle of Skye where he had the reputation of being one of its most outstanding salmon fishermen. He could write; in fact I have vague recollections of reading a book of his in which he described, with literary power, an expedition which they had to hang on to a ledge almost by the skin of their teeth, and were only able to keep themselves alive by drinking the blood of a slain goat.

He had an unhappy knack of coming into your room when you were not there. In fact he once reprimanded me about this; I thought this a little unfair as I was generally there for much longer hours than were strictly necessary. On another occasion I had recovered only one new compound from a certain mixture; I told him so; but a day or two afterwards he came up to tell me I had told him a lie—by this he meant a scientific lie—for he had recovered two compounds from the same mixture. However, I was prepared for his peculiar temperament; my professor at Queen's had also worked under him; he told me of an incident when he had broken a flask so that its contents were distributed all over the bench. As usual the old man arrived at the wrong time; standing behind, he watched as A.W.S. madly tried to mop up the mess; then he said: " Mr. Stewart you'll never make a chemist " !

But Mr. Stewart did make a chemist; and the old man was a very great chemist, a Fellow of the Royal Society, and the organic chemist at U.C.L. when Sir William Ramsey was at his peak. I had entered the college as a Ph.D. student: when I mentioned this to the professor one day, he said: " Ph.D. fiddlesticks ! You do the work and the degrees 'll come " ! As most of his own degrees were honorary, this outburst was not surprising, but for me the idea was a little unrealistic. However, a few years later he was to pass my Doctor of Science thesis, so may be his remark was meant to be a stimulus rather than a denial of the value of degrees as a whole.

Sometimes one learns more from unofficial than from official teachers. I hadn't been at U.C.L. very long before I became friendly with one of the best chemists I had ever met. He was a Ramsey Fellow lately returned from Holland, where he had taken a Ph.D. degree at the University of Leydun. To watch this little Englishman, who might have been a Dutchman, at work was a revelation. Jacket off, sleeves rolled up, and with half a dozen operations going at once, he would also be engaged in translating some abstruse paper from English into Dutch. From time to time one would hear " Blast ! " or some Dutch imprecation, and another flask would go crashing into the waste-box.

He helped me in my chemical affairs; I helped him in his love affairs. One day he showed me a letter from an old school friend; she would like to meet him again. Further letters passed, a meeting was arranged. Would I accompany him to smooth the first shy approaches ? The upshot was that the three of us agreed to have lunch together at the Regent Palace Hotel in Piccadilly. She proved to be a nice wee lassie; they fell for each other immediately; and a year or two later were married. After this happy ending there were happy events, and many more brain-childs, from this prolific chemist who became a leading research director. Just before I retired I received a copy of a large standard work on chemistry; I looked at the name of the translator who was none other than my friend of those far-off London days.

At first we lived in a boarding-house in Maida Vale. There were about five Queen's men in the house, two of whom were medicals and three of us were chemists. There were others: a Jap who claimed to be half Scottish, a Chinese student and his wife, two Spaniards, some Boer students, a Jewish family—mother, father, and a very æsthetic son, and a number of spinsters eking out an existence on scarcely adequate incomes. The house was one of a circular terrace arranged around a garden and tennis courts. It was of the spacious Victorian-neo-Georgian type so common in West London.

What a strange and polyglot collection of people ! The two ladies who ran the house, trying to do the best they could for their guests on the lowest possible terms; and the guests trying not to complain about the monotony of their diet; the old ladies striving to keep up a semblance of culture in the midst of the sometimes cultural, sometimes raucous and even immoral activities of red-blooded youth. The Jap was a lover of women, Ju-Jitsu and tea. His attitude to women was mainly concerned with their sexual possibilities, but he was generous and hospitable. If he heard you coming up the stairs late at night he would call you into his room and there, dressed in his kimono, he would insist on giving you a cup of his excellent tea as a nightcap. By profession he was a foreign correspondent with some firm in the city, and by inclination a womanizer with scant regard for the women who responded to his fatal attraction.

The Chinee was a charming person who loved and respected his equally charming wife. He had been a Cambridge student, but, on his marriage to another student, he had been cut off by his father; eventually he had become articled to a city accountant. His wife came down for supper on Sunday; apart from this appearance she remained in her room with the baby. On Sundays I occasionally helped father to push the baby in his pram in Regent's Park. As I made my way through the Sunday morning throng at the lake-side, saying " goo ! goo ! "—or whatever one does say to a Chinese baby—I used to receive some strange looks from Chinese nannies along the way.

As to the Irishmen: one was a pathologist attached to a big London hospital. He was dapper, clever, and cultured; he read Latin and Greek, and was able to help us with our German texts. He was the complete antithesis of the wild Irishman. His room was always neat and decorated with prints of the great works of art. Like most of us he was not heart-free; he was engaged to a cellist student at the Royal Academy of Music. In spite of his scholarship, however, he was no dweller in cloud-cuckoo-land. At this time, when our conversation tended to be more particular than abstract, he was able to keep us informed about much that was going on; in his particular capacity he was well able to do this. He knew the news behind the news.

It would be using a cliché to say that the other Irish medical man had an accent—a Belfast accent—that you could cut with a knife; it would not be a cliché and nearer the truth to say that he had an accent that could cut you like a knife. He had lately come back from the States, where he had been working on a fellowship; and his accent had not been improved by a slight American overlay. He, too, was clever. According to our landlady he was so clever that he had written an important scientific article sitting on the edge of his bed one night. I could well believe it.

Unlike the rest of us he was not a research man, he was job-hunting, and therefore had more leisure which he used in reading immense quantities of Irish history. He told me once that he thought the English were on the way out and that the next great nation would be Ulster—not Ireland but Ulster. The way things are going now it looks as if it may take a long time for this to happen, unless Ulster becomes such a difficult place in which to live that eventually the whole population leaves *en bloc* to live in and dominate some other country ! Since those days the same man wrote many books and articles on his favourite topics. Anyhow, like most other men of his nationality, he loved a good argument; for this reason and others I found him to be good company. Sometimes of a night he and I would go down to Hyde Park Corner to listen to the

soap-box orators. One of these was a Mormon missionary
with whom my friend got into discussion about the problem
of evolution. At one stage a Cockney girl beside me said:

" Oah woant you speak 'is voice is awful ! "

With this compliment in mind, I had to join in the discussion
more than I had been doing hitherto; but the soap-box orator
got the better of us; for at one point my friend asked him if he
had ever seen a certain very thick prehistoric skull in the
British Museum.

" No," replied the orator, " but I see one now ! "

Ah well, it was as good a way of passing time—if one had
time to pass—as any other; which reminds me of another
Hyde Park Corner orator. I think he was speaking against
patent medicines—who asked us if we had ever heard the
story of the man who had swallowed a watch and had been
taking certain pills ever since—to pass the time away !

Passing time ! Looking back now with appreciation of the
long hours we worked, I wonder how we managed to find so
much time. Maybe it was because we were younger and
needed less rest, or could it have been that there were no cars,
no radios, and no TV ? After dinner we would often go down
to Lyons's Corner House in Piccadilly where, for the price of
roll, butter, cheese and coffee, you could listen to excerpts from
grand opera by the Carl Rosa company, performed on a small
stage on one of the many floors, on each of which they had
some form of music for the musical and the unmusical.
When funds permitted we went to the theatre. Two plays in
particular stand out in my memory: the first production of
Bernard Shaw's " St. Joan," with Sybil Thorndyke playing
Joan. Never shall I forget the scene in which Shaw's cold
satire and dialectic suddenly gives way to sheer poetry: the
scene on the banks of the Loire when the page calls out:

" See ! There ! There she goes ! "

And Dunois says:

" Where ? Who ? The maid ? "

And the page:

" No, the Kingfisher. Like blue lightning. She went into
that bush."

I still find it difficult to read this scene without emotion. The other play was the immortal musical fantasia, " The Immortal Hour," with Gwen Ffrangeon-Davies singing the principal part.

But more than anything I recall my lonely wanderings amid the mazes of London's little streets. Once having seen the great show-places, that was enough; for me the old inns, the quaint corners, and smaller churches, the places mentioned by Dickens and many other great writers. Visits to these off-the-beaten-track places were for me the highlights. And there were the occasional red-letter week-ends when we two would meet under the clock at Charing Cross, afterwards to have a half-crown lunch or dinner at " The Fifty " in Soho with perhaps a visit to a park, cinema or theatre afterwards. More often, however, it was to go to Croydon for the week-end where we would be entertained by my fiancée's kindly relatives. How well I remember the grey-haired, long-faced, pipe-smoking school-master with his rare capacity for understanding, talking to me and I to him in his book-lined—it might be more accurate to say his book-enveloped—study. Much to the discomfiture of his wife we often talked until the grey London light began to chase the shades. His wife complained that he didn't get enough sleep; she was probably right, as he would often read and work all through the night; but he lived and worked until he was nearly ninety. Considering he had spent a part of his life half-starved in a prison camp in Germany he didn't do too badly !

A certain longing for a more independent home life ultimately drove three of us to rent a flat in Hampstead. A woman " did " for us during the day and, as we lunched at our colleges, we had only the evening meal and breakfast to prepare. Maybe we were psychologically better in the flat, but our digestions probably suffered from a surfeit of sausages and other easily prepared dishes. In consequence I used to walk across Regent's Park, and up the Euston Road to Gower Street whenever it was possible to do so; and in the spring evenings we sometimes hired a jolly-boat for a pull across the lake. All this and some tennis helped to keep me reasonably fit for a summer when the temperature rose to 90° F., and I was doing " combustions " in a basement with a furnace registering thousands of degrees.

One of my friends in the flat was a pianist, so we had many a musical evening. I still associate Chopin's Nocturne in F with Nicholas Nickleby, 'flu and fog; for I was reading the first, suffering from the second, and breathing the third while he played. Either the playing was effective, or the nursing by my two friends, for I recovered in due course.

Soon the three of us were to be separated: one to become a Government chemist, one to go to the Gordon Memorial College in the Sudan. As to myself, an invitation to join the junior staff at Queen's was an invitation I could not, and would not, ignore.

CHAPTER VI

DONS AND DOCTORS

A S happy as a sand-boy I returned once more to my well-loved university. Why shouldn't I be happy, after all? I had two first-rate colleagues and two chiefs whom I liked, admired and respected. With considerable experience behind me I had acquired some confidence. I was on to a fairly good line of research, and I knew the direction in which I wished to go. I was interested in lecturing and teaching; I knew I had a fairly strong carrying voice; and I thought I knew how to interest others. There were, of course, large gaps in my knowledge, but I felt these were unimportant because they could always be filled in when the necessity arose.

I suppose I was still at the zenith of my physical and mental powers. Belfast may not have been the world's cultural centre, but for the young man of zest, there were many ways in which his zestfulness could be satisfied. From the Mourne Mountains in County Down to the basalt-topped limestone escarpment of the Antrim coast, there was some of the finest and most accessible coastal scenery in the world. Fishing, walking, riding, golfing, hill climbing, and swimming—all these could be enjoyed easily, and at a cost within the scope of the most modest pocket—and one's pocket was certainly modest on a mere £250 a year with few perquisites other than the occasional tuition or invigilation fee. And for those who liked female company from time to time, there were dances galore at which one might meet lots of naturally pretty, and pretty natural, girls.

The country had now entered one of its more or less settled phases. One could go about one's legitimate business without let or hindrance. The Government of Sir James Craig had been firmly established, and established with good intentions. We appeared to be entering a new era of hope. Maybe many things went on under the surface of which we, in the relatively peaceful cloisters of the university, were more or less unaware. Catholic and Protestant students mixed unselfconsciously and, officially at least, there appeared to be little discrimination; in fact, I cannot remember the word being mentioned at this time. Games and social activities knew no bounds or boundaries; and, when crossing the Border, few would have considered they were entering an alien country. The sound of the gun in Belfast or in Dublin was no longer a familiar sound.

And I was glad to be back in the laboratory again amid all its sights, and scents, and sounds: the bubbling and jumping of liquids in glass vessels, the Bunsen's roar and the rose-red glow of fiery glass, the smells of alcohol and almonds, of iodine and iodoform, of esters and ethers. Above all I loved the eager questioning student life; those who were avid for learning; those who romanticized learning; those who learned because they thought they ought to; and those, with a little ability and a little money, who came to the university to have a good time. All those and others were represented; all were young people on the threshold.

Our work included a few lectures a week, supervision of practical classes, laboratory organization and research. Above all I enjoyed the informal discussions and work with students; the personal help you could give as you walked around the laboratories; their problems became your problems; and you understood their problems that much better because you had so recently been through the same mill. It is a truism to say that in all branches of life one must take the rough with the smooth; and this is as true in academic life as in any other. Most of my lectures were on organic chemistry to second-year students; I enjoyed these, but I did not enjoy a course of lectures on metallurgical chemistry which I had to give to first-year engineering and science students. Also, I had to undertake the work of the lecturer for a short period during his absence. This meant facing a hundred—two hundred maybe—medical students. When I went into the theatre for the first time there was a roar of cheering like the sound of a storm breaking on a beach. Suddenly it subsided; and I had to cut into the silence with a voice which seemed to me in the circumstances to be almost feeble and tremulous.

One would have thought that with all this science and scientific reading, little time would have been left for more reading of a general nature, but this was not the case. In fact I began to read widely, and I rarely let a Saturday morning pass without calling at a well-known book shop near the Castle Junction. For a time I was very keen on H. G. Wells: *Ann Veronica, Kipps, Mr. Polly* and, above all, his fantasies of possibility: *The War of the Worlds, The War in the Air, The Ford of the Gods, The Invisible Man,* and all the rest. At this period the possibilities of science seemed limitless; like Wells and Shaw I saw man evolving and creating, creating and evolving, until out of it all god-like man would gradually emerge. It was therefore my bounden duty and the duty of all of us to assist this process by every means in our power. Science was a religion which almost took the place of religion. However, the failure of the Russian experiment, Nazism, the misuse of atomic power, bacteriology, and psychology were later to raise grave doubts in my mind; and I began to wonder if, after all, some knowledge that passeth all understanding might be necessary before we could hope to turn the sword into the ploughshare.

The influence of my chief led me to study the detective story more fully. On his recommendation I read *Trent's Last Case* and *At the Villa Rose,* and I re-read Sherlock Holmes. These in their turn caused me to go back to the sources of their inspiration. I discovered Edgar Allen Poe, Honoré de Balzac, even Oscar Wilde's *Dorian Gray,* and many other writers of the fantastic, the mysterious, and the horrifying. But I soon became satiated with blood; my mind began to revolt; and I found it difficult to read the most lightly written horror novel; not even the Agatha Christie type in which the on-holiday guests ate a hearty breakfast down below, while upstairs lay the pallid body of a murdered man or woman. But you cannot dissociate horror from literature; even the Bible and Shakespeare are full of it. Perhaps that is why, in recent years, I have turned more and more to the nature poets. I once heard Mr. St. John Irvine say in effect that if you wished to be a great dramatist you should read " Sophocles, Shakespeare, Shaw and me." I read a good deal of the last three at least, but I never became any sort of a dramatist; none-the-less I still believe that wide and discursive reading can beget wisdom.

My professor was a great reader; in fact a professor of history once said to me that he enjoyed the company of A. W. S. better than that of men on the literary side, because his knowledge of literature was so great. He read in three languages everything from the classics to detective fiction; not only did he read but, unlike most of us, he remembered with factual detail most of what he had read. Though he was very deaf, and had to use a hearing aid, he listened to your opinion and often invited it. When he did invite your opinion he never put you in a difficult position by asking you about something of which you might have little knowledge. Nor would he embarrass you by saying: " Have you read so-and-so ? " He was much more likely to open the conversation with: " What are you reading at present, Crowe ? "

I referred earlier to his text-books; these must have been exceptionally difficult to write; they required constant revision year by year; and, to keep up to date, it was necessary for him to read original papers in a number of languages. In spite of all this he found time to write a stream of novels under the pseydonym of J. J. Connington. His first novel created quite a sensation—at least in our circle. It dealt with the story of a financial adventurer; he told me that much of it had been founded on experience. Then he wrote a scientific fiction novel based on " The Nitrogen Cycle." Everything in it, he said, was scientifically sound save for one mistake— had I spotted it ? I hope I rose in his estimation when, by intuition or a good guess, I hit on what I thought might be a scientific error; as it turned out, I was right. There followed a series of detective novels. He told me once, with reference to these that he never let down his readers: all the clues were there, so there was nothing to prevent you from finding out " who done it." This, I think, was both the measure of his success and his failure; his novels tended to be dehumanized, to be too much of a jig-saw; they had little of the emotional element in them. Nevertheless they were sufficiently successful to have been published in a number of different countries and languages.

He was essentially human; he was human in that he had his dislikes and prejudices. Whether because of the war, or because of some unfortunate experience when studying in Germany I don't know, but he was certainly strongly prejudiced against Germans.

"You see, Crowe," he would say, emphasizing his point with the inevitable cigarette in its rough wooden holder, " you see, it's their system, the Ph.D. system, the professor wants certain results and they see that he gets them."

On another occasion he said:

"Where does all the really original work come from? From France or Russia: radioactivity, the Periodic Law? Not from Germany. Oh, yes, they work all right; set a German to count all the blades of grass in a field and he'll do it. But really original work? No! Take Ostwald's theory of indicators — nonsense. I met Ostwald—unpleasant fellow!"

But he knew when he was being unreasonable. If you argued with him he would concede your point, and he would laugh at himself. He had his intense prejudices and his equally intense loves. As one might expect, his favourite author was Kipling, but the unrealism of Yeats and the Celtic twilight group were anathema. He probably modelled himself to some extent on his great and former chief, Sir William Ramsey. Ramsey, he told me, was a fearless experimenter who would try anything on himself, such as having liquefied ammonia gas poured into his nostrils to prove that it had no smell. And there was the " ether dream " experiment when he allowed himself to be given small quantities of ether at a time, while he wrote down his experiences. This was to test the idea that under ether you thought you were about to discover the secret of the universe, and the most unlikely object would be the final key. Ramsey came to the conclusion that the dream was caused by the benumbing of the critical faculty of the brain.

As to A. W. S. as a chemist: he had his critics; in fact I heard him once described as " a journalistic chemist." This was not true, and was said by one who had none of A. W. S's facility for literary exposition. He had contributed a great deal of fact and theory in his time; I heard it said that, had he bothered to move in the right circles, had he been more in the heart of things, he would undoubtedly have been a Fellow of the Royal Society. But he was not an honour hunter; and no man could have been more honest about himself. He told me once that he was a hopeless practical worker, yet his knowledge and intuition were at times uncanny. I remember asking him how one could estimate some rather obscure substance. He thought for a minute and then he said: " Isn't there a method using so-and-so ? " Another time he was chatting to me as I was carrying out a research operation. Said he: " Have you ever tried diazotizing these things, Crowe ? " " Diazotize them ! They'll be oxidized to blazes," I thought. But I tried it; it worked; and this led on to a new line of research with far-reaching results.

More than anything I enjoyed the evenings when he entertained me at his home. Dinner over, coffee would be served in the study; then his wife would discreetly withdraw, leaving us to our conversation. The battery of his hearing aid and the inevitable box of cigarettes would be placed on the coffee table; with toes extended to the blaze, with a background of books extending from floor to ceiling, and a great picture depicting one of the ages of the earth in front, I would listen and contribute to a conversation which could go on until the small hours, but it was never boring. Science, literature, music: all these spheres of learning and culture came under scrutiny. And it was not a case of

> " At arguing, too, the parson owned his skill
> But e'en though vanquished he could argue still."

for all his arguments were based on knowledge, and his knowledge was profound. Though I think he had played the violin a little at one time, he was not a practical musician. However, when gramophones began to improve, he purchased the best obtainable at the time, and built up a library of first-class records. Northing extraordinary about that ! But it was extraordinary how soon he had armed himself with such a knowledge of keys, intervals, harmonies and so forth, as would have put any professional musician to shame.

My immediate chief was the lecturer in organic chemistry. He and I had a lot in common and before long we became close friends. His unfailing, quiet, ready, wit was a constant source of pleasure. When one added to this the qualities of a gentleman whose ready sympathy and understanding were always available, one had most of the ingredients of true friendship. I had more honest-to-goodness laughter in his company than in the company of any other man I ever knew. He was not the hail-fellow-well-met type who would clap you on the back and pin you down to the latest story. No, it was just his little quip about this and that, and his own effervescent sense of humour that kept you constantly amused.

When cars were first becoming more within the reach of the ordinary man, he purchased an open tourer; and, with characteristic generosity, he often invited me to go on tour with him. One Easter vacation we " beetled off," as he would have said, to Donegal, ostensibly to climb the Donegal mountains. This was my first visit to this wonderful county, probably one of the most beautiful in Ireland, for it contains within its boundaries almost everything that is typically Irish: lake-filled glens, rugged mountains, fast-flowing streams, sea-cliffs and silver sea sands, straggling villages, charming people, and places where Gaelic is still the only language known to many.

To leave the lab. in March, to get away from its fumes and smells, and from the research which may not have been going well, into the open country in an open car, was motoring of a type that few people know in these days when you flash along in a stuffy atmosphere, while the scarcely discernible landscape passes at speeds of fifty, sixty, or seventy miles an hour. I suppose we raced through the Barnsmore Gap at thirty ! on a rough road, but what of it ? Let no one imagine that a car in those days was a machine that let you down at the end of fifty miles or so; not a bit of it ! Cars then seemed to me to be just as reliable for what they had to do as most motors nowadays.

First we stayed near Dunfanaghy in a boarding-house run by two genteel spinsters. Like most of their kind, and many others for that matter, one of their chief joys was to know so-and-so who was something; and even more important was to have so-and-so who was something staying at their house. As I felt that I could not at this stage presume on first-name terms with my senior, I used to address him as " Colonel."

The old ladies pricked up their ears at this; one day one of them drew me aside and, in a voice from which the excitement was barely concealed, she said: " Is he really a colonel ? " I hadn't the heart to tell her that he was merely a humble Doctor of Science. They did us well for breakfast; we usually had a sandwich lunch in the mountains; but, whether we were in or out, the evening meal consisted of tea and boiled eggs. As we found this repast somewhat unsatisfactory my friend would move over to the side-board and, stooping down in imitation of a burglar cracking a safe, he would conscientiously rifle the cupboard in the hope of finding even a morsel of stale cheese.

We climbed Muckish and Errigal. Many people from many lands have proclaimed the magic of the mountains of Ireland. One does not need the head and feet of a sherpa to be able to climb them, but when you make comparatively slight physical effort, what mystery, what enchantment, what unearthly loneliness ! Why ? I cannot answer this question. But that this mysterious quality is there has been testified to by numerous writers, poets and travellers. Ghosts ? Fairies ? The abodes of saints ? The last outpost of early Christian civilization ? Explain it as you will, the mystery remains.

But more than mere physical effort was required to enable us to climb Muckish—The Pig's Back. For we proceeded straight across country over moor and bog with the heather up to our knees. Half-way up we were in snow; for a time it seemed that we could neither get up nor down. Breathlessly we reached the breath-taking summit with our hearts in our mouths, the whole of Donegal at our feet, and the Atlantic light so clear to the west that you would almost have thought you could see America. And the same with Errigal, though here we sat astride the ridge-like summit with a great mass of rock sweeping below us into a billowing ocean of moorland.

And we explored all that north-west, marble-impregnated coast of Donegal from Marble Hill to Horn Head, and from Horn Head to Bundoran where we became civilized once again. Here we had a grand hotel to ourselves where we luxuriated in deep hot baths, had a good dinner and a bottle of wine, and were waited on by dark-haired, blue-eyed colleens who, having no one else to wait upon, were only too pleased to play up to the quips and witticisms of two irresponsible scientists from the Black North. In passing let me say that Bundoran is not Donegal, this sea-girt, sand-girt, straggling resort is no more Donegal than London is England. They say the air is good— whatever that may mean—it's a great place for children; there is a *good* sea there, and sure 'tis a grand healthy place altogether. I believe, though I don't remember, it's the first place where I was rolled on a beach; and it is certainly where my grand-father betook himself year after year after the harvest, to rest and smoke a pipe with his cronies.

In those days, before I had the use of a car, treats like this were all too few. Soon, too soon, we were once again heading for the Border. Two home-going incidents stand out in my memory. The first of these in a fair-congested town, as we were literally pushing our dung-splashed bonnet against the sweat-rimed flanks of bullocks and bulls, steers and stores, a red-faced, picture post-card Irishman shouted: " Stop ! Stop ! Stop for a cow, a goat, or a woman ! " Any hardline feminist would have been justifiably revolted at the classifica-tion; to give the man his due, however, I think he thought he was placing women on a pedestal like the goat at the Puck Fair. And then later we had a bit of a discussion with the proprietress of the hotel at which we stopped for lunch. Oh ! I don't know what it was all about, probably the merits or demerits of North and South; anyhow she said: " Sure 'tis the silver bullet will pay in the end." Her point was that the Border would eventually enrich the South, and impoverish the North. Neither has happened ! So where do we go from here ? Back to the lead bullet, or should we do away with bullets, whether of lead or silver ?

In all this time you, the reader, must be wondering what was happening back in The Park. To tell the truth I saw little of it. My whole life had now become so involved in the university that, as often as not, it was a case of the last tram home, once or twice a taxi when I missed the last tram; occasionally indeed I had to walk when funds were short. Often one of my colleagues would say: " Working late to-night ? " And we would work late. Sometimes we had to work late because we were in the middle of a research operation which could not be left. Sometimes we worked on Sundays, especially during exam. times when solutions had to be made up, checked, and re-checked with great accuracy.

And, of course, there were social activities; dances to be arranged, parties, magazines, and so on to be organized. Once we had a sort of pseudo-band the instruments for which were made from laboratory equipment. For one party we had the lecture bench built backwards to the wall to form a stage, and in front we erected a proscenium and curtain. This turned the lecture theatre into a one-night theatre; and here we put on a variety show to entertain the guests at the Christmas party. I cannot say much about the merits of the show; all I can remember of it was dancing Irish jigs and reels with a man who claimed to be a descendant of the kings of Ireland. For a long time afterwards an Irish jig was one of my party pieces; but the last time I did it I pulled an Achilles tendon, so I decided it was not for the over sixties !

For exercise, and to expel the laboratory fumes from our lungs, we played hockey and rugby. The Department of Agriculture had just come into being; these men were almost full-time chemists; so there was a good reservoir of hefty countrymen. Before long they were not only testing for elements in test tubes, but they were also trying to score tries for " The Alchemists " which is how we named the newly-formed rugby side. We played teams from other faculties; out of this an inter-faculty competition developed; this was soon to become an integral part of the life of the university. Sometimes I wonder if students have as good times now; I doubt it; in those days so much had to be started from ground level. Now everything is laid on; so that there is little left to do other than to make protests !

But to come back to The Park. I was to find now that I had little in common with many of the friends with whom I had grown up. I was steadily becoming more of an intellectual; many of them had become men of affairs, businessmen, accountants and so forth. In those days to go to the university was the exception rather than the rule. Thus I was, to some extent, thrown back on others with like interests. One of these was an older man who lived with his bachelor brother, spinster sister, and mother, in a house with an ever-open door.

The mother was a Victorian. It would be wrong to say she dominated her family; it would be more correct to say that she was the central core around which the family revolved. Like most other Victorian women, from the time she became " old " she sat in her silks and satins and shawls at the fireside. When a mother dominates a family, the family don't love her; but it would be quite wrong to say that this mother was unloved by her family; I never knew one of the five to say a hard word about her. Her one passion was croquet on the lawn in front of this old Victorian house with its rambling garden running down to the stream's edge. Silver-haired and clothes-cluttered, she would raise her mallet in the air in jubilation when she won, or in frustration when another player's ball was in her way. When one of the " boys " asked for her advice she would draw from the well of her experience some of the water of life. And her experience was far from limited, for she was the widow of a police officer; in their early married life she and her husband had been based in Liverpool; and I remember her telling of how she would go out at night to the local pub. to draw a pint of porter for her husband when he needed to relax.

The spinster daughter, slight, energetic, full of " crack," and always interested and sympathethic about the affairs of others, looked after the two " boys " at home, and the mother, like a mother. Sometimes I would drop in to find that the brothers were out: " Ha ! Ha ! Ha ! Willie," she would say with the sort of energetic giggle that preceded her statements. " Go in there, warm yourself, and talk to mother while I make a tart." Tarts were her speciality, and were produced for all meals except breakfast. Supper usually consisted of tea and a tart. One night the rest of the guests had gone, thinking that I had departed with them she came in rubbing her slight hands after the cold night air at the hall door and said: " Well, boys, what did ye think o' the tart ? " When she saw me she was taken aback, but immediately saved embarrassment by saying that of course she was including me as one of the boys. But the boys and the mother thought the world of her, and listened to her with rapt attention when she sang to her own accompaniment, such Victorian ballads as " Dry up Those Tears " in a voice that was worthy of better things.

The younger " boy " at home was a trained pharmacist; given the opportunity he might have been a scientist in a wider field than that of compounding medicines for a doctor in the city's sordid heart. His great hobby was graphology which he, like others, tried to make into a science. I still have a signed copy of a book he wrote on the subject; and, for a time, he was called in as expert witness in court cases demanding the recognition of handwriting.

The older man was thought to be delicate, though he lived to be ninety-three ! In spite of his great age his health was never good. When a comparatively young man he had a break-down just before his final arts degree examination. At various times he had pneumonia, pleurisy, and a duodenal ulcer. Few winters passed without his succumbing to those little ills to which the flesh is heir; all of which goes to show that longevity is not necessarily associated with general health. But whether in good health or in bad, his sense of humour never deserted him; the twinkle was always present in his eyes. It is difficult to describe his sense of humour: it was pertinent, quick, quiet, and kindly. He had a lean face, long grey hair, and he was as slim as a lath. He could draw well, and was an actor of merit.

Being of the rolling-stone type, he gathered neither moss nor money; but his life was intensely interesting, for he found more interest in the environmental circumstances of his job than in the job itself. He acted with the old Ulster Literary Theatre in the time of Harry Morrow and Sam Waddell, brother of Helen Waddell and author of *The Drone.* Later he was invited to join the Abbey Theatre in Dublin; and, about the same time, he became a master in some kind of a reform school—though anybody less suited to such a post could scarcely be imagined. When in Dublin he met many of the great literary figures, including such people as Yeats, Synge, Lady Gregory, and the renowned Countess Markievicz. In such an environment it was natural that he should espouse the Nationalist cause; yet though his Sinn Fein sympathies found little favour at home, it

is a tribute to his good humour and his family tolerance that no
apparent friction arose within the home circle. No doubt his
influence helped me to widen my vision, and gave me greater
understanding of those whose traditions and background might
be different from my own. I think he also stimulated a love
for many of the Irish playwrights and poets with whose work
I had hitherto been unfamiliar.

His homing instinct soon brought him back from the Celtic
twilight to the harsher light of The Park, the ascendancy, and
the Ministry of Labour. As usual, the latter gave scope to his
flair for observing and sympathizing with the human dilemma.
He loved to describe some of the characters who came into the
office for interview. One of these was a girl who had just been
married:

" On the dole ! " said he, " in the name of fortune what
prompted you to get married on the dole ? "

" Och ! " she replied, " sure it was all the go ! "

Then there was the time when the office was situated beside
a house, the inhabitants of which had a rather unsavoury
reputation; he had a parcel of fish on his desk to be taken home
for " the tea "; but, when having his own afternoon cup, the
cat from the unsavoury house commandeered the savoury fish.
When he complained they said:

" But how did ye know it was our cat ? "

" Och ! " said he in exasperation, " sure it had a yellow
streak."

And a story he loved to tell, and one we loved to hear, was
about the time something was being done at the pipes outside;
he heard the following conversation between the plumber and
his helper:

" Did you touch thon spanner ? "

" Ah did not ! "

" Ye did ! "

" Ah did not ! "

" Well, don't do it again ! "

The beauty of this story is in its characterization. Here was
the typical, unbelieving, realistic, North of Ireland man,
as unbelieving in his personal relationships as in his relationships
with the people of another faith and another political outlook.

On Saturday nights J. G. Abbey and I would go on the prowl. After a relaxing drink beside a roaring fire in the bar of the old Royal Avenue, we would browse among the books in the unique Smithfield Market in the hope of picking up first editions; from thence to a theatre, or possibly to the now defunct Empire to witness the dame-like antics and listen to the broad Irish witticisms of Jimmy O'Dea. J. G. was a bachelor who loved to look at the colour and comedy of human life, but he never became fully involved in it; thus the ogling girls of Chichester Street left him unmoved. In his semi-professional days he came into contact with many charming and delightful girls; they liked him; everybody liked him; but there it began and ended. Not indeed that he was oblivious to female charms; penuriousness may have held him back from romantic involvement; and I think he had too much respect for women to regard them simply as purveyors of carnal satisfaction.

Mention of J. G. Abbey reminds me of one or two others with whom Abbey was also friendly. In those days the rostrums of our university were dominated by characters, such as the long-haired, monocled, Grecian professor of Greek, who is reported to have said to a difficult class one day: " Gentlemen, I am tired of casting pearls . . ."; and he forthwith stumped out of the room. Then there was the dark-haired, bearded, play-writing Professor of Economics who would order two slices of bread and butter and a plate of soup for lunch; taking a bite out of the bread he would use the semi-circle as a kind of eye-glass through which to survey his fellow diners.

Our table at lunch usually consisted of a famous rugby international assistant in the anatomy department, a forthright barrister secretary of the university, and one of the most remarkable and colourful characters who ever graced the laboratories and lecture rooms of Q.U.B. He was a small bald-headed slight man with gleaming eyes that caught and held your attention. Even at this time there were few capitals in Europe that this former Paris art student, turned anatomist, didn't know, and in which he was not known. He was at University College, London, when I was there; one day I met him in the Charing Cross Road; he buttonholed me and with

the traffic streaming by on either side of us, he gave me a
dissertation on his research. He loved animals, and had such
a remarkable way with them, that he would walk fearlessly into
a lion's cage without turning any of his scanty hair or the
lion's prolific mane. In later years he became so much
interested in circus life that he toured Europe to collect
" turns "; and, when he retired, he devoted himself entirely to
the production of his famous Christmas circus.

The story I am now about to relate happened at a time when
there was a great deal of interest in spiritualism. Sir Arthur
Conan Doyle, one of spiritualism's great protagonists, was
billed for a lecture to be given in Belfast in the near future.
In the circumstances it was not surprising that the subject
formed the main theme of our lunchtime discussions. Most of us
were sceptical except the anatomist who suddenly thumped the
table so that the glasses shivered on the marble surface and said:
" But I am a medium ! "

Looking at those strange twinkling eyes of his one got the
impression that he was pulling our legs, but not a bit of it.

" Yes," he said, " I am a medium and, in fact, the spiritualistic
people in Belfast have tried to get me to join them, but I
refused."

" Come on, tell us more about it," we said.

" Well," he replied, " it was like this. During the war,
when in the R.A.M.C., I was drafted to a hospital in France.
On the evening of my arrival I was introduced to a nurse, a
Belfast girl. Walking along the corridor that night on my
way to bed I saw, framed by the end window, a nun who
crossed herself and disappeared. Meeting the Belfast girl again
at breakfast, I asked her how she had slept. ' Oh, very well,'
said she, ' but I had a rather strange experience. I saw a nun
in the corridor.' Later, talking to the old man in charge, he
told me that the place had been a convent; it had been sacked
at the time of the Revolution; and had been haunted ever since
by a nun who had been buried in unconsecrated ground.

I said:

" But look here, you were an artist. You are a highly
sensitive, imaginative, man; surely what you saw was simply
a sort of visible projection of your imagination ? "

"No! No!" he said. "I saw this nun as clearly as I'm seeing you now. Besides, this wasn't the only experience. One night when I was working late for a certain examination, I looked up and there was my aunt who had died a couple of days before, framed in the doorway."

Well, he saw what he saw; no one can prove that he did not see those things. Reality to one need not necessarily be reality to another: no more than the mind of Beethoven implies that we could all have Beethoven minds.

I don't think this man had ever defined his religious views other than to say he believed that mankind was evolving toward immortality. He died a short time ago; much to my surprise the announcement indicated that he was a Roman Catholic; whether he had always been one, or whether he had embraced this faith in later life I don't know.

With all this in mind it was inevitable that we should go to hear Sir Arthur Conan Doyle. I went with a Quaker friend, the senior member of the junior staff. He invited me to his evening meal in a big dark house in the centre of the city. I shall never forget that evening. We dined frugally on potted herrings in that large bare room, to the accompaniment of the clanging trams as they spluttered and flashed on their way to the city centre, a little further up High Street. Then, in that rather grim Ulster Hall, we listened as down on the rostrum this big, walrus-moustached, evening-dressed creator of Sherlock Holmes unveiled for us the innermost secrets of death. For a time I thought here at last is the answer. . . . But !

The great man showed us his ectoplasmic spirit photographs taken in the dark; it struck me that if this substance—ecto-plasm—was capable of photographing itself, like ultra-violet rays, it should be capable of discharging the gold leaf electro-scope, so I forthwith wrote to Sir Arthur suggesting certain experiments. Here was his reply, quoted verbatim from the original letter which is still in my possession:

15 Buckingham Palace Mansions,
S.W. 1.

Dear Sir,

I think you might prove a successor to the late Dr. Crawford. I do not exaggerate when I say that his name will outlast that of most living scientists. His work was radical and vital.

I would recommend to you his three little books to be carefully studied—then Shrenck Notzing's big book and then Geley's last book on Ectoplasm which has to be read in French. If you could get in touch with Miss Golligher you have your material, but it means tact, which Fournier d'Albe had not.

When Ectoplasm is fully formed it is solid and would affect the plate—under a flashlight—as any other solid would do.

When it is vaporous it would lend itself to your experiment with the electroscope.

In the great majority of cases spirit photos—as apart from visible materializations—are direct impressions upon the plate and bear no relation to light. That is my conviction, founded on experience. The actual mediums are very ignorant people and can tell nothing of their own powers. Two cameras have several times been trained on the same sitter simultaneously— one has shown an extra and the other none. We often get them in the carrier without exposure. You are in a land of miracle and photographic laws all go overboard. By all laws a two-minute exposure would leave a black plate. It did in other cases. Not with Mrs. Deane.

> Yours sincerely,
> A. Conan Doyle

May 22 (1925)

It is not my intention to give an account of the pros and cons of spiritualism here. Suffice it to say that I did not proceed with the proposed investigation. Having read the literature I was not impressed by the scientific nature of the researches, nor by the explanations of the results. Fournier d'Albe's investigations conducted in Belfast into the Goligher Circle seemed to me to be fairly convincing—or unconvincing if you like.

Besides I had other things to think about. At about this time I gave my first full dress public lecture. I looked up the transcript of it the other day to see if anything I had said then, in all the naiveté and innocence of comparative youth, was pertinent to-day. The lecture on Electrons and Radioactivity was given to The Chemists and Druggists Society of Ireland. One paragraph is worth quoting:

" I tell you the days of science are just beginning. In days to come war will be no more, and the scientist will devote all his energies to the betterment of his fellow man. When we find a means of tapping the energy of the atom the Golden Age will really have begun."

Pertinent ? Yes ! But how wrong I was !

From séances and science to songs; a big jump maybe, but the less serious aspects of life became more serious when I became a member of The Queen's Jesters, a well-named concert party with a reputation that had to be maintained. The anatomist to whom I referred earlier was the chief jester; and he was as good at jesting and joking as at handling lions and leopards. In fact, if all else had failed he could have been a world-famous clown. We had a violinist, cellist, and pianist who might have gone far in the musical profession had they not turned their attention to physics, pathology, and other things instead.

We toured the province like " The Good Companions," but the concert that stands out most vividly in my memory was one given to the prisoners in the Crumlin Gaol in Belfast. Most of the men in the front row were lifers incarcerated for crimes of violence against the person. When the concert was over the prison governor called on one of the men to propose a vote of thanks. Few men could have done better; he sounded suave, urbane, and cultured. Afterwards the governor told us that he was a graduate of either Oxford or Cambridge imprisoned for confidence tricking. The governor showed us around: men in cells, some in solitary confinement, the death cell, the gallows. Ah, me ! What sadness ! Wings clipped for life for a moment's callous stupidity, or for a complete inability to control some hell-bent urge; but society had to be protected.

To come back to the outside world and happier things. My three years on the staff of the university were moving rapidly to a close; decisions would have to be faced up to and made; first I must face the final hurdle of my doctorate. My researches had been going well; each new substance turned out to have its anticipated composition; and some had interesting physical properties. I remember a friend, afterwards to occupy a chair, saying to me: "But nobody can foretell the value of any piece of research; even to spend your time weighing chickens' livers might have some far-reaching importance." I agreed with him, with some reservations. I cannot help feeling that a lot of what passes as scientific research is done with one object only; that of getting a degree. The results, however, may often remain buried in the archives. I can only hope that what little I did may, at least, have been a jumping-off ground for other more able scientists.

The time for writing my thesis was moving ominously close; none-the-less I enjoyed my last year. An old friend with whom I was very much *en rapport* had joined the staff. He was a musician and a golfer; and as family cars were now available we managed to get around a bit. Neither of us liked to be tied down to a club, but when the opportunity afforded, we would go off for a day's golf at one of the many good, bad, or indifferent courses around our coast. He was a much better golfer than I; however, like the good sportsman he was, he never lost patience with my pulling, slicing, and efforts to get myself out of the various hazards into which my ball seemed to be attracted like iron to a magnet.

I remember one day in that year better than any other. It was the day of the annual Chemical Society picnic. This time we decided on Garron Point on the Antrim coast as a suitable venue. The Antrim coast has been described by somebody of note as the second finest coast road in the world. Not having seen all the coast roads in the world I cannot agree or disagree with this description; but on the day in question I thought— and we all thought—that words were inadequate. Lazily the blue, blue, waters o' Moyle covered and uncovered the gleaming sea-wrack which clawed out over the hard, white, basalt-topped limestone escarpment with a vividness, the like of which could never have been seen on a darker coast. Hundreds of feet above the sea we lay on Garron Point, savouring the fresh cool air from the unsullied sea, and the sweet scents of late spring grass. Then, as the sun began to burnish the whole meniscus of the westward heaven, slowly we wound our homeward way around some of the fabled bays at the ends of the Nine Glens, past the white harbour and white cliffs of Glenarm, past the Ballygally Head, past Blackhead and Whitehead, past Carrickfergus with the history of Ireland, England, Scotland, France and America imprinted in the stones of its castle, and so on until our *cortège* of open cars became caught up in the smoke, and the traffic of our hill-surrounded city.

This was my last break. Now I was working day and night,—often nearly all night—on my thesis; for two months I scarcely lifted my head, and my unfortunate sister, who did the typing, was scarcely able to lift her head either. However, at last the job was finished and the bound, gilt-lettered volume was presented to the Faculty. Though I was pretty certain about our own people, I was apprehensive about the old man in London. Would his report be favourable or otherwise ? So I sat in the chair at the desk in the old research lab. waiting, waiting, and fearing the worst. Then at last I heard footsteps; in came my friend, the Senior Lecturer; as soon as I saw his smiling kindly face I knew that all was well, and I had been granted the degree of Doctor of Science.

Now came the time for decision: what was to be my next move ? Consider the circumstances: industry was at a stand-still; chemists were a luxury whose value British industry had scarcely begun to recognize; people with the highest qualifications were clamouring for posts in the academic world. I had already been interviewed for a university post where all the conditions were favourable to my appointment at the magnificent salary of £300 per annum without increments or pension. I failed to get the job because I was outclassed by others with much higher qualifications, and more experience than I had at the time. I had applied for posts in many parts of the world, and had been interviewed for some but drew a blank each time.

Besides, though I thought I could lay claim to some gifts and talents, I wasn't at all sure that these were such as would enable me to become a great scientist, nor did I feel that I wanted to spend too much of my time as a lonely seeker after truth in a laboratory. As a lifelong lover of the natural world around me, I felt that I would die if I were to spend the rest of my life cooped up in the heart of some black city in the industrial North.

And there was the problem of marriage. As things were my finacée and I could see each other only during vacations;

this was unsatisfactory for both of us; and, while we enjoyed those breaks, we yearned for a more stable existence. Getting married is always difficult; in many ways I think it was almost more difficult in the twenties. It was unusual and frowned upon for a girl to keep on working after marriage; as for hire purchase: you might as well go to a moneylender ! Thus to get married—at least respectably—you felt you would need to have £500 in the bank and at least £400 a year. We had neither.

I had been offered a Musgrave Fellowship; this would have enabled me to continue researching at home and abroad for another two years; I declined it. I liked best the teaching end of my work; I thought I had some ability in that direction. A post in a school should give me scope for my interest in other activities; and I now required a job offering some degree of stability and security. So when I received a wire from the Head of one of England's top grammar schools offering me sixth form work, provided we were both satisfied with the results of an interview at Chester, I crossed over one night, crossed back the next; and the same afternoon saw both of us enquiring about marriage by special licence from my fiancée's kinsman-parson, and principal of a theological college.

CHAPTER VII

LEODIENSIANS

A S none of us were particularly keen on a big wedding we
were married by special licence at my fiancée's home in
another, but more exclusive, tree-lined grassy park. By this
time the old park where I had lived for so long had been broken
up and built up and had lost its character. It now contained a
housing estate on the former green fields between us and " The
Village." Some of the old residents had gone because they
couldn't afford to keep up the older houses. Many of the
residents now were just people in the mass; individuality had
been lost. My own parents had moved some time before into
a new, highly respectable, park within sight of the new, highly
respectable Houses of Parliament.

Immediately after our wedding we entrained for Dublin
and Dun Laoghaire. The following morning we had a rough
crossing to Holyhead; being reasonably good sailors, however,
we arrived in Snowdonia none the worse. We were captivated
by Wales and the Welsh with their lilting accent. Our little
secluded hotel at Capel Curig was ideal for a honeymoon and
an ideal spot from which to explore the mountains all around
Bettws-y-Coed. Scorning the mountain railway, we climbed
Snowdon on foot by the Pen-y-pass; and, from its lofty summit
with so much of this castellated, historical, princedom spread
out below, we felt that whatever lay in front, we should have
unforgettable memories of the past. Nearly forty years later
we were to revisit this place to find it little changed, as we
seemed to have changed little; it was difficult to believe that
nearly forty more years of life's journey had been accomplished
since those days.

After leaving wild Wales we explored the walls of Chester,
and spent a night there—a rather depressing night I remember;
for we had to listen to a woman whimpering in the next

bedroom; besides, our own idyll was coming to an end and we had to face reality. We had little or no money; a term's salary each and our wedding cheques; as for my yearly salary, many young couples would now expect to draw almost as much in a month as I was to receive in a year. Next day we arrived in Leeds with no place to stay other than in its grand hotel. By the next night, however, we had found a more permanent home in a rather frowzy furnished upstairs flat in a place ironically termed Hyde Park. It was an upstairs flat—sizable rooms with big windows—but depressing, for our down-at-heel landlady lived below to the rear with her crippled daughter. It was good, however, to see our own silverware and china out at last, and our brand new coffee percolator bubbling with its goodly brew.

Before many weeks had passed we had moved into a self-contained flat in a terrace near the Grammar School and overlooking the university. Though flat-life in such an area was not our idea of paradise, it suited me very well at this stage when I had so much work to do. Conveniene to the school and its games facilities was a decided advantage; in addition, we were within walking distance of the centre of the city with its arts theatres, concert and picture theatres; all very important in those days of our youth, especially at a time when TV had not yet come into being, and we couldn't afford a radio.

Early married life is fraught with unforseen perils: one false step and a man may be damned for ever; one burnt meal could sow the seeds of a separation. My first false step was to take my wife down town one afternoon for tea; when I put my hand in my pocket for the money with which to pay the bill I found I had none. Fortunately I discovered this before I had to suffer the embarrassment of a pretty waitress standing by while I fumbled. Hastily we held a conference; it was decided that I should use my wife's only coppers in going up to the flat by tram, while she would remain, like an abandoned woman. I arrived back just in time to save her from the unwanted attentions of a lascivious-looking gentleman. The upshot of that was that I was never again trusted about money when we were going out together. On the other hand, my wife, though an accomplished cook, was still in the experimental stage of trying this and that on her husband. Once she thought she would make her own bread with yeast—a good old Yorkshire custom—but she put in all the yeast at one go, and left the bread in a bowl on the radiator while she went off to do the shopping. When I came back to the flat I couldn't open the door because the bread, under the influence of the unnecessary and unnatural dose of fungus, had climbed out of the bowl and along the floor, effectively sealing the door. I teased her so much about this that she never again attempted yeast bread—at least not until the necessity arose during world war II.

Like most other schoolmasters I was not particularly happy during the first month or two in my new surroundings. I remember one of my immediate colleagues—an excellent teacher of physics—telling me that he never liked to meet later the boys he had taught during his first year. I think this is true of all of us. Everything was new to me. I had left school quite a long time ago, and for a fair number of years I had been a specialist. Though some of the VIth form and scholarship work was very advanced—and I spent a good deal of my time at this—I had to re-orientate myself when it came to teaching younger forms; and I was called upon to teach some advanced physics, a subject in which I now felt inadequate. Up to this, too, I had two or three lectures a week and some practical classes; but, to have to lecture for many hours a day with little break between, I found very tiresome, and it was not long before, like most others, I began to—or was compelled to—find ways and means of conserving my energy.

The one thing they don't do when you are training for a degree is to teach you how to teach. Nor do they teach you how to interest the uninterested. Though my predecessor had been an excellent man, I found many of the methods in use objectionable. There was an excessive use of text-books. Read chapter so-and-so, now a test; write a précis; this was the method, the informative method, pushed to its limits. Maybe the Heuristic Method had limited me; I could not get away from it; I felt that everything must be proved, and that teaching people how to think scientifically should be the end product of scientific training. I enjoyed teaching young people, and I enjoyed teaching those on the threshold of university scholar-

ELIZABETHAN STYLE, VICTORIAN PILE
Leeds Grammar School

THE SCYPTICAL CHEMIST

ship; but the long haul in between, the hordes who had to be driven, pushed, punished, and cajoled through the School Certificate, this I found most difficult.

Considering that I now refer to nearly half a century ago, facilities for teaching were excellent. Lecture rooms, laboratorics, apparatus and projection equipment were always available, and a laboratory assistant whose practical ability would have put most of the degree men on the staff to shame. Like P. G. Woodhouse's Jeeves, he was always at your elbow at the right time; and like a good N.C.O., he knew his place; when he had to help you out of a difficulty he made you feel you were conferring a favour on him by allowing *him* to help *you*.

As to the school in general, it was an Elizabethan Grammar School, mainly for day boys. It was run on English Public School lines and was, according to the rules, a public school. Grammar schools, in the original and truest sense, were founded in the sixteenth century to provide a more generous educational background for all and sundry. Up to this time higher education was concerned mainly with the classics, but the grammar schools widened the curriculum to include mathematics and languages. Many of these schools became famous, and a number were incorporated into the public school system, which, whatever its defects, became recognised for many years as providing the best education in the world. This was the category of the school in which I found myself. Each morning we prayed for our noble sixteenth-century founders; what good this did to them or us I don't know, except to remind us of meaningless names.

It was a Church of England foundation with its own chapel, in which services were held on Sundays and prayers were said during at least one morning in the week: on the others prayers were in the Upper School, or we had " House " prayers. Listening to the sermons on Sundays, one rather got the impression that God could be best represented as a close approximation to the best type of English public school prefect; and it was pretty certain that he would have put up a good performance on the cricket pitch. In this country we are often accused of discrimination, and a lack of integration in our educational

I

system. This is true and regrettable; but I am not convinced that we are the only sinners in this respect. I think I am right in saying that there were no Roman Catholics on out staff; moreover, I think it would have been impossible for a Roman Catholic to have been appointed. There were Anglo-Catholics; within my hearing I heard one of these stoutly denying that his views were in any way consistent with the Roman outlook.

The buildings at the edge of a so-called " moor " were old and a little gloomy in—what was then—a gloomy city. The science block, being newer, was somewhat brighter, but when the heating reached this end of the school it had lost most of its heat, and I can remember freezing in the elementary laboratory with its stone floor and glass roof. Having a body which must be warm to work properly, I sometimes found it difficult to control a class, to think for them and for myself, when the temperature outside was sub-zero, and the temperature inside not sufficiently high to provide the right balance between loss and gain of heat. Outside there was a fairly good pitch used for rugby in winter and cricket in summer. There were squash courts, and tennis courts, and later an excellent swimming bath. In fact I have happy memories of one summer vacation spent in Leeds, when I and a colleague for whom I had great affection played tennis, cricket, and squash in turns, swam in the un-occupied swimming bath, and afterwards drank the local beer in the local at fourpence a glass—oh, happy days ! Our poor wives, in the meantime, were suffering the throes of pregnancy; this was the only fly in an otherwise perfect balm of Gilead after the hectic end of the summer term.

Now " dear readers "—as they would have said in a Victorian novel—let me take you with me for a day in this school:

On arrival in the morning I enter by the main door, reserved exclusively for the staff; mount the broad stairway and enter the staff room, where men are draped around, the oldest—always known as " old so-and-so "—with their backs to the mantelpiece effectively concealing the fire from the not-so-old. " Good morning, Paddy," some may say, for schoolmasters, like boys, are quick to place nicknames on their fellows, and mine was obvious. Prayers in Upper School, gowns hastily donned, and hymn books quickly withdrawn from pigeon-

holes in the adjoining masters' study, and then, as the bell rings,
a rush to the Tudor-like Upper School where rows and rows
of boys are already assembling. The head mounts the rostrum
with his prefects ranged around. Removing his inevitable
" tile " he announces the hymn; a prefect reads the lesson, then
a collect or two; and the Head gives his peroration which,
whether he means it or not, the staff feel is directed at them, and
in consequence they come out breathing unchristian-like
imprecations. " Did you hear what he said this morning ? "
My God ! After all the years I've striven to inculcate some
discipline into this school, to be spoken to like that; it's the
blasted limit ! "—this from a youngish, grey-flanneled, sports-
coated classical master who had not outgrown his public school
head boy manners and attitude.

Along the corridor the " Master of the Week " and the
Senior Master are anxiously prodding boys and colleagues
around the white-lined corners of corridors into their various
form-rooms and class-rooms. My class, say fifth-form chemistry, is seated down the long benches of the elementary laboratory. First I test home-work. During the test I notice a boy
copying. In a moment of exasperation I say: " Down to the
Head, Jones Minor ! " I go with him, knock at the study door,
and am bidden to enter. " This boy has been cribbing in a
test, Headmaster." " Despicable boy ! " says the Head, pressing the bell at his feet. " Stick Sergeant ! " Not wishing to
witness the flogging I beat a retreat. In five minutes or so the
boy returns smiling and holds up his fingers to symbolize the
number six. Though I don't agree with the punishment, it is,
after all, the Head's school; his methods are not my business,
so I keep a still tongue. Anyhow the precipitancy and dramatic
suddenness of the action of one not prone to this sort of thing
has a salutary effect; and I never again have to take similar action.

The class goes on. I question and solicit answers. I perform
experiments, draw diagrams and give notes. I try to lighten
things with occasional jokes which I find these Yorkshire boys
quick to appreciate. Sometimes I overhear a joke from them.
While demonstrating vaporization or something of the sort
I say: " See that mist in the flask; that's caused by alcohol
vapour." At once I hear a boy say: " Must be a Scotch mist,

Sir ! " Some individual experiments down on the benches to illustrate the points under discussion, and the session ends with the ringing of the bell for " Break."

Masters move along toward the staff room fumbling in their pockets for pipes and tobacco, or cigarettes. In those days such a civilized custom as coffee at break was not thought necessary for masters, so the only thing for it was school gossip in a smoke-filled masters' room. You could, of course, go down to eat chocolate and drink milk with the boys, but I felt in need of some more stimulating beverage, and eventually started a tea club in my little departmental room. From then on break had more significance.

After break come with me to meet my sixth scholarship set—maybe not more than half a dozen who will sit for various Oxford or Cambridge college group scholarships trying, each in turn, until successful. One of these boys is a big strong fellow; he doesn't like me very much since yesterday, a half-day, when I refereed a house match and gave a bad decision against his house. Another is a small Jewish boy with a brain—as somebody said " like a sponge "—I have to be careful about my facts, for if I make a mistake, he'll be on to me like a flash. Another boy there, that handsome lad, brilliant, but so soon to be cut off by his own hand while at the height of his brilliancy. And that chap there; forgive me, I'm only human, I'm bound to have favourites; he's a big fellow, good at games and keen on chemistry; I admire him and the feeling is reciprocated, I believe ? He gets his scholarship and many years later I am to hear of him from an inspector with whom he had been in rooms at Oxford—this after I had been back on my native heath for a long time.

The bell rings; the end of morning school at last ! Now we have an hour and three-quarters; too long a dinner-hour, so long, in fact, that it is difficult to begin again; but we have to do this only three days in the week; for the other three days, including Saturday, are half-days devoted to games. We go down to dinner—or lunch if you like—to find one of the older men doing the carving; he has done this for years, and he does it with the same gentlemanly ease as he shows when swinging a golf club. He is one of the few men who has been around the world—as a tutor at a time when gentlemen's sons went around the world with a tutor—he plays golf and he drives a car. How does he do it? No one knows but it is whispered that he has private means Being the senior member, though not the Senior Master, he sits at the end of the table.

Opposite sits old Travers, the history master, the very embodiment of Mr. Chipps. Without fear or favour he passes comment on all and sundry. The Government of both school and country come under the fire of his wit. Though the most conservative of men, politically he is a socialist. He tells young Gregg, the English Master, that the English know no history; but, looking at me, the Irish *do* I reply that in the North we know about 1690; there our history begins and ends. There is an argument about the advisability of a coalition to combat the depressed state of the country. " Nonsense," says young Gregg, " a coalition is a dictatorship." " You are a political child," retorts old Travers, glancing at his watch, for he has asked some boys around to his flat for coffee—the flat opposite ours; I can still see it with its crossed college oars and colours, a faded honour cap, and the manuscript of his monumental work. The unfeminine room so desperately in need of the feminine touch, not so much to tidy it as to give it warmth. In spite of his irony and criticism, all his unexpressed affection is for the school and his boys; if there is a match in the afternoon he'll be on the side-lines.

But there is no match this afternoon, for it is a long day: a sixth-form practical-much the same as at the university: analysis, organic preparations, or maybe a physical experiment— determination of molecular weights or something of that nature.

After school what is there? Ah, yes, a " House Tea ! " I am scheduled to sing at it. After a half-hour break we go along to the dining hall to eat sandwiches, and jellies and cream. A short speech from the house master, in which he refers to the splendid spirit of the house, implying that it is superior to that of any other house, is followed by an equally short speech by the Head in which he thanks the House, by honouring him with an invitation to its excellent tea. Looking down at his uneaten jelly he says that jelly immediately makes him think of culture; and that this house in particular, and the school in general, is remarkable for its cultural activities, etc.

We repair to the Upper School. A handsome young man is M.C., and a very remarkable young man this: we note the brown scar down one side of his face where German liquid fire had seared around him. He was sixteen then and a sergeant. He had been buried alive in his trench, and brought home paralysed from the waist down; but one day a psychotherapist said to him, in effect: " Rise, take up thy bed and walk "; and he walked, and from then on he never looked back. Now he is the most energetic of young men. See him prance up and down the stage, now dancing, now singing, now playing the piano. Listen to his quips and rhymes about everybody and any topic of school life. Whether he is singing

" You start at the foot of the ladder
And slowly rise up to the top "

or ragging me about " The Wearin' o' the Green "; or " Jelly," the Scoutmaster, about his short pants; he is at all times the life and soul of the party, as well as being little short of a professional; and he can turn to straight acting with the best. Young boys and the High School girls rave about him—and why not ? He can send a cricket ball to the boundary; make a dashing run along the wing in a rugby match, or put up a good show in the centre of a soccer pitch. Yes, a truly remarkable young man !

Soon he will call on old Griffith to sing " Strolling Down the Old Kent Road " or one of the other cockney ballads at which he excels. Old Griffith is the art master; he had known Sir John Lavery, and once he had seen Mr. and Mrs. Patrick Campbell on the verandah of a hotel in Switzerland: " two of the most beautiful people he had ever seen," he said. Old Griffith is more than an art master; he is a fine actor and producer. Sometimes he would so contort his face in the masters' room, in imitation of some character, that he would set the whole lot of us roaring with laughter. "Dr. Haughton Crowe for a song !" and I give them " Father O'Flynn " or, in even lighter mood, " Phil the Fluter's Ball." They love it, for it is new and a change from " Ilkla Moor."

Home at last with maybe some work to prepare or correct for the next day. And so to bed—a busy life but a full one.

Saturday was as busy as any other with possibly a visit to Sedburgh, St. Peter's, York, Wakefield or Bradford with a team, though this did not happen very often. Sometimes I sang in the choir in chapel on Sundays, or occasionally I might be called upon to read the lessons.

Of my other colleagues a few stand out in my memory. One was the school chaplain who was all that a school chaplain ought to be; he was a Christian in the best sense of the term: tolerant, understanding and sympathetic. Though he made no secret of the fact that he hated teaching, he was an excellent teacher, and a man who understood boys. There were two young men with whom I had much in common: one was very musical; and the other loved music. Both were scientists; and one was to become headmaster of a school from which, by sheer coincidence, one of my own staff was later to be appointed. I have already mentioned the biology man. We were to become great friends; and I recall with pleasure a day when the two of us set off to a heather-covered hill known as Beamsley Beacon. In the heart of the Yorkshire Moors, on that lovely June day, we saw the great German gliding ace, Herr Kronfeld, cleaving the air in an engineless machine. I resolved then that one day I should fly: I *did*; but not in a plane without an engine.

I do not know what happened to all of these men, but I do know what happened to my biology friend; in succeeding years we met in our respective countries to cast a line together on flowing streams and, though his excellent qualities may not have been fully appreciated at the top in my time, eventually they were appreciated, for he acted as headmaster for a period before retirement. What happened to all of the others I cannot say; to you who played " The Londonderry Air " on the first Sunday we attended chapel; to you who, though shot through both knees in the first world war, could hit most bowlers all over the field, and whip the ball from the scrum like a twenty-year-old; to you who would often invite me to your flat for a welcome after-lunch coffee while you played your favourite records and mine. Oh, yes, and I mustn't forget Monty the merry mathematician, and mathematicians are not always merry men; and then there was the soldierly-looking senior master as dignified as his name. How glad we were when he took the rostrum at prayers for he brought dignity and respect to his temporary position. It is not inevitable that a man of distinction should produce a distinguished son; but this man's son, a pupil at the school in my time, became a foreign correspondent of international fame.

Whether I have been fortunate in my school sergeants, or whether all school sergeants are heaven blest men, I don't know, but the sergeant at this school was similar to the one I knew as a boy. He was everybody's friend and the enemy of none. A fine upstanding highlander from the Black Watch, with a voice to match, he would cope with authority, with young masters, and with boys, without toadying to the first, repressing the second, or offending the last.

Like the sergeant at Inst., he could be encouraging without being obsequious. For example, one day I was talking to a boy in the room where he worked—a sort of " no man's land "— after the boy went out he said: " You know, Dr. Crowe, I can just see you as a head." But it was at a school camp that you saw him at his best, whether putting up a marquee in a high wind, or cooking hundreds of eggs, or having a pint in " The Craven Heifer," he was the soul of good temper. There was always soup to be had at his stove after an energetic day; and many a night, in spite of our tiredness, we talked the night away until the first rose-red flush of dawn began to creep silently over the tops of the mountains and along the dales.

Those camps: the first in particular stands out clearly in my memory, possibly because the weather was excellent that year. How delightful to leave Leeds at Whitsuntide; to get away from the murk and the smoke; to journey along the quiet Wharfe River, past Ilkley and then deeper and deeper into the dales, into the Craven limestone, under Ingleborough and along Ribblesdale to Ingleton, where we found a line of white tents all ready and waiting for our reception. This lovely country with its exquisite centuries-old villages, its bubbling streams, its green dales, its limestone walls, its scars and crags and potholes, how did this strike one by comparison with the native heath ? Hard to say; I have never been good at making this type of comparison for each country has an individuality not easily

A TERRIBLE COMPOUND—A COCKNEY, A YORKSHIREMAN AND AN IRISHMAN
In the Dales

defined; and I suppose away down deep in all of us there is an attachment to the soil on which we were nurtured; an attachment which tends to make us ignore the defects, and see only the beauty coloured by the homing instinct. Possibly in our own country there is greater variety with its ever-changing views of landscape, seascape, mountainscape, and lakescape; possibly on its mountains and moors one feels more of that lovely mysterious quality referred to by many writers. Yorkshire is snug and secure with the security of centuries of peace, but this very snugness and security makes it seem almost smug. Some of our towns and villages look as if they hadn't been here yesterday and might be gone to-morrow; Yorkshire villages look as if they had been here yesterday and to-day, and might be in existence for evermore.

However, here we are in a camp beside the unstill waters of the rippling Ribble. Here is a crystal-clear pool unwarmed by the leaf-filtered sun. Here are natural diving platforms of carboniferous limestone from which we plunge into the clear icy water. Perhaps to-day we are off on a long hike among the Three Peaks: Whernside, Pen-y-Ghent and Ingleborough. Back with appetites like elephants we make short work of Sergeant's Irish stew and plum duff. But the day is not over yet. Soon our indispensable young master is going around whipping each of us into renewed activity, for there is to be a sing-song in the marquee. Before long we hear the unresonant tinkling of the piano in this unusual sound-absorbing canvas hall. Even the most staid are singing the popular songs of the day: " Miss Annabel Lee," " My Sweetie walks down the street," or possibly the evergreen " Tipperary." Old Griffith, in charge of the party, sings " My Old Dutch." The boys do their turns in song, and dance, and mime. Some of the senior boys have asked me to write a detective play similar to one I did for a House Tea; but, not being good at reeling things off on the spur of the moment, I decline; instead I sing " The Gentle Maiden " followed by " The Garden Where The Praties Grow." But as usual the life and soul is our M.C. and pianist; with a flair amounting to genius he can turn every incident into rhyme, song, or humorous quip.

So it went on: excursions to Walham Cove, and Walham Tarn—made famous by Charles Kingsley—trips to Gaping Gyll, games of mock football and cricket, and visits to " The Craven Heifer " of an evening where once my Northern Irish conscience was a little shocked to find some of the senior boys at their pints. Though it was customary even then to allow prefects to smoke in their common rooms; and, at some of the public schools, light beer was on issue, I thought then, and I still think that young people in the full zest of their young vigorous energy can get so much out of life that the so-called vices are unnecessary. By putting off the time when they find indulgence a necessary escape from life's cares, both their pockets and their health have nothing to lose and everything to gain. I hope I am neither a square nor a kill-joy, but I say all this with the wisdom—and the mistakes—of sixty odd years behind me.

Soon, all too soon, camp was struck; and we were back to smoke and grime, laboratory fumes, preps and punishments, work and worry, and the last bolts to be pushed home before certificate examinations in July. It may not be the case now but at that time in Yorkshire results were, in the final analysis, the main factor when judging the success of a teacher or his pupils. You could give all you had to a school and its pupils, but failure to get a pupil over the School Certificate hurdle was damning. The end product of the system didn't matter; thousands must have been pushed through who would have been better without any label; and who were probably put off learning for the rest of their lives. I am not suggesting that pressure and encouragement, particularly the latter, may not be necessary at some stage, but this should not involve a highly pressurized competitive system for both master and boy.

During all this, what had been happening on the domestic side ? We put up with the flat for a time; whatever the time was, it was long enough for two young people accustomed to the green fields at our doorstep. Eventually we found a house at Adel on the rim of the country. The landlord told us it had been built to specification of a retired schoolmistress who said it was " 'er dream 'ouse." It was our dream house too, but the dream lasted only for one year at the end of which the landlord suddenly decided that he wanted it for his daughter;

we had been fooled into being a stop-gap. The result was that we had to take a much bigger and more expensive house in the same district; but it was a nice house, as modern houses go, surrounded by open country, and built on a piece of virgin moor with the original heather still growing in the back garden. At that time I was singing Moira O'Neill's " Songs of the Glens of Antrim," set to music by Stanford, so we called the house " Loughareema " as it lay " so high among the heather." It was convenient to the school playing fields, tram and bus routes, and the beautiful little Norman romanesque church at Adel. And above all we could travel northwards, north-westwards, or north-eastwards, keeping in open country all the way: through Blubberhouses, and away on northwards to Grassington, to Ilkley, the Pennines, and the Lake District, by Wetherby and Harrogate, and eastwards to the sea at Scarborough—all these were now possible when we had money and time.

Our first-born, a son, though not born in the house, knew this as his first home. Most fathers, however detached, know the mixture of fear and excitement when they hear the cry in the night that heralds events which they are as powerless to control as the coming of the dawn. And I think most of us know, too, the strange mystery of seeing and holding for the first time a child of our flesh and blood. I find it difficult to put into unsentimental words the feeling that here was the focus of one's life; this is what it was all about; this event was not only important now, but for ever afterwards. Life would never be the same again; its horizon had changed; and a new dimension had been added. Flesh of my flesh, blood of my blood, there is a mystery here, an inexplicable mystery. Why should this baby be any different from any other ? Pride or property ? No, I don't think so ! I have owned broad acres since then, but no invisible chords bound me to those broad acres, such as now bound me to this wriggling miraculous bundle of dust and ashes made flesh by the strange alchemy of nature.

Soon Loughareema was to become a focal point for all our friends from near and far; they were all around us, a sort of

Queen's Club. How did we come into contact with these people ? Sometimes by accident; for example, when waiting for the bus one morning I found an old college friend standing behind me; he was living almost beside us. Sometimes we met by design when people wrote saying they were coming over; but most of these Irish social contacts were made through a local Ulster Society, of which I was a foundation member and secretary. The aims of the Society were social and non-political; almost anyone who wished to do so could join irrespective of religious persuasion or political affiliations. The Society was one of the first of its kind; later many similar associations were formed, all over England. Its main inspiration emanated from two men: a former Cookstown man who came to Leeds at the age of nine, retained his Cookstown accent in his Yorkshire surroundings until I came to know him in late middle age; and, in spire of it—or maybe because of it—was later to become a Leeds City Councillor; the other was a Presbyterian minister, later to become a Moderator of the General Assembly.

Lord Moynihan, the distinguished surgeon, was one of our presidents; and of the many guests of honour one Ulsterman stands out very clearly in my memory. I have always been interested more in personalities than in persons, more interested in minds, modes, and manners, than in families and fortunes. The personality of this man, the great lawyer and judge, Sir Malcolm MacNaughton, was as rough and rugged as the wild Atlantic-riven basaltic coast of North Antrim, from which he emanated. He smoked heavy tobacco in a large hooked pipe; and before getting up to speak I noticed him drawing in an explosive charge sufficient to burst the lungs of an elephant; this he expelled in a great cloud almost coincident with the first words of his speech. As I had to sing at the event, and was probably concentrating on my songs, I am afraid his words made little impact. However, a little later I heard him make a short impromptu and somewhat withering speech. We were travelling home by the same ship from Heysham; he happened to be in front of me in the queue at the purser's office; there appeared to be some difficulty about his berth; the purser said gently:

" Have you anyone in with you ? "

" Good God, man ! " was the lawyer's exasperated reply, " who the hell do ye think I'd have in with me ? "

But our other contacts were more affable. There was a big Fermanagh man whom I first came to know when I was on the staff at Queen's; he was an agricultural student. Often of a Sunday he and I would tramp the moors to the " Surprise View," which always surprised us no matter how often we saw it, this fine view across Wharfedale. From there we went down to the local to meet parson and doctor, farmer and farmhand; my friend, in his capacity as a lecturer in agriculture, was hail fellow well met with all of them. In the meantime his current girl friend, a Scot from the Department of Agriculture, would be at home attired in her mini-kilt, nursing the baby, helping in the kitchen, and above all, fairly making the place ring with her laughter, and my wife's sides split with her salty jokes. This merry, bright-eyed highland girl, equally merry as a grandmother, became the wife of a famous professor of agriculture who was also to join our circle. Now they are frequent visitors at our home here in the County Down.

But we were soon to say a last farewell to our big, bluff, Irish boy from the County Fermanagh. Later we went back to Ulster, and he to the South of England; but the war cut short his promising career, for one day, crossing a bridge with his men in North Africa, this great soul of a man was swept away in an undiscriminating torrent. Before this, however, he and I had one memorable holiday; we travelled on a strawberry boat to Holland where we visited cabarets and castles, colleges and cafés; ate a breakfast more like a lunch, and lunched on a coffee, and eventually arrived at Hull so penniless that we had to await an opportunity to dodge down the gangway in case we might be dunned for a tip. What is a memory if it cannot be shared ? I have mine of canals and windmills, and of oceans of red, yellow and blue flowers; but the one who might have shared this memory with me lies in corrupting clay.

Mention of Hull reminds me of another, a colleague at Queen's, whom I mentioned earlier. He became a reader in chemistry at Hull, and often came to us at week-ends. He was witty company; we saw eye-to-eye about most things save

one: my wife's chocolate cake became famous and I must
admit it was chocolate cake with a difference; but I couldn't
eat it for breakfast; he could ! Then his brother came to Leeds
as Lecturer in Pathology. He and his physicist, violinist wife
became inevitable week-enders and, as he was an outstanding
amateur pianist, we had wonderful times together, sometimes
spending all day on Sunday around the piano. I remember the
joy with which this now internationally famous Professor of
Pathology would accompany me in Mendelssohn's " The
Roamer," or Schubert's " Der Erl König "; the more difficult
the song the more he liked to play the accompaniment.

Before this I had acquired a little local fame as an amateur
singer; but some good friends thought I should have my voice
trained by none other than the famous teacher and musician
in Yorkshire, Sir Edward Bairstow. Among those friends was
a skilled accompanist and pianist, a Welsh lady, wife of a
member of our staff, and a little Yorkshireman, a tenor member
of the Leeds Philharmonic whose cheery countenance and
never-failing on-pitch leads were known to many of the great
conductors including Sir Thomas Beecham himself. This man,
a joiner by trade, who was always to be seen on the side-lines
at rugby matches cheering the school to victory, and who had
to go underground at the first blink of summer sunshine
because of devastating hay fever, was to use his influence with
Sir Edward Bairstow to grant me an audition.

This was eventually arranged. The great man thought I
had " a nice, easy voice," and soon I was in the throes of vocal
and musical exercises, and song-singing. What I valued most
from these lessons was learning immense amounts of music,
of songs, and of poetry, much of which I committed to
to memory for all time; and the voice-training proved to be
a great asset in my work, because I could now speak throughout
the day with little effort; also I found later that I could easily
make my speaking voice heard at the back of a large well-filled
hall. Yes, I commend voice training to every teacher !

Sir Edward Bairstow, a great personality and a great man,
but a man one never felt close to because of a temperament
which one day could be charming, and the next the reverse.
There were many stories about him: that on one occasion he

told the festival sopranos that " they were like a lot of donkeys looking over a wall "; that on another he told the organist, a lecturer in music, that " he should come down from that instrument and leave it to someone else who could play it." Once as I went in for my lesson a charming looking young woman was coming out; he said to me: " Do you know who that was ? " I said: " No." Said he: " That was dear little Elsie Suddaby. You know, when she came to me first I told her to go home and do some physical exercises. Now she has just been across to one of those French teachers who is the fashion at present. She told Elsie that her voice was perfectly produced; she could do nothing for her." Then he added proudly: " You know she has never had a lesson from anyone except me."

When I was doing Schubert's " Der Leiermann " he said: " You want to listen to old Sir George Henschel's record of this song." Later I took his advice and sang the song à la Sir George Henschel. He said: " It's too rigid; you must have been listening to old Sir George Henschel; you should listen to Plunket Greene's record ! " He never tired of telling me stories about the famous Irish singer, Mr. Plunket Greene, to whom almost every worthwhile song at the time had been dedicated, and for whom Bairstow had acted as accompanist. Once I asked him: " Was it true that Plunkett Greene often sang out of tune ? " " Not out of tune," he replied, " off pitch perhaps; but it didn't matter because of the brilliancy of his interpretation."

Like Cicero, his prescription for success at the art was " Actio, actio, actio." Once at the end of a lesson he said to me: " Now *I* must practise," and he did; in fact he was never idle: if I arrived a minute or two late I would find him marking examination papers, composing, or practising. He would have had one practice all day, but as I couldn't very well sing chemical or physical formulæ to my pupils, I—and he—had to be content with the minimum. In spite of this, however, my repertoire was soon to embrace most of the Irish songs of Stanford and Herbert Hughes, Schubert Lieder, The Dichter-liebe Cycle of Schumann, Korbay's Hungarian Songs, Parry's English Lyrics and a host of others. Bairstow considered that

an artist must be a performer; in fact must have the urge to
share his art with others. He told me that when he was young
he used to insist on playing for his nannie when he couldn't
get anyone else to listen to him. And so before long I was
singing in school, at the Ulster Society, at workingmen's clubs,
in hospitals, and in many other places. Good for me?
I think so; at least it brought me into contact with a variety
of people.

But our Yorkshire days were soon to come to an end, though
not without some regrets. For some time I had been applying
for headships without success. I had some ambition; I wanted
to improve our financial position; the homing instinct was
strong; and I felt that, if I were to become a head, I could do
better on my native heath. Besides, though I liked the school
and most of my colleagues, I was not happy with the system,
nor with the never-ending, and often justifiable, complaints
about authority. One by one many of those I had known were
leaving as soon as suitable posts were available; and so it was
not long before I was to join the exodus.

Banbridge ! We had known of this place from our earliest
days. You may remember that in the first chapter I mentioned
a boyhood friend who had died young. His mother came from
Banbridge; so both of us felt that we knew the town almost
as though it had been our ancestral home. When I heard from
my old headmaster that the post of headship of Banbridge
Academy would soon be vacant I felt—knew almost—that
my *magnum opus* was in sight. I applied, was called for interview—but so much would depend on the interview a
friend told us; it would'nt be just plain sailing. Anyhow I
crossed by Heysham, and drove to Banbridge on the morning
of my arrival in Belfast; while my poor wife remained in Leeds
anxiously awaiting the result. When she saw a strange black
cat sitting on the gate-post of Loughareema she ceased to worry.
Neither of us are superstitious, but since that day we have
always felt happier on seeing a black cat !

As for Leeds, there is little left to tell. We enjoyed that
summer of 1933, not because we were leaving—though we
would scarcely have been human had we not felt a little light-
hearted at the prospect of a change—but it was a brilliant

summer—the only good summer during our Yorkshire days. When we went home at Whit to look for a house it was so hot in Banbridge that one scarcely liked to leave the cover of the car. It became a little cooler in July on our plateau at Lawnswood between Airedale and Wharfedale. When my sister and brother-in-law came over to stay with us the weather was so good that we did little other than play clock-golf in the garden, save at week-ends when our friend, the pathology lecturer, took us in his little Austin Seven on farewell picnic tours of Ilkley Moor, Ben Rydding, Blubberhouses and all the rest.

At a certain stage of life, friendships seem to be made only to be broken by separation, for we are all impelled to go several ways without sentiment. Though we disliked leaving our many friends, to have remained where we were would have meant disruption anyhow for if we hadn't left them, they would have left us.

So came the day when we shut the door of Loughareema for the last time. The furniture had gone; now we were setting off in my sister-in-law's car, heading for the Lake District and Scotland to Stranraer, from which port we set sail for " The Blue Hills of Antrim." On the way we looked at Haworth; standing there at The Vicarage, looking down over the valley below, I reflected on the fact that we were returning to the place where that strange, eccentric, tragic, father of genius had his roots, and to the very town of Banbridge in County Down where he had worked as a weaver's assistant. Unfortunately, when we came to Grasmere, Dove Cottage and Wordsworth's grave in the lovely old churchyard, could claim no connection with the great nature poet other than that intense love of earth, air, sea, and sky, and the mystery of simplicity.

K

CHAPTER VIII

BANBRIDGEANS

MENTION of Wordsworth makes me go back to the unforgettable day of the interview when, as I watched a rainbow in the morning, I could not say with Wordsworth that

> " My heart leaps up when I behold
> A rainbow in the sky."

for I had other things to think about; and, though my heart was leaping, it was not because of the rainbow. But it was an April day, with great deep masses of cumulus cloud piling up from time to time, to be followed by a downpour of hail and rain that made the Bann water boil like a witch's cauldron.

All this I observed from the long windows of the old Assembly Room when my turn was called. With the other half of my mind I must concentrate on giving right and sincere answers to the questions. Was I in favour of compulsory games ? Was I ? Definitely not ! I had seen the absurdity of such a system: boys compelled to play, and even to watch games in which they had not the slightest interest. The very term " compulsory game " was a contradiction. Find out what boys or girls are interested in; if possible give them every encouragement to follow their own bent. Good ! that was the answer they hoped for. Most of the boys and girls were the sons and daughters of farmers who did not wish their offspring to come home so tired that they would be unwilling or unable to help on the farm.

Was I in favour of compulsory religious instruction ? No ! I had seen the abuse and the failure of this: this forcing of young people to believe in the unbelievable. Religion, to be worth anything, must come from the heart and soul; it must not be treated as a triviality. We should not teach reason in

the laboratory and unreason outside. We must teach young
people to respect all worthy beliefs. These were some of my
unexpressed thoughts. What I said is irrelevant. They knew
I was not in favour. Again I had given the right answer; for
this was an integrated school in which people of both persuasions mixed in happy camaraderie. To introduce religion
would create barriers, distractions, and diversions. It was felt,
and rightly felt, I think, that any gain by introducing religion
would be offset by a considerable loss to the life of the school
and the community.

I left the room; there was a short interval; then I was called
in again. I had been appointed ! I was introduced to each and
all: one or two solicitors, some businessmen, one or two
teachers or ex-teachers, and some women who, no doubt,
eyed me to see if I possessed the social graces. Then there was
tea. During tea I overheard the following conversation:

" Playin' golf this evenin' ? "

" Not bloody likely ! Ah'm for the river. Just the evenin'
for it," was the reply.

Rough talk no doubt, but natural; and, as my eyes strayed to
the window once again, I saw that it was "just the evenin' for
it": this April evening with its intermittent bursts of sunshine
and rain, shower and shadow; these, I knew, were the weather
conditions to bring out nymph and dun and spinner; on such
an evening as this the unwary golden trout would snap at any
piece of gaudy fur and feather within reason and season. I had
taken up fishing, during a school vacation, a year or two
before; in those days, however, a fisherman in Leeds was like
a thirsty man in a desert: distance, expense, and time made the
sport so difficult that it was impossible for the likes of me.
Here the facilities were all around, available for rich or poor.
Faint echoes of that dim past began to stir in my mind: The
Park, the Gilnahirk River, the Comber River. I was the boy
again dibbling for the occasional trout in the occasional stream.
Here I was, back in it all with the green fields, the woods, and
the streams almost within a stride or two; back in this airy land
with the unencumbered air blowing fresh and free from the
Mournes, from the hills of Down, from the Armagh hills, and

from Lough Neagh, without one smut to sully its virgin freshness.

But my day-dream was quickly dispelled. A voice at my elbow said:

" Of course ye know here a headmaster has to work. There's no sittin' in an office all day. Ye'll be teachin' all the time like the rest o' them. But remember, ye've got a good staff. If ye take them the right way, they'll do well for ye. Ye may find the lab's not too well equipped. I let it run down a bit, for I knew the next man might have his own ideas as to what would be required."

The last couple of sentences were said within earshot of some of the Board of Governors, as though to warn them of the ensuing expenditure. I looked at this slightly bent man with the high-pitched tenor voice, the reddish face, the pince-nez, the high collar, and clothes not *à la mode*, but Victorian; and I warmed to him. Difficult to follow, I thought, because of the obvious affectionate regard in which he was held in this, his home town. Throughout the interview he had been on my side, gently steering his Governors in the way they ought to go; and telling them from time to time what to say, or in what ways they must not bind me. They were businessmen; he was a teacher, and he saw things from a teacher's point of view.

My predecessor's statement that I would have to work left me unworried. By work he meant teach; in this small school with its tight economics, and with Ministry regulations allowing of little compromise, it was, of course, necessary that a head should shoulder a full share of the teaching burden. I didn't mind this; I was used to it; therefore it was not difficult to continue in the same path. But I could see that there would be scope here for reorganization, and new organizations. This appealed to me, for I had always liked clearing jungles; I never enjoyed trying to improve what could not be improved; this smacked too much of change for the sake of change. I sensed that here would be many unsophisticated boys and girls who might require some measure of sophistication. While one might not wish to overlay their naturalness, one knew that most would eventually search for their daily manna in other fields where they must bear themselves as citizens of the world.

Was my assessment right or wrong ? I am not sure; but knowing the kind of world that was to evolve around them since—
where manna is easy and lesiure long—I think I may have
been right.

As I mentioned earlier we were to return again at Whit to
look for a house. What a Whit it was ! Never did Ireland's
green fields look so green. Never did spring flowers bloom so
outrageously on meadow, and marsh, hill and heath. And it
was a spring for us, a new world, a fresh beginning; this after
all, is the secret of life and living; this succession of rebirths.
Even the Bann seemed to have been reborn, for it ran down
from the Mournes like a clear spring; under the " Water
Bridge " it was so clear that the great trout could be seen
darting this way and that in search of worm or grub, nymph
or fly. How well I remember the caretaker conducting me up
to the top of our " undistinguished red brick building "
ostensibly to show me the laboratory, but in fact proudly to
point out the game trout, almost as numerous as the fat greedy
carp in the lake at Fontainbleau.

Then my predecessor brought us over to have tea under the
trees in his old-world garden, at the back of his Georgian
terrace house. He pointed out his best roses; then brought us
to the top of his meadow-flanked hill, from which we could
see the great meanders of the Bann, the wheeling gulls, the
red brick building, and further on the backyard of the original
Squeers-like boarding school, the eighteenth-century Banbridge Academy, where the boys were punished in " The
Dunce's Room "—still to be seen—and no doubt served with
brimstone and treacle in due season.

The old man beside me was as much a part of this scene as
the Bann Water itself, for the stream of his life had been almost
intermingled with its flowing waters. Here he had lived and
moved and had his being. Save for his college days in Dublin
and some early teaching in Belfast, all his days had been spent
here. He knew everybody in the town and they all knew him.
Proudly, from our station on the hillside, he pointed out the
the great houses, at the same time telling me about their
inhabitants. Of one he would say: " A decent man; if you're
in any difficulty with school finance he'll help ye out." Of

another: " Be careful of him; ye never know what way he'll turn." And of a woman: " Och, she's all right, but Ah wouldn't like to be married to her ! " Somebody else would " talk the hind leg off a donkey but would do nothin'." Another, " a grand chairman; be sure to keep him on your Board." And so it went on; before long I was well apprised of the oddities, idiosyncrasies, and virtues of them all; but to give him his due his words more often praised than blamed, for he was proud of his people.

The preceding conversation is imaginary; I am not sure that he did say these things at this time, but they are typical. In my book, *In Banbridge Town*, I described the man in some detail; as many people thought this was the best thing in the book a few quotations here would not be amiss:

". . . His character was like a piece of rough-hewn Mourne granite; he would not have fashioned his doctrine to the varying hour, no more than the granite would be changed by wind or water."

" It would be wrong to call him a little man, for he was not little in stature, intellect, or outlook. Being slightly stooped, however, he did not give an impression of height. His face was florid; his eyes behind his pince-nez had an alert roughish twinkle; and his drooping moustache was stained with nicotine from his ever-smouldering cigarette behind which he walked— as somebody described it—' like the children of Israel behind the burning bush ! ' The most surprising thing about him was the sudden appearance of a sharp, jutting, aggressive chin which seemed to be there as a defence against his normal equanimity; in fact a warning that he could be aggressive— even ruthless—when necessary.

" His clothes were not Saville Row cut; boots, baggy trousers, a watch on a chain, high collar surrounded by an old-fashioned spread of tie, and a soft hat pulled well forward. Thus, I saw him day after day crossing the Water Bridge on his way to the Imperial Hotel for a pre-prandial with some of his cronies of whom he had a multitude; for few men were better known, not only in Banbridge, but throughout the length and breadth of the province. Indeed I was often surprised at the people who said to me when I told them of my appointment: 'Ah, yes, you will be succeeding Brice Moore down there.'

" He spoke with a rather high-pitched voice; was a sympathetic, understanding listener, and his own remarks were frequently punctuated with that dry, pawky—and in his case, Puckish—humour so characteristic of his native country. . . . Though some of his most intimate friends belonged to the highest ranks of the Church, both Roman Catholic and Protestant, he told me once that when they asked for religious instruction to be given in the Academy his reply was: 'All right, if ye want to give them religious instruction, I'll throw the school open for ye at eight o'clock in the mornin' and ye can go ahead until nine.' Then he paused and looked up with one of his Puckish twinkles as he said: 'None of them came ! ' "

" Though his breadth and skill as a scientist were limited by the circumstances of his training, as one inspector said to me: ' It was wonderful how old Brice put them through it ! ' His classroom performance was probably not spectacular, but logically, and with native wit, he drew the best out of his pupils. . . ."

This was the man I was to follow; it was not easy, but he smoothed the way by being most helpful. Our immediate problem, accommodation, was largely solved by his help and advice. Should we take this house or that one ? It wasn't a case of simple preference. I believe it was the Irish writer, Lynn Doyle who, in one of his books, referring to the life of a country bank manager, pointed out how careful a new manager had to be about placing his business. Should he deal with this or that trader ? He had to be so careful not to give offence, in particular to any of his clients. So it was with us, even when choosing from the limited number of available houses.

Eventually, however, we chose to rent one half of a large residence in the process of being separated into two. It was a romantic place surrounded by great trees. The Bann, though not the best part of it, the stretch below the town, ran through the grounds. Near by was Huntly Ford, which William of Orange crossed on his way to the Boyne. The house had originally been built by the Dunbars and was of Regency design. It was said that the last of the family had died while distributing alms from the side window to the "hungry-forties" famine victims. In the seventeenth and eighteenth centuries the chief evening occupation of the local inhabitants was prodding for pearls among the silt and stones of this part of the river, which used to be so full of trout—according to the report of an old-timer—that you would have had no difficulty in filling a basket on a Saturday afternoon. Unfortunately, in our time factory effluent had played havoc with both pearls and trout; in fact, even the pollution-resisting perch and pike seemed to find the highly oxygenated waters above the town more to their liking.

The immense sitting-room with its great French windows opening to the garden was so immense that, when our furniture was dumped in the centre of the floor, it looked like a tiny island in the midst of an ocean. We wondered how in the name of fortune we could ever fill the place, but by some means or other my wife was able to perform a five loaves and fishes miracle; so that what seemed so little gradually expanded all over the house, the addition of the nicely-covered box here and there being used to fill up the odd blank corners. Staining ! staining ! staining ! throughout the remainder of this hot summer until term began, I can remember little other than staining floors, except for the odd intervals when I was glad to retreat to school to try to bring order into the laboratory chaos, or to become acquainted with the details of organization, and the minutes of previous meetings of my Board of Governors.

My sister-in-law, who had a science degree and had deft fingers, like her older sister, came to my aid in the laboratory, so that before long acids and alkalies, solvents and salts, Bunsens and Buchners all had their places, and all were arranged in neat and shining rows; while down in the office my secretary, a downright country woman from County Down, helped me to wrestle with facts and figures, arrangements and regulations. This lady knew the country in which she had been born and bred; she knew all the boys and girls, their characters and what had made them what they were. In those days I didn't know Ooley from Balooley, Dechomet from Donagh-more, nor Ballyward from Ballydown, but she—God bless

IRISH ARCHITECTURE—HUNTLEY LODGE

her!—was able to put me to rights. When I was about to make some awful bloomer about regulations—which would have undoubtedly brought down the wrath of the Ministry of Education on my ignorant head—she would say with scant respect for my exalted position: " Och ! but ye can't do that," or ye'll be in throuble with the Ministhry ! "

And in our exalted position they said we must have a "maid"; and a maid was very necessary in this great house with a child of three and another pending. The first didn't stay very long for she said the house was haunted by the ghost of Johnny Morton; she had seen him. But the second, from the County Tyrone, was made of sterner stuff; she stayed and saw us through our difficult times. But she didn't understand about the telephone; she thought it was some kind of a blower; you lifted it at one end, you spoke and were heard at the other. Unfortunately, the other end for her was England where she had a sister. And as the conversation probably ran something like this:

" Hello, Maggie, is that you ? "

" Aye, it's me; is that you ? "

" Aye, this is me; how are ye doin' ? "

" Fine. How are you doin' ? "

and so on. It was only when our telephone bill reached an exorbitant amount that we realized what was going on.

We had a large garden, more than we could manage; we needed a " man "; we got one, and he remained with us until he could no longer cycle from his own place to the house we were to occupy later. Old Jemmy became a part of the family. Once, talking about money, he said to me: " Ah wish Ah had yer purse, sir." At that time I was trying to make ends meet with the magnificent salary of £500 per annum ! He was not very keen on " the Papishes "; and always donned his sash and marched with the boys on " The Twelfth." I suspect, however, that in spite of the belligerent look on Jemmy's face when he spoke of the Papishes, he had many friends among them, for I cannot imagine that Jemmy would have been unfriendly with anyone. He maintained that one day he had saved the " babby." Always lively and curious, our baby girl had managed to get herself over the side of the pram, and in doing so had become entangled in the straps. Jemmy, finding her in this position, had calmly, coolly, and courageously dealt with a situation that might have daunted many an experienced married man. Jemmy was unmarried, but as he put it, he " lodged with a wumman."

I think it was to relieve us from our first chaotic Sunday that we were—with characteristic kindness be it said—invited to join the large Sunday family party in the other half of the house. And it was a relief to get out of the chaos, not only of furniture arranging, but also of alterations. Brick dust and sawdust may be all right in the right place, but not as an accompaniment to Sunday dinner. Besides, at one point the man in charge had driven a nail through a water-pipe; when Moses tapped the rock causing water to gush forth, he could scarcely have produced a bigger sensation. Many and varied were the remarks and imprecations from the hard-working workmen who, to give them their due, were going all out to allow us to get organized as quickly as possible.

So to go through the wall into the baronial-like dining-room, with its fine high ornamental Georgian ceiling and long windows, from which one could see the great beeches along the Bann, was pleasing and restful. But our host was far from restful, his tremendous dynamic physical and mental energy never subsided. He had three chief subjects of conversation: horses, hunting and evolution. We heard all about hounds and huntsmen, farmers and fences, fillies and foxes, from this butcher-cum-farmer-cum-horse trainer-cum-huntsman. It all seemed to us, suddenly changing from the intellectual life of a sophisticated city, as though we had stepped into the pages of Donn Byrne, whose books we had been reading in the hey-day of their popularity.

Sentimental stage Irish stuff you might say of Donn Byrne; but you know the romanticized Ireland of the sentimentalists is just as much founded on reality as the reality of the realists. The perverted characters of James Joyce's *Dubliners* represent the real Ireland no more than the ' Yerrah," " Arrah," " Begorra," poteen-making, hunting, shooting and fishing types of Somerville and Ross, or George A. Birmingham. Such types still exist, even in the Ireland of to-day. You can still hear the flowing talk as an accompaniment to the flowing pints in pubs. You can still see the turf coming down from the mountains in the donkey's creel, or even the milk being brought to the creamery in the same fashion. Horses ! horses ! horses ! They are mad on horses and will discuss them for hours. Thank God it is so; when we cease to see stage Irish types there'll be nothing to typify on the stage.

Not, indeed, that our friend or the company belonged to the types mentioned, but they all had something that could only be defined by the rather vague term, *Irish*. Our huntsman had something of his puritanical, William of Orange influenced ancestry about him. In spite of his saddle-loving nature he neither drank, smoked, nor gambled. But his obsession with evolution was only equalled by his obsession with four-legged animals. Indeed the latter led to the former. He told me that at one time he was almost a salvationist. Suddenly the idea of organic evolution dawned on him; he read about it for four, eight, or even twelve hours a day, to the neglect of everything else. From being obsessed by the fear of God, men of God began to fear him. Local ministers attacked him at lectures; he flung back at them; and I imagine they were no match for him, either in adjectives or aggressiveness.

However, he taught me to ride, or at least to ride better than I had ever ridden before. If you wish to see the full glory of the dawn go out on horseback on a morning in early winter when the first frosts have made the emerald fields of County Down sparkle like jewelled daggers. Many a time I did that in those early days. Many a time I galloped on a beautiful horse up the hill to Lisnaward Fort; and from this ancient background I saw the sun-tipped Mournes like haloed giants of some kingdom not of this world. Green, pink and saffron spread over the land, chasing the little mists of morning from the bedewed valleys and chequered fields. Sometimes I think it was the release for body and mind of these early morning canters that enabled me to withstand the initial worry and frustration of my new charge.

And, of course, there was a certain amount of both worry and frustration. Any man with any degree of sensitivity knows full well that when he takes over such a post, staff, parents, governors and pupils are weighing him up. Let him make one false step and he may find himself in a morass; so he must tread softly, feeling the ground at every step until he knows that he is on a firm footing. Being young and a little impetuous, I didn't always do this, though I should have been warned; for on appointment my own former headmaster had written to me advising me to take advice from my predecessor about "the little personal interests and influences and cross-currents to be expected in every small community. I opened the Grammar School in Larne, so *crede experto*."

What manner of school was this? Well it was far removed from the hedge schools which may have been the inspiration of its origin. The hedge schools, as their name implies, were usually conducted in a lean-to at the back of a hedge at a time when Roman Catholics, and denominations other than the Church of England, were prevented by law from conducting schools. The schoolmasters, excluding the charlatans, were, for the most part, inspired teachers who literally, at the risk of their necks, were determined to pass on their knowledge. Many were men so well versed in the classics that they educated the Irish peasantry to a degree higher than that of the land-owning aristocracy. The result of all this was that a tradition of voluntary education was established. This was able to come to the surface after the Catholic Emancipation Act of 1811.

Many Irish schools, especially those in small provincial towns, originated through the efforts of some local, more or less qualified, gentleman, who "set up his plate," as it were, and offered to teach, and often board, the sons of the surrounding gentry. My school was founded in this way in the year 1784, when a certain James Withers conducted a small establishment in the town. This was afterwards bought over by a famous character, Mr. Andrew Mullan. His forceful, original, and eccentric personality made such an impression that, even in my time, the Academy was sometimes referred to as " Andy Mullan's School." Not infrequently I would be addressed as " Master Crowe," no doubt as the direct professional descendant of Master Mullan.

Andy Mullan became a legend, not only after his death, but during his lifetime. One of his former pupils, who earned the

distinction of becoming Moderator of the Presbyterian Church
of England, the Very Reverend Dr. J. B. Meharry, has left us
this account of him:

"Like most gentlemen of his profession, Mr. Andrew Mullan
was of somewhat uncertain temper, and scholars anxious to
read the atmospheric conditions likely to rule during the day
were given an unfailing chart to aid them. This, strange to say,
was to be found in the particular kind of hat which he wore.
A soft hat signified normal, and was received by the scholars
with smiles and even congratulations. If he appeared in a silk
hat—easily ruffled—they knew he was riding the high horse,
and that at any moment a storm might develop, so a more
sober spirit had to be adopted. But if Mr. Andrew Mullan
appeared in a red cap, symbol of the executioner, then, with
blanched cheeks and heavy hearts, the scholars looked forward
to the issues of the day, knowing all too well that summary
castigations were in store for them. Notwithstanding his
eccentricities and severity, however, he had a zeal for knowledge and had at heart the advancement of his pupils. He
aimed at making them studious and, to a large extent, self-
reliant; the mixed school created mutual respect of boys for girls
and girls for boys; chivalry was instilled into them and, above
all, a fine religious atmosphere free from all sectarianism,
dominated the entire proceedings."

That Andy Mullan set a difficult precedent is without
question; and, in spite of his eccentricities none would deny
that he was in advance of his time. It has taken nearly a century
for many to awaken to the realization that segregation, either
of the sexes or of people of different religious outlook, is not
good for boys or girls, or for the community as a whole.
But Banbridge Academy was to maintain the tradition through
the years right up to the present time. Other headmasters
were to follow, of greater or less distinction. There was the
Rev. J. H. Cooke, B.A. who, after some successful years as a
progressive headmaster, gave up his charge to take on another
in Rhyl, North Wales. Evidently, finding pastoral activities
more to his liking than schoolmastering, he gave up looking
after the young to look after—and be looked after by—those of
maturer years; not indeed that he required much looking after;

for his son told me that at eighty-five he had written to say that " he was keeping up his Latin and Greek, and was finding French particularly easy." After incumbencies in London, he finally settled down in Western Australia. However, the most outstanding of the other headmasters, not so much in his own right as in his progeny, was Mr. Robert Dodds, M.A. whose son, Professor Eric Robinson Dodds is—for he is still very much alive—a Greek scholar of international distinction.

But this expanding school could not expand much further in the little old—still existing—boarding school in Library Lane; and so it spread into the so-called Temperance Hall, until by-and-by, with characteristic Ulster talent for making a little go a long way, a building was erected to serve three purposes: a public library, a technical school, and an academy. By this time a Board of Governors had been appointed; and the old school had become a " direct grant " school; it had to exist solely on Government grants and pupils' fees.

It was thus I found it. Never shall I forget my first staff meeting in that tiny narrow room with its old fusty desk at right angles to a long table. This little cell served as head-master's study, staff room, and general no-man's-land for all and sundry. It was in this that I first met my staff at embarras-singly close quarters. It was here that I first discussed with unnecessary formality much that I could have discussed, and would later discuss, without formality; for we were a small family circle in such close daily association that formal meetings were about as necessary as embroidery on a suit of dungarees. What transpired at the meeting? Of this I have no clear recollection, save that I did make some suggestions, some of which were received with reluctant enthusiasm, and others somewhat coldly. I suppose there was the inevitable fear in the minds of some that this new man might be hell-bent on sweeping the Augean stables, and he had better be prevented from removing men, oxen, and muck. But they need not have worried for, truth to tell, I was as shy of them as they of me. On the whole, I found everybody most helpful without being obsequious, and they were, for the most part, anxious that my transition into this new world should be made as smooth as possible.

Previous to this I had met the Principal of the Technical School, who informed me with great seriousness, that I would be well advised to go over to Rathfriland to see the parents there " in case," as he said, " they might go elsewhere." I confess this was a new idea, that one should go around touting for one's pupils. Still, as he was a man of longer experience I considered it might be well to adopt his suggestion. When I took over the school there were exactly 119 pupils on the rolls; on reading through the minutes I had discovered that the financial position was precarious; our bank overdraft of £200 per annum had been going on for some years, and had now reached such an alarming amount that the Ministry of Education had instituted an enquiry. Economies had been suggested; it appeared to me, however, that expansion, not economies, was the answer. So it was important, not only to retain all our existing pupils, but also to gain others. Each pupil carried a grant of, on average, £12; to this was added fees of approximately the same amount. The Ministry of Education also paid the incremental portion of salaries, but the basic salary had to be paid by the school. As each pupil attracted a sum of roughly £40, it did not require very complicated economics for me to see that an additional ten pupils without increase in staff would soon offset our liabilities.

So I visited " Rathfriland on the Hill," the beautifully-situated hill-top town, where Patrick Brontê had sought his pupils a century and a half earlier. I should contact Dr. X; a decent man, he would be able to help me. Arrived at the house of Dr. X, I rang the bell.

" I'm Dr. Crowe, the new head of Banbridge Academy," I said.

" Come in, come in, Doctor, you're welcome," said the kindly, motherly-looking woman who opened the door. " I suppose you want to see the Doctor; he'll be in in a minute."

The room in which I found myself would, I think, have shocked " Janet " of Arden House. I remember it as a sort of surgery-cum-study-cum-living-room in which the normal appurtenances of all three jostled each other for space. The smell of iodoform mingled with the house smells in a way that might have disturbed the senses of a senior surgeon. Some of the good lady's brood clung to her apron strings, giving an impression that, whatever its faults, here was a home into which love entered.

Soon the Doctor came in like a breeze.

" Och, sure, Doctor Crowe, Ah've heard a lot about you. Ah hope ye'll be successful in Banbridge."

I explained the reason for my visit.

" O' course, man ! O' course ! I'll take ye round. But we'll have a cup o' tea first."

And we had a cup o' tea—a real good pre-war full-flavoured well-drawn Irish cup of tea.

" Now, then, let's see. There's Paddy Murphy, Mrs. Oliver, Tom Mulligan, an' we'd better run out to Ballyward to see Jack Crothers," said the worthy Doctor.

Before long we were on the rounds. Most of the parents were extremely affable: " Of course Tom, Dick, or Molly would be going back to the Academy. Not a school like it in the country." A few were a bit doubtful, inclined to bargain with me. Was I likely to increase, or could I see my way to decrease fees ? In one house, a little old pub, we were invited to sit down on logs of wood; and " what would we have ? " was the inevitable question; but both doctors wisely declined. A few told me not to be afraid to put on the pressure, nor to spare the rod when necessary. It must be remembered, of course, that those were the days of the great depression, when most farmers and many tradesmen were deeply in the red. There was little or no financial aid for education, and so these financially encumbered parents felt that they must get full value—or at least what they thought was full value—for money. Anyhow, when I parted from the Doctor—also a parent— I considered my morning had been well spent.

But to come back to school. No modern teacher would have put up with conditions as they were at this time, nor could any building have been less well adapted for its purpose. Access to the various rooms of various sizes was by way of concrete and banistered stairs with little or no corridor space; thus the congestion was so intense as to be dangerous. Two small lavatories with hand-basins were situated opposite the entrance door; these had to suffice for staff, and boys and girls.

Part of the building was occupied by the town library, the main office by the Technical School, while at night the whole building was used by night school students. With the exception of laboratory apparatus, the Academy possessed nothing, not even a typewriter nor a telephone. Calls had to be made from the Technical office with the principal or members of his staff standing by. Such arrangements were fraught with explosive potentialities; yet, though each day there were frustrations and differences, it is fair to say that explosions rarely occurred; and that if the set-up did not work very well, at least it did not work very badly. It had some advantages, for example responsibility for the building was in the hands of the Technical authorities, and a certain sharing of staff could often be satisfactorily and economically arranged.

But the " Tech." was not the only rented accommodation. We also had the use of an old elementary school across the road. This was the property of the Unitarian—or to give it its correct name—the First Banbridge Non-subscribing Presbyterian Church. We referred to it simply as " The Dunbar," because the fine Regency Church and the school had been founded and maintained by the generous donations and legacies of the locally famous Dunbar family, which had also given its unqualified support to the " Remonstrant Synod of Ulster," and its Unitarian principles. We used the building to house the superior children of superior families who were unwilling to allow their offspring to hob-nob with the hoy-polloy of town and country. Perhaps it is a little unfair to describe the attitude of all those parents in this way; for some genuinely considered we could offer a better education by better methods than those adopted in the large new primary school: a view with which I could only concur, especially when I remembered my own early experiences; which is not to say that there were no good teachers in the primary school: of course there were.

There was one small playing field approached by a narrow cinder track along the river bank. Save on the few occasions when there was excessive flooding, the field had the distinct advantage of being dry; it was on a bank of alluvial sand deposited by the river on its meandering course. Here it was that our young people played with uninhibited joy and energy their unorganized games. That no one fell into the river was a tribute to their sturdy common sense rather than to any precautions taken to prevent this from happening. When wet they repaired to the so-called " Assembly Hall " where, with equal uninhibited energy and joy, they played the old folk games such as " The Farmer Wants a Wife " or " Down on the Carpet."

Of course there were organized games, chiefly rugby football and hockey; these, in spite of—or maybe because of—the difficulties, were played with rare enthusiasm. Changing facilities were almost non-existent; a class-room served as pavilion, and the cloak-rooms, with their cold water supply, were the only available places in which to wash. Fields had to be borrowed or rented from the local clubs; but as they were always anxious to receive inoculations of fresh young blood, they were only too pleased to allow us to use their facilities. Each match was a social event for which arrangements had to be made well in advance. Fields had to be booked; permission had to be obtained from the Technical School for the use of the kitchens; and arrangements had to be made with the girls and lady staff about the provision of sandwiches, cakes, and tea. I was always courteously invited to these after-match teas; and I enjoyed them. And why not ? All this fresh young life; and a type of school life to which I had previously been unaccustomed. Moreover, I felt part and parcel of it all. I had a feeling of belonging such as I had never experienced before. This was my family; and these were my boys and girls—or *ours* if you like, for my staff, pupils, boys and girls, and all those who had gone before, belonged to a unit, to Banbridge Academy, and *ipso facto* to the town which had given this integrated unit birth.

Our small staff was a dedicated staff. It had to be, for they got little out of it in those days when salaries, opportunities, and extras were extremely small. There were no extra payments for extra duties; people did these either for the boys and girls, or for the activity which was nearest to their hearts. Going back in memory once again to that first day when the staff were ranged around me at the long table in that narrow room. Who were they, and whence came they ? What

manner of men and women were they who were content to
devote their lives to the advancement of this relatively small
and privileged group of County Down boys and girls?

Maybe I see them differently now, and maybe my assessment
of them has improved with the passing years.

There was the English mistress; she had so little use for
hypocrisy or affectation that her own naturalness almost
amounted to affectation, but this County Down-ness of hers
enabled her to draw from her pupils the very best that was in
them: they knew her; they confided in her; they knew she
was on their side; and they also knew that she was interested
in them as human personalities. She possessed that greatest
trait of a great teacher; she was more interested in the success
of her pupils than in her own success, which does not mean
that she was so altruistic as to be completely uninterested
in herself.

There was the lean, dedicated, delicate, almost ascetic,
idealistic classicist. He was always trying to change the winds,
but did not necessarily like the winds of change. In spite of his
own " thorns in the flesh " he was an unrepentant believer in
mens sana in corpore sano to be obtained through the mediumship
of Latin and hockey. His sense of humour and imperturbabil-
ity in the face of authority often saved him from being unduly
vulnerable to the east winds of the weather or of fate.

In contrast, our maths. man was, as mathematical masters
tend to be, the extroverted man of the world, golfer, and bridge
player, and pretty certain that mathematics makes men—or
women for that matter. He alternated between saying black
and white to a degree that made one wonder if mathematics
were, after all, the royal road to reason, but he was reasonable
in seeing and laughing at his own eccentricity in this respect.
He was a determined and forceful teacher who certainly helped
to make some good mathematicians.

But the teacher of French was also forceful; by dint of something, or some quality, she was able to compel the rawest and
most difficult boy from the heights of Ballyward or Dechomet
to learn what, to them, must have been a most difficult language
sufficiently well to pass at least the first examination known
then as " The Junior." Naturally two forceful teachers on the

same campus were liable to cross swords at times, especially as regards the amount of homework that could be extracted from their pupils.

Lastly that morning there was the dean's daughter, who had all the ladylike qualities, cultural associations and sense of vocation that a dean's daughter ought to have, especially when responsible for placing the feet of the sons and daughters of gentlemen on the right path. She was the preparatory schoolmistress. There were other teachers, of course; those mentioned were only types of the most outstanding personalities at the time; others will come in as our story progresses.

The only school servants in those days were the caretaker and his wife. He was a big florid beefy man who presided in a cubby-hole in the entrance hall. There, between times, he would make nets, tie flies, and in general make preparations for his next sortie on the river, which ran around the school. " Got six yesterday," he would say to me, " on the spinner, comin' at it like mad; money for jam ! " But in spite of his love of fishing, he was a man of uncertain temper. Leaning on his brush of an evening amid clouds of dust, I would often be assailed as I came down after a long session in the laboratory. " Look at thon chair ! " and he would show me a chair that had come unstuck after decades of heavy wear and tear by young people of two schools. " Lot o' young hooligans, these boys." Maybe they were—some of them—but I felt they had to take an undue share of the blame for breakages. Once during the first snow of my first winter, when snowballs were hurtling about, as I was passing on my way to class, the caretaker hurled some abuse at me about the snowballing. When I told him I was not prepared to accept this from him he said: " Who the hell do you think you are—the Prince of Wales or what ? " At that moment I felt very far from being a person of such high standing. However, it wasn't long before he came to apologize, saying he hoped I would forget about the incident, which I *did* and, indeed, by the following Easter we were fishing the Bann together.

In contrast his silver-haired little wife was the gentlest of souls. Before the days of school dinners she made tea at the lunch break. In spite of her gentle nature, or maybe because of it, she never seemed to have any trouble. Often one would see the two of them crossing the bridge on the way to school, himself in front strutting along like a " paycock," while his little wife trotted along in the rear. But she was the stronger of the two. Once she told me that he had been a powerful drinker; she had got him off it, but since then he had " a terrible temper." Yet he had the patience to make things; he was, in fact, a great man with his hands, and he often proudly showed me the results of his handiwork. Though no reader himself, he acted as librarian, and he controlled the books as though they were his private property. He had even been known to refuse books to some of the lady members because he thought they were unsuitable reading for tender feminine minds.

Through the mellowing haze of the years it is perhaps a little difficult now to see our boys and girls as I may have seen them during the years of trial and trouble. One forgets so easily the petty irritations, the frustrations, and the disappointments when one probably expected more from youth than youth was capable of giving. But I see them now as, on the whole, a decent lot who had their own trials and difficulties. Few boys and girls now with all their facilities—special buses to bring them to the school door, mini-buses to bring them to matches, good equipment, good class-rooms, good dinners, and all the rest—could realize the difficulties that our pupils had to contend with when I began at Banbridge.

By bus or train, by cycling, by walking, and sometimes by at least three of these methods they would arrive in the morning, from the Mournelands, from the Bannlands, and from the lands of Iveagh; from town and townland with names like poems and as old as Christianity. From Ballyward and Bally-gowan, from Dromore and Dromara, from Loughbrickland and Rathfriland, Kilmacrew, Kilpike and Blackscull, and from Katesbridge and Banbridge; from all these places these ruddy-faced energetic farmers' children, or children of country teachers, preachers, and merchants would come in; some reluctantly and others inspired by Ulster-Scots-Irish tradition for learning and getting on. Contingent number one, from Ballyroney direction, would come in by train at eight o'clock in the morning; contingent number two, the Bannsiders, at nine; while the Rathfrilanders and others would not arrive until nine-twenty. Departures in the afternoon took place at various times also, so that I almost had to get down on bended knee to ask a teacher to take classes during first or last periods.

Analysis of the characters of these young people would be difficult because they were so individualistic; few had that civilized veneer and that stereotyped accent that one finds in the so-called public schools of England, or indeed its hybrid "Malone Road" counterpart, so often adopted in similar schools here. With few exceptions they all used, in varying degree, the ancient Elizabethan—but now often despised—accent of their forebears in the County Down. One had to get used to this, especially when it was very broad; for example, I asked a boy one day why he was late; he said: "Please, sir, Ah keeame in a wee keart," which, being interpreted, meant that he had come to school in a small cart—doubtless a slow method of transport. There was a certain roughness of manner, too, which I had to try to smooth down a little. Occasionally there would be a knock at my door; on opening it I would be greeted with: "Miss X says yer to come down to Lower I to quieten the boys." Naturally, such a peremptory order in the middle of the elucidation of some difficult scientific problem, was somewhat irritating. However, I soon learned that the roughness of manner was simply rustic shyness; and that the request had not been couched in quite the same terms by the teacher concerned.

Two-thirds of our pupils were the sons and daughters of farmers. They often came from excellent farms; those that did were usually of good calibre, especially the girls. Probably a girl had to be fairly good academically, otherwise she would not have been sent to us; for the farmer allowed his girls to continue at school with some reluctance; and had to be persuaded that she would do better away than about the house. With his boys his outlook would be more lenient. "Sure a wee bit o' education 'll never be lost on him," he would say, even though it was intended that the boy should come back to the farm. Some indeed never left it; a few might milk a dozen or two cows by hand before leaving to catch that early train; and many had to work hard when they returned home. On the whole, I would say that the farmers' sons who did best, from our point of view, were those who came from the better farms, and therefore did not have to exhaust their energies on too much heavy work. Though this was not always the case. One boy, who later took a good degree at the university, was to be seen early in the morning, before school, delivering buttermilk from a donkey-cart. He worked in a loft by the light of an oil lamp.

Three farmers' sons of those early days stand out in my memory. One entered the Royal Navy, became a commander at least, and was eventually made a Freeman of the City of London. Another gained a first in chemistry, and was appointed to a short-term post at Queen's similar to the one I had previously held. Later he entered the army and served in the Far East; on demobilization he became a research student at Cambridge, where he obtained, not only a Ph.D. but also a rugby blue. I met him recently to find him little changed in spite of the fact that he had become an international executive in one of the world's great oil companies. About the same time a third boy had a similar academic career; ultimately this one was appointed to a chair in biochemistry after he had made a significant and valuable discovery in the field of animal pathology. Every school can boast of its great men: I mention these examples to show that the sons of the farming community in my experience, are fully capable of reaching the higher flights in the academic and professional worlds.

Though the sights and sounds to which many—in fact, the majority—were accustomed were twin horses ploughing the sweet Down earth, the clatter of milk cans, the clickety-clank of the reaper on harvest fields, the sheep dog's warning bark, or the farmer shouting, " High there, Sammy, come up here an' give us a han' on this stack ! " There were others who would listen of a Sunday to father's deep voice cajoling, comforting, and exhorting his flock to follow in the way of the Lord. The tinkle of the shop bell and the call of " Shop ! " the quietness of the country bank house, the doctor's telephone, and the schoolmaster's or schoolmistress's irritability: all these were environmental for many. Impressions without statistics may often be erroneous, but my impression now is that the sons and

daughters of parsons and schoolmasters were more likely to be
good material from our point of view, especially at this time
when examination results tended to be of such vital importance.
It is a natural corollary that those brought up in an environment in which scholarship, education, and academic attainment
are admired, are more likely to attain scholastic success, than
would be the case in homes where such abstracts are treated at
the worst with contempt, and at the best with patronizing
tolerance. Anyhow I think I am right in saying that in those
days, before mass education, we produced, or helped to
produce, more doctors, teachers, and preachers, from the
families of teachers and preachers than from any other strata of
our society. It has often been said that one swallow doesn't
necessarily make a summer—true enough ! but it can point the
way; one of our boys of this early group—a boy from a parson's
family—soared until he became a Cambridge professor.

As to the girls, I recall the best of them as being strong,
healthy, often good-looking, intelligent, and above all,
practical—especially practical even when not particularly
intelligent. The result was that many entered the more
practical professions such as nursing and domestic studies;
some became elementary teachers; a few went to university
to take arts degrees; and one or two became doctors. The
" K.S." people, as they were called, were those who aimed
at becoming King's Scholars by way of the " Senior " with
some special qualifications. If accepted they went on to Stran-
millis Teachers' Training College. When they " came out "
they usually became teachers in country elementary schools in
their own districts. And not a bad life either, for most became
almost essential to local life; many married farmers and continued to teach, thereby adding much-needed funds to the
family purse; others married young local schoolmasters. How
much better off they were than those of higher academic
attainments, who became teachers in some girls' boarding school,
where there was little outlet or opportunity to mix with those
of the opposite sex.

A picture of this small country academy, as I found it, might
best be given by a description of my first speech day. It was
called the " Academy Party," and it was a party in the fullest

sense of the word. Anything more unlike a speech day now could scarcely be imagined. The contrast represents a difference between two generations, one of which passed with the second world war.

I talked the matter over with our Senior Mistress. " How about inviting Dr. Helen Waddell to distribute the prizes ? " She knew her well; in fact, the distinguished authoress was an old friend. I was greatly taken with the idea, for I had already made up my mind that, as far as possible, we should invite those who had contributed directly to the artistic and intellectual life of the people, rather than those in official positions. In this way I hoped that our pupils might be stimulated to admire genuine worth, talent, and learning for its own sake. Up to then I had known only vaguely of Helen Waddell. I knew of her as a classical scholar, authoress of one well-known novel, *Peter Abelard,* and of many translations of Latin lyrics. I knew little or nothing of her local connections, so that I now remember with great pleasure that lovely late autumn day when the Senior Mistress and I set off to find the farm and home of her sister and brother-in-law in the townland of Kilmacrew. There, on a garden seat looking out over the well-kept and progressive farm of the scholarly clergyman, farmer we discussed the project. As I watched the autumn leaves make their slow descent to the ground, I could not help thinking of this symbol of rebirth, and I felt that no matter what difficulties might be ahead, the continuance of the school was as certain as the eternal cycle.

Of course Helen would come ! They were sure she would be delighted; she would be at home at about the time, just before Christmas. They would write immediately. And they were as good as their word for, in due course, we heard that she would be happy to distribute the prizes, and to talk to us.

At last the great day arrived. The decorations were draped around the Temperance Hall, the bunting, the holly, the mistletoe and all the rest. Hundreds of sandwiches were cut and made, buns and biscuits, cakes and cookies, tarts by the hundred, and tea by the gallon, all had been prepared. Prizes had been purchased and set out; a programme had been

arranged. Invitations had been issued to *all* but not to *sundry* ;
for the sundry came anyhow; but the *alls,* which included
every very important person in the district, had to be specially
invited to sit on a platform so overloaded with the important
and self-important, that one wondered how it could withstand
the strain.

And Helen didn't arrive ! Imagine my chagrin ! This was
my first speech day. Eight o'clock, five past, ten past, a quarter
past ! I stood at the door of the Temperance Hall in a fever of
nerves while inside the hum in the hall grew until it sounded
like waves in a storm. Ah ! at last ! What was that ? The
sound of a motor cycle above the storm on that wild December
night ! And in out of the storm she came to throw her arms
around our Senior Mistress in greeting, and to shake hands
with me, all the while full of apologies for what had happened;
the car in which they had started off had broken down, so she
had no recourse but to come in the side-car of a motor cycle—
a form of transport now almost unknown.

With little time in which to recover our equilibrium we were
on the platform; the chairman had made his opening remarks
introducing the speakers and the new head, and calling upon
me for my report. " Now for it," I thought, as I rose slowly,
and with considerable flutterings against that seemingly empty
part of my anatomy in which butterflies are reported to flutter
on such occasions. I knew that, as the new man, I was under
close observation; and I had to make a speech about past
achievements and future plans, knowing little about either.
However, I got through with it, but of what I said I have no
clear recollection. On the lighter side I remember referring to
the black cat that had haunted our garden on the day of my
appointment. I hoped this would be a good omen for myself
and for Banbridge, and I suggested that a suitable crest for the
school might be a black cat rampant on a red background.
In a more serious vein I probably said that while I respected all
that had been done in the past, I felt that perhaps too much
emphasis had been placed on examination results, and I hoped
we might be able to extend the social side of our activities,
so that our pupils might be good mixers as well as good
scholars. I thought that mere learning was not important;

it was much more important that learning should help to produce men and women of greater understanding and wisdom.

Before getting up to speak Helen Waddell, with grace and thoughtfulness, turned to congratulate me on my speech. Then she held us spellbound while she talked about things present, things past, and things to come. With what poetry she repeated the familiar names of the towns and townlands of our countryside as she said:

"All this countryside that Banbridge lies at the heart of, names that are themselves like an old folk-song or a come-all-ye, Closkelt and Ballyroney, Annabawn and Drumgooland, Loughbrickland and Donaghmore, Ooley and Ballooley, Kilmacrew and Ballygowan and Dromore; these are the names that I heard from my aunts around the fire, and these are the houses where my great-grandfathers went courting my great-grandmothers."

And how near she brought us to the great, and how prophetic her vision when she concluded with these words:

"The last century saw the machine conquering nature; is this century going to see the machine conquering man? It will depend on one thing only: the spirit in which man uses his vast new incalculable powers. And on the possibilities before that spirit the most significant and stirring thing that has been said in our time came the other day casually, at lunch from Bernard Shaw; he was arguing with a great biochemist on vivisection the biochemist's view was that it was a cruel necessity. 'Cruelty,' said Shaw, 'is never a necessity. If a thing is wrong it is not even expedient. Shut that door for ever and let the spirit of man set itself to find another door, and it will find it, for there is nothing beyond the power of the spirit of man.' Another door than cruelty, another door than poison gas, another door than war! It may be that some of you here are destined to find it."

Alas! we did not find it; nor have we yet found it. And one is prompted now, forty years on, to cry: "How long, O Lord, how long?"

But to come back to less serious things. A programme followed—not very ambitious in those days: the usual formal

singing of songs, and some dancing—not Irish. Oh, dear, no !
That would have been a gesture much too nationalistic to have
been accepted by the audience ! Then there was tea, when my
wife and all the ladies joined in feeding all the ladies and
gentlemen, adolescents and children, of the town; for the
formal business of the evening being over, the numbers now
suddenly began to swell to far greater proportions. Soon all
the playboys and playgirls, including myself, were involved
in the old folk games: " The Farmer Wants a Wife," " Down
on the Carpet," " The Grand Old Duke of York," " The
Lancers " and all the rest. By midnight the whole town was
there and the fun was reaching its height; the prep school
children were literally dancing between the legs of the adults.
The more sophisticated attempted to foxtrot, waltz, or one-
step, but their efforts were not very successful in face of the
demand for games, games, and more games. It is hard to
believe that long, long before I retired all this had gone by the
board, and even the younger members of the school could do
little more, and wanted to do little more, than wriggle and
contort and gesticulate to the music of some ear-splitting dance
band or pop group.

As this book is largely autobiographical and, *ipso facto,*
concerned with myself, my reactions and ideals, I need make
no apology for pausing at this point to consider how I now felt
about the whole business. Had I been wise in accepting the
post ? Was I suited to the job ? Was I likely to make a success
of it ? What ideals had I, and could I carry them into effect ?

It is hard to be precise in such matters because every job in
life, especially those in which others are involved, has a content
involving different, and even opposing, qualities. That I liked
the work in general goes without saying, otherwise I would
scarcely have written this and other relevant books. Because of
the smallness of the school the work was intimate, friendly and
human, and it was among people whose problems I knew and
understood. I liked teaching, especially young people on the
threshold of science, and older people on the threshold of life;
in the early days I had to teach nearly full time so it was
important that I should like teaching. I was interested in
people, in their psychology, background, in their make up, and

and in what made them tick; and so, on the whole, I enjoyed the relationships with parents, pupils and staff. In so far as administration and organization involved personal relationships with people I was happy, but when they involved numbers in a card index or something quite impersonal, I was not happy, and much inclined to leave such jobs to others who were able to do them better than I could. School finances, too, were a headache in those days of so-called independence. Those long lists of unpaid fees, how they used to worry me! Farmers were constantly in the red; and to have to pursue them for payment, was a side of my responsibilities that I detested.

This first speech day did one or two things for me. In the years to come I knew that public appearances of one sort or another would be my lot. Though I had never enjoyed this type of duty, I now knew that in this respect at least I could face the future with some confidence. Here, too, was a means of expressing oneself, one's beliefs, and one's ideals, more freely that in private conversation. Here at least, at the end of the year, one had a chance to rise above petty criticism; one could explain and expound; and whatever criticism might be made of immediate decisions, the long-term results could be made manifest.

On the practical side it was evident that the school was too much restricted to the subjects necessary for the passing of examinations, and the rigid requirements of the Ministry. Obviously, as I mentioned earlier, finances must first be put in order; having achieved this we must increase our scope by the addition of another language, and another science. But a much more difficult task would be that of trying to enlarge pupils' vision. The stick was still being used far too freely up and down the country, not merely as a punishment for the more objectionable type of offence, but as a method of teaching. I felt I had a duty to try to eradicate this so that our pupils might learn without undue fear; and learn so to behave as to be socially acceptable human beings. And, while I realized that the earning of a living would be vitally important, I thought I must try to recapture in some measure the educational ideals of the originators of education. I could have said of the people around me, as Ruskin said in his day:

" They never seek, as far as I can see, an education good in itself. Even the conception of abstract rightness in training never seems reached."

Abstract rightness in training ! A little difficult to define, perhaps, but I thought then, and I still think, that an education that tends· to inculcate ideas of justice, tolerance, kindliness, and thoughtfulness, and one that does not seek for the true, the good, and the beautiful, is an education that has failed.

It might be a little incongruous in these days to talk about reaching for the moon, but the metaphor will do as well as any other. Maybe I was reaching for the moon, none the less my moon-madness was not as mad as might appear; for, as the years passed, and as the succeeding chapters, I hope, will show, at least some of the ideas and ideals that I and others had in mind then, gradually began to assume more tangible form.

At this time there were two public examinations, based largely on the old " Intermediate " system. These had come into being at the time of the division of Ireland into two communities; they had changed little since. Both were group examinations with certain compensatory clauses allowing candidates with minimum marks in a subject to carry over marks to another subject. The first examination was known as the Junior Certificate, the second as Senior Certificate. The senior examination could be used for entry to university and colleges generally. Examinations for bank and civil service, while usually separately conducted, were based on the senior syllabus. The Junior served little or no useful purpose save that a pass in it gave some status to those leaving school at fifteen or sixteen. There was a time when it could be used for entrance to pharmacy and, with some limitations, to Trinity College, Dublin, when Trinity students had to take a freshman examination known as " Little Go," and sometimes an arts degree, before proceeding further. Results of both Junior and Senior were published in " blue books." The publication of these was awaited anxiously, and often with nervous apprehension throughout the long summer vacation. Many a minor, and even a major, tragedy lay beneath the pages of the blue book. For many a parent it was an end to hope for there was no redress. There it was: failure in a key subject ! You were

downed and damned academically for all time; at least unless
your parents could allow you to have another go, which
wasn't always the case.

There was an entrance examination conducted by each
individual *secondary*—as they were called—school. This was a
farce and excluded none, for no small direct grant school could
afford to turn away fee-paying pupils. Papers were set by the
staff, corrected by the staff; and, where necessary, candidates
were given an unofficial second, and sometimes a third, chance.
Complete failure did not usually result in refusal to accept
pupils; if they still wished to come they would be placed in
Form I; and would qualify for a preparatory school grant.
The result of all this was that the spectrum could range from the
very dull to the very clever; and, as numbers were small at this
time, one might get this range in one form. This was good for
the dull, and had little effect on the clever—at least that was my
impression.

Games were played with great enthusiasm by those who
played games; the numbers who did so represented no mean
proportion. Boys usually played both hockey and rugby
football, and the girls hockey. Because of lack of facilities
attempts to introduce other games—tennis and cricket—met
with indifferent success. Enthusiasm for hockey outweighed
that for rugby for two reasons: there was a strong hockey
tradition in the town, and the boys knew their chances of
winning the Schools' Hockey Cup were good, whereas their
chances in the rugby competition were negligible. Though I
thought I had matured sufficiently not to become unduly concerned about the winning of team games, I must admit that on
the occasion of the cup final I was a boy again; I could not help
being swept off my feet by the infectious enthusiasm, and by
the feeling, right or wrong, that a certain degree of school
prestige was involved.

Sometimes I travelled in the bus with the crowd of boys
and girls—they sang their way to the match, and they sang
their way home again, while red and black scarves fluttered in
the slip-stream like proud pennants. I stood on the touchline
impervious to cold or damp, because my excited blood circul-
ated almost as freely as though I had been out there in mid-field.

Sometimes I had to carry on polite and desultory conversation with my opposite number from the opposing school, but I wanted to be a lone wolf to enjoy the circling sticks, the clever passing, the brilliantly evasive run, and the ball surely netted at the vital moment. This didn't always happen, but it is true to say that in those early years the school nearly always figured in the final game; and not infrequently were the proud purveyors of the cup to the Bannside. And, of course, the Bannside loved to receive the cup; for town and gown in those days of fewer schools and smaller population was a closely-knit unit in which the success of gown was also the success of town.

Time moved on and the school moved on. At the end of each year I was able to report progress. Our financial difficulties began to ease, but never to disappear because, as numbers increased, there had to be an increase in staff. I was glad of this, of course, as it meant that we were able to widen our scope by introducing new subjects, first priority being given to physics, though we had no special facilities for the teaching of the subject. At this period, and indeed up to the time of my retirement, the regulations about staffing were an anachronism. These were based entirely on numbers, and bore little or no relation to the requirements of individual schools. You were allowed one teacher for each twenty pupils, and one more. Any teachers above this quota were described as unauthorized staff, and were paid a minimum basic salary without increments. These regulations, presumably based on a time when any teacher could teach any subject, made it extremely difficult, and at times impossible, to provide for the needs of individual pupils in small schools.

Dear me ! The worries and frustrations ! How we overcame them I don't know. Sometimes one had to cope with the unreasoning and unreasonable parent, with the rigid inspector who was incapable of turning a blind eye; with a member of staff who rightly felt this or that subject was not for him or her, but who would reluctantly take it on to help us out of a difficulty; or with the boy or girl who wished to do one subject for which it was impossible to make provision, and might thereby be prevented from entry into some college or profession. These were trials and troubles common to all of us who were

THE NEW OLD SCHOOL
Banbridge Academy as it was

headmasters of small provincial Ulster schools in the twenties and thirties. All these difficulties could only be overcome by expediency and compromise from hour to hour, day to day, term to term, and year to year. And perhaps I should add that some inspectors *were* able to turn the blind eye, and that our small Ministry and its officers were always accessible without formality, so that as a last resort one could carry one's troubles to those in the highest authority, even to the Minister himself.

To say that I travelled the road of time unflurried and unworried would be to deny what every headmaster knows to be the truth; but the years passed happily enough, for we seemed to be doing something new and making progress all the time; and at the end of each year this progression was epitomized on speech day. When this function came along one forgot the valleys of despair and saw only the heights of success. By this time the old Academy party had disappeared, a step that brought me some unpopularity until the public, in general, became used to the new idea. Things could not have continued as they were, because the school was now growing so rapidly that if we had not divided up the party into two or three functions, the party would have burst its bounds, or the walls of the Temperance Hall.

Of these functions one that stands out clearly in my mind was in 1937. I had invited Mr. Lynn Doyle, the well-known Irish humorous writer, author of *Ballygullion* and many other stories of Ulster country life. In the first instance I think I asked him to come on St. Patrick's Day, March 17th; but in that particular year St. Patrick didn't oblige by " turning up the warm side of the stone." In fact, he did the reverse, for he poured on us the full fury of an Arctic blizzard. A few nights before, it snowed, and snowed, and snowed until Bridge Street, Newry Street, and The Cut resembled more than anything else a road through a backwoods town in the Klondyke.

On that evening I had asked my secretary to do some work for me at Huntly Lodge. As the evening advanced so did the snow until rails and roads, lanes and lines were so packed that any hope of reaching Dromore that night was as remote as Franklin's hopes of making the North-west Passage. But my

M

secretary, with characteristic County Down stubbornness, insisted that "she'd be to go," and no amount of inducement would persuade her to stay the night. So I had no recourse but to get out the old Citroen, which coughed and spluttered into reluctant life, but refused the hill as stubbornly as my secretary refused to remain. Eventually we ploughed on foot through the drifts to the station to find that trains were as few and far between as the stars in the wind-swept, cloud-torn sky. Never shall I forget that dreary cold wait in the dreary station for a train that didn't arrive until after midnight had boomed from the Town Hall clock. How she made the last of her journey to her country home, I don't know; but she made it, and turned up the next morning. As she kicked the snow from her boots outside the old staff room, she looked as unperturbed as if she had spent the evening warming her feet at her own fireside.

There was enough, and to spare, to keep her occupied that morning, for we had to send messages all over the country by letter, by telegram, by telephone, and by grapevine, letting our small but outspread world know that Speech Day had been postponed until near the Easter vacation. But when it came it was worth the delay. Who could have made a more suitable guest that this literary figure who knew his County Down, and his County Down people, so well that his *Ulster Childhood* has become a classic, and whose *Spirit of Ireland* is an emanation from his own Irish spirit ? As Arthur Emerson, the late editor of the *Banbridge Chronicle,* and I sped along the valley where the O'Neill forces had made their stand against Sir Charles Poyntz for Queen Elizabeth, I remember Emerson saying with reference to Lynn Doyle: " Och, sure you couldn't tell where that fellow might turn up ! " And indeed you *couldn't,* for there had been some mistake about his place of arrival. Eventually we tracked him down mooning about in the Goraghwood Railway Station in which he had arrived about two hours earlier. But he was quite unperturbed for he was interested in everything, in the " cracks" of the railway porters, in the conversations of the desultory passengers, and in the wide landscape sweeping away from beneath the great quarry above, to the Mournes and the sea at Carlingford Lough. He was interested in all these things, because he loved them so passionately that a two-hour wait at a lonely station in the heart of the country, was simply an opportunity for further observation.

As Emerson manœuvred his high-powered car at breakneck speed—he was a fast driver—along by the Scarva Canal, he pointed out this or that item of interest, the Humpback Bridge, the Danish Dyke, Shark Lough and all the other things in this lovely quiet sheltered valley which has changed extraordinarily little throughout many decades. Each time I motor along it now I am relieved and overjoyed to find so little change in this fertile land, since that afternoon when Emerson, Lynn Doyle and I journeyed along it on our way to Banbridge.

Lynn Doyle—Leslie Montgomery—was a charming guest at Huntly, and his speech that night—lightened by his sparkling humour—was one of the most outstanding I can remember. He said he " hated school like poison, for it was an old-fashioned school where you had to get up at seven, wash with cold water in a draughty shed and, as there was one towel, it was a case of God help the younger and the weaker members. But as they were half-starved he did learn to cook, and he reckoned he could cook sausages and fry or scramble eggs with any woman in the hall ! " He ended his speech by saying: " At the present moment you children may be thinking, ' I wonder what that ould fellow is blethering about.' Well that ould fellow is not an ould fellow at all; he is very much what you are—full of joy and life—but when he gets a good thing he has this additional advantage, he knows it. Live with the times, look out on this beautiful world around you with enjoyment, and then you will be able to see that these ould people you look to as living in a sort of semi-misery are having a darned good time."

Good medicine for the ageing ! I never forgot this speech. When I retired it was constantly in my mind. Nor did I ever forget the party at Huntly that night. It included an old friend, Rev. Dr. Andrew Gibson, M.C., later to become a Moderator of the General Assembly—a man as popular in Cork as he had been in Flanders, and in Leeds, where I first met him—Emerson and one or two others. With a " wee jorum " inside us the conversation soon rose to the heights, and reached a stage when it must inevitably go on into the small hours. Soon we became obsessed with a subject dear to the Irish mind—politics—and I can remember how well Doyle forecast much of what is happening at the present time.

The following morning he had a love affair with our little daughter—we now had a daughter born soon after we returned to Ireland—and the affair was reciprocated for she fell in love with him. Hand in hand the pair walked around the garden under the old beech trees by the river until it was time for the Dublin train, and we had to part with this pleasant Irish humorist for ever. As an interesting postscript I should add that his bank took exception to some statement he had made in his speech about the indifferent education of new entrants to the bank. He wrote a public apology in which he stated in effect that this was the bitter end as far as relations with his bank were concerned; and that he could only look forward now to a lonely procession to his grave without even a single bank clerk to walk behind the hearse !

The busy years passed by, punctuated by both work and pleasure. I remember my father once saying to me that holidays were not very important in so far as one's life work was concerned. It depends on the work. I regarded holidays as being very important; partly because one was affected by the general spirit of a school and young people: the working up to a peak at the end of term, and then the sense of release; and partly because here was an opportunity to get away from the life of a school for a little, to mix with more mature people, and to occupy one's self in completely non-academic pursuits.

Our first holiday after we returned home was spent at nearby Newcastle in the County Down. We went there with our newly-born baby daughter, accompanied by a maid and a nurse. Imagine in these days anybody in our position being able to do this; it would be impossible now on five times the salary I had then. This was the first holiday I had spent in the County Down resort since I was a child. Overshadowed by the great giant beehive of a mountain where Saint Dominicus prayed—and, according to local legend, still prays—it had remained much as I remembered it. There was the promenade with its wind-blown trees, the long, long, stretches of silver strand extending from Donard to Dundrum, the Demesne with its green stream leaping over moss-covered granite boulders, Maggie's Leap where Maggie leaped from a bold, bad, man with her unspilled basket of eggs, and the Bloody Bridge, where the bloody Con Magennis massacred his unsuspecting prisoners who thought they were on their way to freedom. We ate bilberries on Bingian's side; caught blockin at Maggie's Leap; and dived from the harbour wall into the fretting wavelets of the green sea. And my friend of yesteryear was there, the lecturer from Queen's. One night we went fishing from a boat in the Irish Sea, but a storm arose, and we had to make a hasty landfall among the rocks by the Bloody Bridge to avoid being sea-sick, if not shipwrecked.

The holidays I remember most in those early years were two we spent in Donegal. I believe it was in Coronation Week that we went to find a place on the North Donegal coast. And we found it; no more ideal spot for a family holiday could have been imagined: a little grey bungalow in a marble-sided cove with silver sand to the door, and the little rocky hillocks and foothills of the Donegal mountains streaming away to the rear like green waves on a billowy sea—all absolutely private, with private coracle on the beach, private fishing from the rocks, and an infinite number of trout-filled, and sometimes salmon-filled, streams and lakes in the hinterland. You stepped straight into the main room through the door, and there the red glowing turf fire was always burning, so that whatever the weather you could be warm and snug.

To catch great fish from the rocks with the salt spray stinging your cheeks was sheer joy. In a stream bubbling through boulders and over marble shingle I caught my first salmon; and up in a mountain lake one day with a wind blowing from the mountain at my back, I found golden brown trout rising in a ring a few yards out. I thought that something like a black spider was being blown on to the lake; and I was right, for every time I dropped a dry black spider over a rising fish he took it. I talked to a wild Donegal man when I was fishing up there. Said he: " I was in the last war." I asked him what he thought about it. " Och," he replied, " sure 'twas the best picnic that ever I was at ! " Whether the word *picnic* was just a figure of speech or not I cannot say, but I could not help thinking that anyone who regarded the 1914-18 war as a picnic must have been living under pretty poor conditions at home.

On this, my second visit, I had no reason to discard my earlier view that Donegal *is* undoubtedly one of the most beautiful counties in Ireland. Here again I saw with joy its lake-filled valleys, wild rock-bound coast, and that strangely clear view of mystical blue mountains offset by a green that seemed to colour the air. And the thatched cottages ! hundreds of them dotted over the dry-walled, outcropped, peaty wasteland of the west, gripping the hillsides as though they were limpets on the rocks. Out of the clear blue from the mysterious land across the bay, one day a currach drew up on our beach and two men stepped out, one with a wooden leg and the other with a patch over his eye. Did we want any fish ? Of course we had to buy some; and they had to have a cup of good strong tea before making the hazardous journey back in their frail craft. This was only one of many visits from the two, whom we obviously dubbed " Long John Silver " and " Captain Cuttle."

We had a maid with us in Donegal; she came from " Tyrone among the bushes "; good, hard-working people come out of Tyrone; she was no exception and, as well as being hard-working, she had all the friendliness of the friendly people of Tyrone. She rarely wanted to go out of an evening; she would rather stay with the family. On the way home we must go to see the uncle who had reared her. Going through Newtownstewart she proudly pointed out the Bank House in which she had served as a maid for some time before coming to us. She had left the job because she didn't like Montgomery's ghost which was said to haunt the house. This was a reference to the notorious police inspector who had done to death his friend, the bank manager. The trial, which went on for a long time, resulted in the conviction of Montgomery who was ultimately hanged. All of which reminded me of a remark made by one of the senior members of my Board of Governors, a member for whom I had great respect and affection. The night before the meeting lightning had flashed and thunder had crashed all over the land, and torrential rain had caused the river to rise until the school stood out in the flood like the prow of a ship on a storm-torn sea. " Like the night Montgomery was hanged ! " said the governor. This was the first time I had heard the expression and, I think, the first time I had heard of the trial. It appeared that on the night following the execution there had been a terrible storm which many people thought was an angry visitation from the hierarcy of heaven.

I cannot describe all of our pre-war holidays. Any attempt to do this would extend this book beyond its intended limits. In any case it might give the impression that a headmaster's life was one long holiday. This was far from the truth. In fact few holidays were uninterrupted by some disaster, such as the unexpected illness, or resignation, of a member of our staff. When this occurred advertisements had to be inserted, and meetings and interviews had to be arranged. Indeed, as time moved on, I seemed to become more and more involved to an extent that it became difficult to snatch more than a very short holiday. Perhaps this was bad organization on my part, I don't know; but I was never very good at drawing rigid lines such as " I will be available at certain times and at no other " ! Maybe this was all to the good, for I found that most of my staff were as prodigal of their spare time as I hope I was.

But I do remember very clearly one other holiday. This was spent in the heart of the famous Glens of Antrim, immortalized by many poets, the most popular of whom was Moira O'Neill whose " Songs of the Glens of Antrim," though sometimes adversely criticized by the highbrows, were thought good enough for the music of Stanford and Harty, and good enough, too, to bring back the sound and feel of the mountain tears of Ess-na-Larach, or the beauty of " Corrymeela and the blue sky over it " to thousands of exiles all over the world. Senti-mental poetry maybe, but sentiment is as necessary to the soul as food to the body and, when we lose all sentiment we lose our souls. Many distinguished men have written of the Antrim Coast Road. H. V. Morton, in his book, *In Search of Ireland*, states that " On a day of brilliant sunlight it is finer, to my mind, than the Cornische Road in the South of France." Other, and possibly greater, poets than Miss O'Neill, have written with the nine glens as background. John Hewitt, for example, who later was to be one of our distinguished guests at the Academy, wrote:

> " And yesterday as I came down
> Where Oisin's grave-stones stand,
> The holly branch with berries hung
> Rose upright in my hand."

One of our own staff, Kathleen Kevin, was also inspired by this famous prehistoric grave near Cushendun in her poem, " Oisin " :

> In Tir na nOg the blue seas shimmer,
> Through snowy branches swaying low,
> Sweet winds from seaward whisper softly,
> " Will Oisin go ? "

Ossian, or Oisin, was a legendary Ulster hero.

But of all the words that have been written about the Antrim Coast Road and The Nine Glens, none stick in my mind like those of Moira O'Neill, and it was near her rambling, white Regency house that we chose to spend the lovely summer of 1935. Though we were happy there at Lurigedan's foot, and bathing on that white-shingled shore, and I was happy catching small trout in big streams, and occasionally big trout in small streams, the rumblings of impending trouble in Europe were already to be heard.

My holiday was interrupted, for I had been asked to go as a delegate from Northern Ireland to a League of Nations Union conference at St. John's College, Cambridge. It was at a time when that terrible triumvirate of Hitler, Goebels, and Goering had thrust their ruthless way to ruthless power. The Union was split from top to bottom over the pacificism issue, but the Chairman—Lord Cecil—with quiet patience and consummate skill, managed to reconcile both views at the opening stormy meeting, so that the conference was saved from disruption at its inception. Of the many distinguished speakers the one who stands out most in my memory is Professor Gilbert Murray, the renowned Greek scholar, poet, and worker for peace: maybe his voice is dead, maybe his doctrine is dead; but I wish there were more people in the world ready to listen to voices such as his. At the end of the day exiles from Europe's seething cauldron of idealogies, distinguished musicians and exponents of the arts, would entertain us while we sat on chair and rug in the peace of this great college hall watching the evening sun glinting on gleaming spires, quiet backs and sweet lawns. It was all so peaceful, and we hoped so peace-making, but so futile when judged in the light of events soon to follow. And yet I don't know; maybe the ideas and ideals expressed then are slowly but surely penetrating the reluctant minds of men all over the world.

But if the development of the world was going in the wrong direction, developments at school were considerable. Though as yet we had made little progress toward new and better buildings, staff had been increased and finances had improved to an extent where it was thought it might be possible to make a reasonable bargain with the local authority. An additional mistress had been appointed to the Prep. School; she was to serve with great ability and loyalty up to the time of my retirement and after. Later we were joined by an art mistress who not only revivified the art department, but also created a dramatic society second to no other similar school society in the province at that time. In fact she cadged, cajoled, wheedled, inspired, directed, and in general went through all the necessary exercises in the book in order to produce beautiful and successful productions of many famous plays. And she did it all without a proper stage, or properties, or any of the paraphernalia that most directors would regard as essential to production.

The pair of them—her sculptor husband and herself—had a cottage in the heart of the blossom-drenched, fruit-growing country of Ulster in the County Armagh; there they entertained the intelligentsia, proletariat, the *bourgeois,* and the aristocracy of county, country and city. There one might meet artists and artisans, poets and policemen, wranglers and writers. Through a haze of sherry you might find yourself discussing quatrains with Louis MacNeice, Presbyterianism and poetry with W. R. Rodgers, or ballads and legends of Mourne with Richard Rowley; or, for that matter, science with a scientist, farming with a farmer, art with an artist, or songs with a musician. They would all be there at one time or another, either together or separately. And they were all, or nearly all, citizens of no mean city; they were no mere dilletantes; they were, if not all internationally famous, at least locally famous or good exponents of their several arts and sciences.

As one would expect at this time, the two were far left—in theory at least. Just before going away for a caravan holiday with a hired caravan, the husband arrived in our garden with a friend. He was always interested in—and, be it said—rather proud of, what his friends were about. On seeing the caravan and car in front of the house, by way of introduction, and including car, caravan and me in one sweeping arc of his arm he said: " One of these non-intervention chaps." The reference was that I, being a capitalist caravan owner, would naturally fall in with the " non-intervention " policy in the Spanish Civil War. The friend to whom he introduced me was a one-armed pilot who rejoiced in the nickname of " Ballocky Bill." Ballocky Bill was either on his way to, or had intentions of going to the war in Spain, but was later caught up in world war II in which he died. On another occasion the sculptor and I were discussing government ! Said he " What we want to do, Bill, is to get rid of all these lords and ladies, and all the half-educated robots of the Commons; instead we should have a government of artists, poets and scientists, and all the real thinkers." Though his conception was a bit Platonic, perhaps he had a point and maybe this is the direction in which we are heading.

But the evening I remember most was the first of a summer vacation. Knowing my liking for fishing, he had " trysted " with a county lady for the use of her lake and boat for the evening. It was typical July weather, uncertain from one day to the next, and from hour to hour, blue sky and thundery showers, thundery showers and blue sky in swift alternation. Two English army officers from Armagh barracks had accidentally arranged to have the boat at the same time, so all four of us went out together. It proved to be one of those coincidental meetings that so often happen on this small island of ours, for one of the officers proved to have been at an English boarding school with one of my colleagues of the university staff days; in consequence I was able to reunite these former schoolmates.

Can you imagine four men in a boat with a wee dram to keep them warm, on an exquisite little private lake, in a richly endowed land with woods and shrubs sweeping to the yellow-flag-margined lake ? Can you imagine all this with free rising fish, and the notes of the old mansion bell stealing from time to time across the scintillating raindrops on grass, and wood, and marsh marigold ? If you can imagine all this, then you can imagine what it feels like to be in heaven; for, I swear it, we four thought we were in heaven from the time we left the little pier until we landed with our catch of golden fish.

Caravanning ! When we went on a caravan holiday it was an adventure not to be compared with the modern version, when you usually go to a site with every modern convenience, and many inconveniences, laid on. In those days you could wander willy-nilly wherever your fancy led you. And as often as not fancy led you to the lake's edge, the sea's edge, or by the banks of a bubbling brook. On that last summer before the face of Europe changed for ever, we set off—herself, myself, Michael, Alison, and Judy, the dog—with a heavily-laden caravan, too heavy perhaps for our twelve horse power Fiat. We managed, though at one stage I remember being turned back by an imperious policeman in a street in a small town; as I couldn't reverse the outfit I had to suffer the indignity of unhitching and turning the caravan, while all the rest of the traffic hooted and blew their horns. Later a broken universal joint caused a delay spent at the back of a public-house in the west. We had to remain there until a new part could be obtained from Dublin; it came speedily and the repair was executed with an efficiency that could scarcely be matched in these days.

Eventually we parked in a field beside a mountain stream at Mullaghmore, near Sligo. A kindly uncle in Sligo arranged for me to fish in a pool owned by the Pollexfens, famous relatives of W. B. Yeats. And there I fished in the Celtic twilight, and I thought of " The Wild Swans of Coole," and of

" We seek for slumbering trout
And whispering in their ears
Give them unquiet dreams ";

and I sang " Down by the Sally Gardens "; and was happy,
for I soon found that my pool would bathe more than a
star; it held big shining salmon. I hooked one; he bolted
and sawed through the cast around a rock on the far side.
Then I hooked a second; he repeated the performance; but this
time, keeping a tight line, I walked through the shallows above
the fall and found to my surprise that he was still on when I
reached the other side. Unwrapping himself, he made for
the far clear bank where I was able to manipulate him better.
Eventually, encouraged by the plaudits of a small number of
onlookers, I succeeded in landing him. That was the first of
many fish I took from the pool; it was the best salmon-fishing
I ever had, or indeed, am likely to have.

But the clouds were lowering, literally and metaphorically.
It rained that summer as it had rarely rained before; and the Nazi
grip on Europe was tightening inexorably. So we thought it
might be better to be on our homeward way; and on the way
homeward I can remember one last night by " the winding
banks of Erne." It had rained all night. In the mists of the
following morning I just dropped over the wall separating us
from the lake to have one of the most enjoyable swims I could
remember. My shivering return to the warm caravan was
greeted by the smell of good Fermanagh eggs and bacon
sizzling on the pan. Far-off happy days, it all seems now like
the memory of another age ! And it was another age, before
the dawn of the nuclear menace, multiplying motor cars,
protest marches, hippies, yippies, pops and drugs, and God
knows what !

If war were to come there would be almost insoluble problems to be faced at school; I knew that. With our inadequate
cramped buildings; I could not then foresee how we could cope
with an inevitable sudden rise in our numbers; nor did I know
where we could get staff when the number of available candidates must fall to a mere trickle. Formerly it had been a matter

of choosing one from upwards of fifty, with parents and parsons
and friends in general trying to persuade us to discriminate in
favour of their particular protegé. Now all this would be
changed, and in fact, was already in the process of changing.

At home another had been added to our community: an
Austrian refugee from the Nazi tyranny. She—poor lady—
had lost everything wosth living for: her professor father, her
cultural surroundings, her beautiful Vienna, her music, her
home, many of her possessions, and above all her peace of mind.
Though she had come ostensibly to help in the house, anyone
more unsuited to helping in the house could scarcely be
imagined; she was much too old to adapt herself to a new way
of life. I have written much that is complimentary about the
town of Banbridge, but I don't think it matches up to Vienna !
What she thought of it all I don't know; but I do know that she
was a very good musician, and was able to play accompani-
ments to my singing of German Lieder with great skill.
Also I was soon able to carry on a slow conversation with her
in German; and I think her presence had some influence on
our son, afterwards to become a linguist. Later she was to
join a sister in London, but she died there of a cancer, no doubt
precipitated by the unhappy circumstances at the end of her
life when, normally, she would have been going into peaceful
retirement.

We began the year 1938-39 with high hopes; we ended it
nearly in despair. Before this time the Governors of the school
had decided that our position was now strong enough to be
able to say to the Down Education Committee—as the body
was then called—" Look here, the school is in a good position
financially, we'll hand over our assets to you provided you'll
build a new school." The thing was phrased a little more
tactfully, but this, in effect, was the offer. A deputation
consisting of our chairman, one or two influential members of
the Board, and myself, met the august assembly of very
important persons in Belfast and, hey presto ! the matter was
arranged. It was agreed that there would be no interference
with the internal affairs of the school; and that we should be
able to carry on as an individual unit in much the same way as

heretofore; a policy that was adhered to faithfully nearly up to the time of my retirement.

For months afterwards I was to have many meetings and appointments; these were always pleasurable and hopeful because achievement lay ahead. Nearly every afternoon was a trip of exploration over the green fields of the Bann Valley within the perimeter of the town. On these trips I was usually accompanied by the Committee's Surveyor, who proved to be an agreeable companion and, more important, he had the necessary technical knowledge. One had to take into account, too, all the local cross-currents, the pressures of interested parties. To give the local people their due, however, I must place on record the fact that little pressure *was* exerted; and when it came to a final decision it was based entirely on the best interests of the school. Eventually we decided on a high dry plateau on the Scarva Road.

In those days more was left in the hands of a headmaster than is the case now. Not only did he have to teach, organize, and take an active interest in every side of the life of the school, but he also had to be a sort of financial wizard, combining the attributes of a man of business with his academic attainments. I am not suggesting for one moment that I was good at all of these; but it was left to me to make a suitable bargain with the owner of the land, or his agent. The agent in this case resided in a little old house—The Toll House—at the outskirts of the town. Day after day I journeyed on foot up the hill, past " The Cut," past the Downshire Arms, to the house on the other side of the main road to Dublin; and here in a Dickensian setting I would try to make the bargain. My antagonist, or protagonist if you like, with his courteous manner, high collar, and steel-rimmed glasses, the clerk on his high stool with ledgers and pen, the evening light filtering through dusty windows; all these combined to give an impression of old-fashioned integrity.

So we bargained, the agent doing his best for his client, and I doing my best for the school authorities. I think we finally agreed on £1,100 plus expenses as the purchase price for about eleven acres. The price was accepted by all concerned, though I regretted that the Committee would not purchase a few more acres directly in front; this flat ground would have made an excellent cricket pitch as well as ensuring the preservation of all the land in front of the proposed building. As things turned out it didn't matter very much, for Hitler was soon to put paid to all our hopes; and there were those who said: " You'll never see your new school now, Doctor."

CHAPTER IX

HOME GUARDS AND HIGH FLYERS

IT certainly seemed as if we would never see our new school for, as the black-out curtains went up and the depression of the " phoney war " descended, methods of destruction rather than construction became the order of the day. I think we must have closed school on the afternoon of that final, fateful broadcast when we heard the quiet, grieved and broken voice of Chamberlain say: " Outside the storms of war may blow and the land may be lashed with the fury of all its gales, but in our hearts there is peace." Then lightning seared the black sky, thunder crashed all around, and our little girl wept. I dare say Chamberlain had found the right words to express what was in our minds. This terrible thing had been in all our thoughts for so long: this conscience problem—war, appeasement, pacifism; whether we must try to stop the terror in Europe by bringing to our own kith and kin the terrible arbitrament of modern war. These were the problems that had worried our consciences for years. Now the problem no longer existed; the answer had been found; the matter had been taken in hands by forces almost outside human experience. But in my mind, and I am sure, in the minds of many members of my profession, there was the nagging thought that some fine boys whom we had helped, stimulated, and inspired, and whom we had come to regard as personal friends, might soon have their lives cut off before they had begun to fulfil their early promise.

However, to work ! To work ! To work ! Things had to be done, and done quickly. Already numbers were climbing; not that there was any massed rush of refugees to Banbridge, but many people had friends in England who were only too pleased to send their young people, or come with their families, to the comparative safety of the town by the Bann River.

EVENING SUNSHINE SCANS BALLIEVEY'S SCATTERED LANDS

So I placed before my authorities and the Ministry a scheme for the erection of a temporary wooden building, and a few improvements to the Dunbar School. They sent down inspectors from the Ministry to try to dissuade me; fortunately I was adamant, with the result that in due course the building, with two class-rooms and a small headmaster's room with a telephone and extension to the old staff room, were erected. This was heaven, and a haven to which I could repair at times when I needed peace to deal with personal matters and problems. And here at last was a piece of property for which we were directly responsible; something that we could lock up at night; something to call our own.

The war changed many towns. Few more than this small market town in the heart of County Down; and here I quote from a talk on " Schoolmastering in War Time " which I gave for the B.B.C. soon after my retirement:

" Hitherto the only disturbance to the concentration of our pupils had been the rough calls of drovers as they prodded their fleecy or sleek beasts across the water-bridge to the fairs, which in those days were carried on up and down the length and breadth of the main street. Or a boy's attention might be distracted by the golden flash and splash of a brown trout, as it leaped upward toward an Olive or a Black Gnat or some other delectable morsel.

But now, what a contrast ! The rough voices of cattle drovers were replaced by the raucous voices of troops on the march singing ' Roll Out the Barrel '; while the bellowings and bleatings of frightened cattle had become the frightening crash of tanks and Bren-gun carriers as they rolled across the water-bridge. Now the attention of boys was no longer distracted by the glint of sun reflected from the back of a brown trout, or from the wings of a gull as it encircled our river; instead new and more powerful distractions were the glint and roar, and flash of the latest engines of destruction. As for the girls it became difficult to keep their attention on the glamour of history, poetry and science, when outside was the glamour of soldiers from England, Scotland, America, Wales and Belgium."

N

And now to illustrate further how we coped with the problem of increased numbers resulting from war-time displacements, another extract from the same broadcast:

" As time went on we did improve accommodation, first by a wooden hut, then by a Nissen hut and by renting some rooms at the back of a church—not a teacher's paradise, I can hear you say—and it was not ! Indeed I was frequently asked to come across to the church rooms, either because both teacher and pupils were nearly asphyxiated with smoke, or the roof had fallen in, or the girls were standing on the desks to escape the mice ! Add to this the distraction of German prisoners—or were they, as some said, Russians compelled to fight for the Germans—working in the station yard below; and you have an environment not just ideal for academic education."

Each evening the lugubrious face of the caretaker would come over to make some complaint; but to show me that his sympathies were on my side he would add: " Ye couldn't watch them, Sir, ye couldn't watch them ! " And he was right. How could you watch them in such an environment ? How could you prevent ceilings from falling when they had probably been there since the Regency, and in any event had not been put up to withstand the vibrations of heavy-footed fourth, fifth, and sixth formers ? It was at about this time when we were nearly distracted for want of accommodation and staff—there were now only two men left, myself and one other—that a local lady chose to say to me that " the name of the school was mud." Unfortunately, one rarely thinks of the right reply at the right time, or I might have said that if you leave mud alone it will settle, but if you keep stirring it up with a stick it will remain.

But we survived, and more than survived; for I think in those days we reached our highest peaks, both academically and on the sports field—which might mean nothing. Or, dare one say it in these times—could it be that the spirit of man is, after all, more important than his environment ?

The other day I was talking to a very intelligent and very charming former pupil, who had married a very important person, and who was a very important person in her own right. She paid me and the school the greatest compliment it had ever

been my pleasure to receive. She had come to us for war
reasons, and had been to other schools; she remained with us
throughout the war, until she obtained a university scholarship.
In effect, she stated that neither I nor anyone else could quite
understand what the school had done for her. It was like a
conversion; it was a complete release of her heretofore inhibited
personality. We had opened up for her new vistas and new
pathways; and, for the first time she had begun to realize the
real joy of learning for its own sake. I think this is the substance of what she said, and I make no apology for quoting it
here; for if the things she said were generally true, then I and
those who were with me at the time need have no fear that
" we had left undone those things we ought to have done."
    I said that we had also been more successful at games than at
any other time. This was true especially now that we had a
playing field of our own; the site originally purchased for
the school had been put to good use as a sports field. One day
a well-wisher, a kind lady, sent word to me that if we would
cut them down, she would let us have four straight long fir trees
from her plantation. It was a lovely autumn afternoon when
four of us set out into that country near where Hugh Brontë
must have courted his beautiful Alice McClory; and where,
Patrick Brontë may have wandered with his passionate red-
haired pupil. But romance was far from our minds as we sawed
and chopped until each monster of the wood fell among
the sweet-smelling fallen leaves. One went the wrong way,
so that it blocked the road until we were able to get it clear.
Fortunately no military convoy appeared, otherwise we might
have been arrested as members of an illegal organization. Anyhow the posts were soon tractor-borne to our fields where they
were stripped, seasoned, painted and erected. They were still in
use when I retired, though they were then on another field
referred to by the boys as " Mount Misery." For a pavilion on
the Scarva Road site we used the very large strong packing case
in which our Austrian refugee had transported her belongings
from Vienna. With a door and windows put in by our manual
instruction teacher, it made a good enough shelter. Many a good
game was played on this field. Though we never came anywhere
near winning the rugby cup, if we survived the first round we

regarded it as an outstanding achievement. This we did on the new field, and gave the much more powerful Portora Royal School a run for their money in the second round; but—more important—the captain of the team in this match was later to be selected to play for Ireland. We won the Hockey Cup in the year war broke out; and kept it in storage until the end of the war. Both boys and girls continued to play hockey, though all the cutting, mowing and rolling of the ground had to be done by our own efforts. In spite of all the difficulties enthusiasm ran high, and I can remember one match in which I played for the staff against the school; I believe I scored the winning goal, and thereby created what I hope is still an unbroken record !

But of far greater importance we—the family—had to find a new home. Where ? Houses had always been scarce in Banbridge and, as in every other place, the exigencies of war time had altered what at best had been a difficult situation, into one that was almost impossible. We intended this time to go into a smaller place, a quiet place somewhere in the heart of the country and yet not too inconvenient. Would Fox Lodge do ? We thought it might be a possibility; so, on a lovely blue and green April afternoon, we journeyed along the Bann, across Lisnaree Bridge, and up the hill to where this old farm-house looked out over the sweet green fields and luscious meadows of the Bann Valley; but for some reason or other we were not satisfied. And so we made our way across the twenty-acre field, through the hedge, and into the bramble-cluttered orchard of the great house of Ballievey known locally as "The Castle." We picnicked in the orchard and then ambled down to the house which we had named " Watendlath," because it made us think of the famous farmstead in Walpole's *Rogue Herries* saga. At the time we had not seen Watendlath.

But the pleasant young man who greeted us was neither a rogue nor a Herries, though the original owner of the house, if not a rogue, was certainly unpopular, for we were later to be told that the locals used to burn his effigy at the cross-roads. By a strange coincidence, I had met this young man away back in our Leeds days, when he was a textile student in that city. His father, the owner of the property, and the other members of his family, had gone back to Belfast where his father had business interests, but he—the son—had remained to carry on some farming activities in the meantime.

Having explained to him that we thought Fox Lodge would not suit, he said: " But would you not take the big house ? " We looked at each other; such an idea had never entered our heads. It was a huge place with acres of garden, basement, attics, and heaven knows how many rooms between. We raised objections. " Och ! " said our young friend, " sure you can shut up the rooms you don't want." I mentioned the garden. " Work whatever you can and leave the rest." And the paths ? " Och, get them scuffled once a year." It all sounded so simple. Light ? There had been a supply worked from a turbine at the old mill below, but with the collapse of the linen trade this had been cut off. " Sure what's wrong with lamps ? " said our friend. Water ? There was a supply from a small reservoir in the garden. When this dried up ? " No difficulty at all, you just have to pump water by hand up to the tank." No difficulty ! Once I remember pumping two thousand strokes to fill the tank !

Still we were young; and with the optimism of youth, we thought we could tackle the place. Anyhow we were pretty desperate for a house; and so we made, as things turned out, one of the best decisions of our lives: we would take the place, renting it in the meantime.

Let me describe briefly the house as we saw it that day. A completely unspoilt Georgian country house, it stood on top of a high terrace overlooking the Hall Green and the valley of the Bann leading up to Banbridge. Its perfect Palladian doorway was surrounded by its many-windowed, ivy-covered façade. Inside was a fine hall with Adams design archways, and a wide stairway with its exquisite mahogany banister curving gracefully upwards. Below stairs was a great flagged kitchen with an old-fashioned range; and there were all the other appurtenances of a house of the period: buttery with ceiling hooks for hams; wash house, speaking tube, and old wire bells that made a wonderful jangle throughout the house. Outside there was a courtyard surrounded by farm buildings, and beyond, another yard with steward's house and more farm buildings.

On either side of the hall were the spacious living-rooms; the one on the right with an added bow window of greenish Waterford glass looked out toward a jungle of holly trees, a great copper beech, rhododendrons and laurels, and beyond— trees, trees, trees, as far as the eye could see. At the back of the stairway there was a minimal bath-room, with a bath calculated to scrape the backside off you, and a small lavatory with a round window like the porthole of a ship. Behind the left-hand living-room there was another smaller room fitted out as a modern chemical laboratory. Each of the two floors upstairs had three large bedrooms and two small rooms, one of which, the upper one, was a useless attic.

The old garden on the south side was nearly overgrown. Pear trees pushed their blossomed branches through the windows; escalier apples surrounded vegetable plots; and on the hillside plums, apples, and pears fought for existence against the insidious inroads of ivy, brambles, and nettles. Further up the hill a four-thousand-year-old oak, ash, and beech surrounded " forth " stood in its water-filled moat: a monument to our early agricultural heritage. And away across the fields one could trade the sinuous grace of the Bann streaming down from the blue line of the Mournes on the far horizon.

What a beautiful place ! we thought, as we looked out over the fields on that April afternoon. And what a wonderful place for our children ! Even if it kills us we'll live here !

Soon we were to move in with Biddy the dog, Daisy the donkey and, last but by no means least, Bella from Tyrone, who, being as strong as a horse, could have done the work in anything from a cottage to a castle. And then there was the man whom we inherited with the house. Though he lived not very far away, since he had " left home " at one time to go to another place—also not very far away—he had forfeited his inheritance and therefore he spent most of his time at " the castle," where he kept some ill-fed cows and a few other beasts on our " set " land. Between milkings he worked for us. At milking time one would hear swish ! swish ! swish ! as an unrich accompaniment of streams of thin milk to your man's

unrich baritone singing of " Shall We Gather at the River"
interspersed with "The Maid of the Sweet Brown Knowe."
He had a little room in one of the out-houses. Here he boiled
eggs, made cups of tea, and entertained his lady friend—
a colourful lady from Loughbrickland. Once I had " a bit of a
barney " with him and threatened him with the sack. " Och,
no ! " said he, " ye wouldn't do that ! Ah may not be married
but Ah've a wumman to keep ! " But he had one redeeming
feature: he was very fond of children, though the warm fresh
milk he sometimes gave them must have been alive with every
conceivable breed of bacteria.

Soon we were sawing wood, pumping water, clearing nettles,
cutting down ivy, weed killing, staining floors, scrubbing and
painting, digging, delving, and planting until at last the great
place, though never reaching perfection, was at least habitable.
When I look back now I wonder how it was all accomplished;
for our children were young, my wife had charge of a voluntary
canteen for the troops; I was Gas Intelligence Officer, had a
unit of the Air Training Corps, and had charge of our local
Home Guard. Though at this stage of the war there wasn't
much to sing about, I and a choir of Banbridgeans were singing
for victory all over the country.

And it wasn't long before our big house was discovered.
When our friends were at loss as to know what to with their
children, so that either they could get away to the war, or their
children could get away from the war, it was a case of " send
them to the Crowes, my dear." And they did send them, with
the result that there were boarders at Banbridge Academy for the
second time in its history. And young officers would come along
entreating us to take their young—and sometimes pregnant—
wives; thus we became, not merely a boarding school, but
almost a maternity home as well. Sometimes there would be
a cry in the night when I would make a hasty dash down to the
Fiat car, with the omnipresent fear in my mind that it might
not start, and that things might begin to happen before we
could make the journey over frost-bound roads to the hospital.
It was on such a night that Carol was born. She doesn't
remember; we *do* !

But we had our good times and bad times. One Christmas Day, for example, even in those war years, I can remember the big table at its full length fairly groaning under a weight of good things, while all around the board were the beaming faces of those released for a few hours from the business of making war. The old, the middle-aged, and the young found enjoyment together in those days before the term " teenagers " had been manufactured by those for whom it was big business to make such distinctions.

Looking back now I think it would have been unfair of me to have left home and school and family at this time. Why then did I apply for a commission ? Maybe I was caught up by war fever, or perhaps it was the depression caused by another kind of fever: the endemic jaundice so prevalent at the time. The human mind is so complicated that it is often difficult to analyse motives; perhaps it is better not to analyse them too closely in case what we see might make us think too little of our own characters. However, the army authorities said they would grant me a commission provided the education authorities would give me leave of absence. This the latter refused to do, so I had no option but to serve at home as best I could.

I applied for entry to our local Home Guard unit—or Local Defence Force as it was first called. I heard nothing for some time, then one evening I was met on the lovely little suspension bridge connecting the wooded heights of our home with the other side of the Bann. There, as I stood looking at the peaceful Constable scene of the old bridge, the old mill, and the sleek cows grazing in the yellow-flagged water meadow below, I was approached by an equally peaceful-looking grey-haired countryman who told me " Ah'd betther report at the Hall that night." He said this in an esoteric way, almost as though he feared that, if he weren't careful, the information might be reported to the German High Command! Or, what is more likely, centuries of our own little troubles had almost inbred this secretive manner.

Promptly at eight o'clock I reported at the local Orange Hall as instructed. There were few, if any, when I arrived. One by one, as time wore on, Isaac, Pat, Jim, John, Joss and so on came stiffly in, and sat down on the benches around the walls. As most were tired countrymen there was little conversation except for the occasional crack and leg-pull. After what seemed an interminable time the officer in charge, a big solid slow Ulster countryman, said: " Ah suppose ye'd betther have a rifle and uniform; an' then we'll do a bit o' drill." I got my rifle and uniform and we did our bit o' drill. But at the end of the parade, I felt somewhat depressed at the thought that these methods would do little to repel the Hitlerian hordes should they ever attempt the passage of the Bann.

As time went on, however, I began to respect these men more and more. I was now in command of the Home Guard. My opposite number in charge of the original police section, though gentle and slow in manner, proved to be absolutely reliable; he knew everybody and every district; not even a cartridge could have gone astray without his knowing where it was. The general run of the men, too, though not super-ficially, efficient, had a natural flair for the mechanics of weapons, and in particular for shooting; they loved the competitive element at the butts and most could show a good card.

Training, now in co-operation with the regulars, soon became more intensive. Many of us went on courses which were a good deal more serious than the kind of thing humor-ously represented in " Dad's Army." At one of these I was in an officers' dormitory when a sergeant came in singing Schumanns " Du bist wei eine Blume" in German; he had obviously been celebrating something or other. When I recog-hized him as a master at my old school, who had been a captain when I was a full private in the school corps, I couldn't very well order him out.

But I must not digress too far, or I could easily find myself writing a Home Guard journal. Training became more and more intensive: we had big exercises and small ones, hand grenade throwing, rifle grenade firing, anti-tank exercises, and sometimes exercises involving both the Army and the Air Force. There was the battle of Shilling Hill, the battle of Eliza's Hill, neither of which are recorded in the history of World War II, but those who took part in them—Corbet

men, Banbridge men, and men from Katesbridge, and Ballyward, and Ballyroney, in fact from all the ballys, and hills, and
bridges in the area—these men will remember. For me, as for
them, it was all good fun; it was diversion; it was exercise;
fortunately it never became more than this, but if it had done
so no doubt these men would have rendered a good account
of themselves.

Sometimes the military sent regulars to lecture on specialist
subjects. Once they sent a cockney sergeant to lecture on gas.
In the course of his talk he informed the men that chlorine
smelt of musty hay, and phosgene smelt of bleach. As politely
as I could I ventured to suggest that perhaps he had accidentally
reversed the odours of the two gases. " Ooh, naow ! " he said,
" I've just come back from a course and it's all chainged
naow."

But the Home Guard did not fully satisfy my desire to take
a more active part in the war effort; so when the Air Training
Corps idea was mooted, I agreed to form a unit. It was to
consist of two flights, one of town boys—mainly Technical
School boys—and one of Academy boys. My senior master—
one for whom I had great affection, and one who was with me
in all my projects—agreed to train the town unit, while I was
to take command of the whole, and look after the training of
the Academy flight. Though we had little training both of us
were commissioned. I attended some courses. The first was
at Torquay, in Devon. As a course it was most unsatisfactory;
the organization was bad; they knew little about us, and scarcely
knew what we wanted. In the mornings we did a lot of square
bashing under blue, hot skies wearing full uniform with gloves
and gas masks. As the regular R.A.F. officer in charge had no
objections, we decided to remove our tunics, but an order
quickly came down from H.Q. saying that " gentlemen could
not drill in braces, belts must be worn." Accordingly some of
us succeeded in purchasing belts in a local haberdashers.
I remember the purchase especially well because Tauber, the
great tenor and Lieder singer, who had thrilled me when I
heard him singing " Der Doppelgänger " in Belfast before the
war, was in the same shop choosing a tie. The following
morning, when we went on parade with our new belts, an order

came down from H.Q. saying the previous order had been a mistake; it had been rescinded, and gentlemen could now drill in braces !

Came the day when we flew for the first time; it was a beautiful day in mid-summer when we set out, resplendent in new uniforms, for a temporary aerodrome in a clover field near Lisburn. As we were the first unit to fly, and the first to be uniformed, the publicity people were anxious to make the most of the occasion, so we were met by press photographers and reporters. The first to approach asked me my name. I said Crowe. Then he asked the name of my Flight Sergeant. I said Gosling. By this I think he thought—as they would say in our part of the world—I was " takin' a han' out of him." Anyhow the following day a picture appeared in a leading Belfast newspaper under the caption: " CROWE, GOSLING, and the other EAGLETS."

But for the Eaglets, and for all of us, it was the thrill of a lifetime. I have flown many thousands of miles since; for a real adventure, however, you must be over forty, you must fly in a tiny light aircraft so that every time you put your head over the side the breath is nearly sucked out of your body by the slipstream; and you must land in a clover field on a perfect summer day with the smell of the clover meeting you as you come down. Following that, I had many other flights, including the long-distance navigational exercise over the Atlantic, and a few when I had the unforgettable experience of balancing the machine in the fluid air, of turning and climbing and finding myself lost in a cold opaque stream of swirling cloud.

It was all experience; but it was the people I met who interested me more than the machines: the young pilot who told me he felt sick at the sight of an aircraft on the ground, because he had seen one of his friends burnt to death; the flight sergeant navigator who was sick in flight—it was always like this with him, he said. Once I was in the same Nissen hut with a young Canadian pilot; he had seen one of his crew cut to pieces by an air-screw. As he was on night flight work he usually came in as I was getting up. The first thing he always did was to look at the photograph of his young and pretty wife; he was terrified that he would never see her again. On the morning I was leaving he had packets of sweets all lined up for me to bring home to my kids. In the midst of all his fear and worry, what a kindly thought ! I never heard from him since, but I hope life, or God, has been good to him wherever he is.

The late Marquis of Londonderry was the Air Commodore commanding the A.T.C. in Northern Ireland. Rich aristocratic men are rarely popular, and he was no exception, especially as he had been an appeasement sympathizer, and had entertained Ribbentrop at Mount Stewart. For all that when you saw this ex-Minister of Education, ex-Minister for Air and septuagenarian setting off into the teeth of a southerly gale to fly solo in a Gypsy Moth from Aldergrove to Mount Stewart you could not help but have some admiration. Also when he did not consider it beneath his dignity to come down to Banbridge one evening to inspect a handful of cadets drilling in the station yard, one felt inclined to think: " Surely this was a man."

Anyhow, in view of his interest in the A.T.C., but against the wishes of some, we decided to ask him to be our guest on speech day. We entertained him at Ballievey. Unfortunately the soup had been inadvertently salted twice; thus it was not a very successful introduction to the main course with which he toyed. But my wife's speciality was a chocolate soufflé which immediately found a way to both his stomach and his heart. So much so that he attempted a somewhat unsuccessful conversation with my wife. He said: " Do you fly Mrs. Crowe ? " As Mrs. Crowe had at this time never seen the inside of an aeroplane, this did not get very far. When he asked her if she grew oranges this was the last straw, so we quickly hustled him to the hall and the platform.

Probably he was suffering from suppressed nervousness, as we all do on such an occasion. Later we entertained him to tea. This time he was much more relaxed. On the way out in the car he gave me an account of the final conference at which the existing Irish political division had been arranged. He told me that after the signing Arthur Griffith shook hands with him and said, with tears in his eyes: " Sure the next time we meet, 'twill be on the floor of an all-Irish house ! " But the more flamboyant, hearty, Michael Collins said: " Sure the next time we meet 'twill be at the Curragh races ! " Thus he exemplified the difference in character between these two Irish leaders.

Perhaps I should have mentioned earlier that before this, against the wishes and advice of parents, friends, and many well-wishers, we had taken the plunge and purchased Ballievey House with its cottages and fifty acres of land. So that this great Georgian house, and the earth around it, had become ours for all time, or at least for the usual nine hundred and ninety-nine years, of which the most of two hundred had already expired. The house at Ballievey—or Baile Aodpbha, Beautiful Town-land—had been built about 1784 by a farmer-cum-linen merchant. It was one of four similar houses, known as Bleachers' Houses, in the area: one almost identical being near the Lagan River at Magheralin, another, the former Bishop's Palace, near Dromore, and a fourth, the famous Sheepbridge House at Sheepbridge, near Newry.

Shortage of petrol and finance were reasons for giving up the car during the war, so we had to travel by bicycle, or by the little train to Corbet which passed underneath our woods, and came to a spluttering, reluctant halt about a mile further on, whence we had to walk back along the line. Coming home was easy enough; but to catch a train on a frosty morning, often meant running on the slippery sleepers in imminent danger of breaking a leg at every step. Then I bought a pony that wouldn't go; that is to say he had a mind of his own, and would draw the trap for a certain distance until he felt a little tired; at this stage no power on earth could have prevented him from turning for home. But at least he served his purpose, which was mainly that of transporting our visitors from the Corbet station. Never shall I forget the day I bought him. I went to Dromore fair with the maximum money in my pocket. For my part I felt like a fish out of water, but I had arranged to meet a man there who was used to such dealings. The owner of the pony mentioned his price and immediately shot out a big powerful fist to grasp mine. But my friend was quicker; he quickly interposed his body, saying: " Och, ye can't bind a man like that ! " If the adventure wasn't particularly successful, at least I came home from the fair with a pony and change in my pocket rather than a gross of shagreen spectacles !

My wife was keen to have hens, so we bought some. We called them the L.D.V. for they were all black like the first black denims issued to the Local Defence Volunteers. At least they gave us some eggs during the bleakest and blackest depths of the war-time shortage. And we bought two cows. We knew nothing about cows. We thought our man *did*, but he didn't bother very much, being more interested in his own. When the man from whom we bought the cows heard that we were complaining about the lack of milk he said: " Och, if they'd give them a bit o' feedin' instead of keepin' them out there standin' with their arses to the wind ! "

He was probably right; but they weren't very good cows; and we soon got rid of them, after we had gained a little more experience of that very susceptible natural machine—the milking cow. Before the war ended, however, we were nearly self-supporting: fruit from the orchard, fresh vegetables, including the inevitable flowery Irish spud, from the garden; eggs, milk, butter churned with the old plunger churn; there were hordes of rabbits on the hills, and big pink-fleshed trout in our own pools, though, as you may imagine, there was little time for fishing; nevertheless in season we often had the odd brace in the larder. Heat and light were our main difficulties; sometimes I think we must have been pretty cold in this large house. Wood alone is not a great heater unless you have large quantities of it. We lit ourselves to bed at night, each with his or her own hurricane lamp to which Pat, a highly imaginative member of our war-time family, gave highly imaginative names.

Though we were spared the worst hazards of war, and even the great air raids left us untouched, there were times when one would have thought we were in the forefront of battle. There were bombing, machine gun and rifle ranges on the Nut Bank adjoining our Hall Green. Nose caps from bombs frequently came singing into the garden, and on one occasion, when I was standing on the river bank talking to another man, a bullet passed between us. Sometimes land mines shook and cracked our windows. One incident that still gives me nightmares was when I happened to notice Pat swinging a silvery object in her hand. As I had just been on a weapons course, I at once recognized it as a detonator; on making investigation I found that she and our son, on their usual ramble, had pulled the object from a one-pound slab of gun cotton which some careless officer had allowed to remain in an old mill ! I made a complaint, but a complaint would have been useless if the mercy of Providence had not intervened to prevent a double tragedy.

But soon the noise, the clamour, and the danger to us were to disappear. Soon the mighty convoys could be heard *en route* for North Africa. And soon there were to be the invasion of Europe, V.J. Day and V.E. Day; and the uneasy peace was to spread into our hills and valleys, and all over Europe and the world. Black-out curtains came down and lights went up; and the little birds battered themselves against Ballievey windows at night for the sheer joy of seeing the lights again. One by one our visitors left us, some to go to colleges and some to return to hearth and home. The Home Guard had been disbanded and, as there was no longer a demand for air crew, our boys soon began to lose interest. After all the fuss, and excitement, and the chatter and laughter of young voices about the house, there was a sudden uncanny silence that left us feeling almost lonely.

Now there came a revival of interest in the things of the mind. People's thoughts began to surge toward the civilized ways of life. What was to happen after the war ? Were we satisfied with existing institutions ? There were debates, talks, discussions, articles in the press, and letters to the press. We must never allow things to slip back, so that conditions could bring about another war. What was wrong with the social set-up ? What was wrong with religion ? What was wrong with education ?

Ah, yes ! Education ! It was the wave of this feeling that caused me to write *New Education for Old*. I felt then, as indeed I had always felt, that we had become bogged down in a morass of examinations, factual learning, corporal punishment, and in a certain traditional drabness of buildings, equipment, and teaching methods that were completely lacking in inspiration.

I therefore made my appeal for a new spirit and for new ideals. We must search for beauty in art, truth in science, and goodness in religion. As far as buildings and equipment were concerned the war had shown that, if the money could be found for destruction, it could also be found for construction. The war had also proved that action rather than books, or both combined, were better teachers than books alone. Factual information was useless if not allied to understanding and wisdom. If public examinations were to be continued, they should be *subject* rather than *group* examinations; a boy or girl should not be dubbed a failure merely because of failure in some essential subject. Better feeding, and better housing of our schools, could work miracles; and I even suggested the possibility of children being sent abroad in school ships.

Though we still lack sufficient idealism and cohesion in our system, I have lived to see much that I suggested come into being.

Dr. Helen Waddell, whom I mentioned earlier, wrote a foreword to this book. I quote here her last two paragraphs:

" The silence that fell on us when G.B.S. finished speaking came upon me again as I read the last paragraphs of this schoolmaster's plea for the children, for something more than utility in education. ' Education is spiritual in essence and therefore it is the spirit of the thing that counts. You may house your boys and girls in palaces, but this will make little difference unless they are taught by princes. . . .'

' Once,' he went on, ' prehistoric man trained his sons in the making of weapons that they might survive in the struggle for existence. Then, even in religion, even in science, came the struggle for power. If we adopt the utilitarian outlook on education, our aim differs little from that of our ancestors, except that we endeavour to clothe our sons and daughters with an armour of bank notes instead of one of mail. . . . If education is to mean anything at all, the breath of God must sweep through it from the turrets and spires of Oxford to the humblest country elementary school. . . . Children, parents, teachers, Ministers of Education, let us desire, imagine, will and create. . . . Let us dream the type . . . that we wish to create."

The crazy diabolic symphony of power was still vibrant overhead, strange counterpoint to the cry of this passionate dreamer. Then accepting, transfiguring, harmonizing both, the echo of a still mightier singing

> " to hope till Hope creates
> From its own wreck the thing it contemplates."

How relevant to our own times !

I was more than surprised at the *succès d'estime* of the book. Many wrote to me about it, including men of the older school. Praise from one's own former headmaster is appreciated by all of us from the humblest dishwasher to the leaders of the land; and when mine wrote to me, I was pleased beyond measure. He said that " I had said much with which he was in complete sympathy," and that " I had made my challenge with startling effectiveness."

Then came the era of atomic and nuclear power. When we read about the dropping of the first atom bomb, even those of us with some scientific knowledge were shocked and surprised. From our earliest days as students we had heard of the dread possibility, but I think few of us realized that the announcement was other than dramatic newspaper headlines about some new type of ordinary high explosive bomb. Leaving aside, however, all the tragedy and horror, there was much speculation at the time as to how the thing worked, so that when I was invited by the Royal Institute of Chemistry to give a Christmas lecture to schoolboys and girls in Belfast, I thought that something about explosives leading up to the atom bomb would be of topical interest.

I called the lecture " Christmas Crackers." Between my able assistants at Queen's University and myself we devised a series of experiments calculated to satisfy my young hearers' desire for flashes, bangs, fire, and fizzes for ever. We touched off nitrogen triodide, burst soap bubbles filled with hydrogen in the air, blew off oxidizing mixtures, examined vacuum tube phenomena, and in general thrilled and enjoyed ourselves. It is almost too obvious to say that the lecture went off with a bang, but the newspapers said it did—at least it must have been successful, for I was asked to repeat the lecture the following year. Thereafter these Christmas lectures for sixth forms became an annual event, so I had the satisfaction of knowing I had helped to initiate a new and stimulating scientific venture.

It was at about this time that I wrote *Man, Mind, and Matter,* a popular approach to philosophic thinking. Again I was influenced by the minor renaissance after the war, and sometimes a little appalled at the general ignorance about the known facts of science and their effect on thought. Also I wanted to try to reconcile scientific and philosophical thinking with religion. Of course my critics said that I had failed in the latter—and they were probably right, for you cannot reconcile the two—but they added that I had a remarkable flair for expressing scientific ideas so that they could be understood by the unscientific. The book was published jointly by Harrap of London, and Mullan of Belfast. During its preparation for publication I had some discussion with a director of Harraps. He said that, though he had found the book so interesting that he had read the typescript into the small hours, being a non-practising, believing Catholic, he could not agree with all my premises nor with my conclusions. When I met him in London a few years ago in the flush of œcumenism, and a general change in outlook, generously, he said: "Maybe you were right after all."

The war was over, and the toll had to be counted. Of the boys with whom I began, one was killed when his fighter plane crashed in England, and another was lost over Germany. Not very many, you might say, but when one remembers that a sixth form in those days might have half a dozen boys in it, it was two too many, especially when there were boys whom I regarded as personal friends. In our own home, during the war, we had seen life come in and life go out, and as our young people went their several ways the vague emptiness of the aftermath turned our thoughts back to the land.

In the years following the war the production of food was still a pressing problem. Grow more was the slogan. If you had land you were required to plough a certain acreage. Gradually we were increasing our cow and hen population. Sometimes of a night, with work finished, I would set out over frost-bound roads, with the moon riding high and casting its yellow light over sparkling hills and meadows, past needled pines, and the frozen Corbet Lough. On the way I would invariably meet a laconic gentleman who would say "Rough!" and pass on his way. At the local there was one who could come in white with quarry dust. "One by the neck," he would say and, raising the bottle to his mouth, he would drain it without pausing for breath. There was another who lived in a shack at the edge of the Corbet Lake; what he lived on no one knew, but he had all the wisdom of a "He Ancient." There was another who took more than one by the neck; in spite of it they said he kept a spotless cottage. He rode a bicycle; when I asked him how he managed to get home after drinking so much, he replied: "Och! sure Ah just walk her!" Then he told me that he reckoned he was a better man than Hitler, for he had stopped the British Army. I asked him how he had done this. "Well," said he, "wan night Ah was comin' home from Banbridge an' Ah fell aff the bike in front o' the convoy, an' the whole lot had to stop to get me out o' the way."

Usually, however, there were more important things to talk about; and from time to time I would pick up bits of useful information. Then one night a man looked at me very hard, and he said: "Docthor, why don't ye grow a bit o' yer own feedin'?"

CHAPTER X

BACKS TO THE LAND

" GROW some o' yer own feedin'." I pondered the matter
as I walked home; and I thought about it again the next
afternoon as I stood at my favourite view-point looking across
from our Well Field to the blue distant dome of Slieve Donard,
and the heavy mass of Slieve Commedagh. Would this be
taking on too much? Men, finance, equipment, all these
would have to be considered. We had been doing nicely from
the letting; the overdraft was down to negligible proportions;
why add to our worries by going in deeply once more? And
yet there were those who said: " Ye'd be betther to farm yer
own lan'. Them boys that's takin' it 'ill take every ounce out
an' put damn all back." Though we had tried to offset this
by insisting on proper rotation and fertilizing, there was some
truth in what they said. Also there was the " grow more "
slogan; and, with our big family—for we still had boarders—we
could do with lots of feedin' for the hens, the cows, and
ourselves.

And so we made the third big decision of our lives; we would
farm our own land. What about help? Our excellent maid,
who could clean and cook, calve a cow, cut logs, and even take
a cow " a-bullin' " when necessary, had gone a-soldiering and
had eventually married a soldier. So we scoured the countryside, even going into the depths of County Armagh, with no
transport other than our bicycles. A journey of forty miles
or so on a Saturday afternoon can be quite taxing when you are
not used to it. While we enjoyed the journey through the
apple orchards of Armagh, we were not particularly enamoured
of some who wished to come and live in our semi-basement;
for it was obvious that in many cases the basement rather than
the contribution to the farm work was the attraction.

Finally, a seemingly suitable pair did accept the job. At first they said nothing about children; there were, in fact, two girls. There was a brother; could we find a spot where he could lay his head ? What next ? But we had reached a stage when we would have consented, not only to father, mother and the two children, but indeed to the whole family connection. They said they would all sleep in the same room, but our moral sense revolted at the idea, and eventually uncle, with his green hat, green cutaway coat, and brown shoes, was relegated to the harness room, where he appeared to be happy enough in front of his log fire.

Things went well enough at first. Father appeared to be a good worker. He could turn his hand to most things, from felling a tree to planting a bed of shallots; but I had my doubts about what might happen when it came to major issues, such as organizing the planting of a field with potatoes. His rather rough, dark-haired, sombre woman appeared to be competent enough to take the edge off the housework. From the beginning, however, it was obvious that uncle was no more than a kindly, humorous, benevolent spiv. He was the sort of man who was always looking for work with no intention of finding it. He always walked a little behind father, and seemed incapable of tackling any job without him. Children loved him, everybody loved him, but a farmer requires more than a kindly drone.

There were few tractors in those days; those who possessed them usually had them " on the country;" that is, they contracted to do the work of others in addition to using them on their own farms. So, as we possessed no implements, I arranged for others to do my work for me. But I didn't reckon on the fact that many others were scrambling to have their work done at the same time; and it was not just a matter of being at the head of the queue. Those who harried the contractor most were those who got their work done first. I had decided to sow seed potatoes, seed hay, and oats. Of these the most vulnerable were the seed potatoes, which could be attacked by frost, fungi, or too much initial growth. And then there was the weather factor; to see the good days passing without a sign of men, tractor, and implements was, as they would say in the

County Down, a " heart scald." As our scanty savings, or the bank's money, were now heavily invested, when someone would come along and say: " Yer spuds is turnin' to mush ! " I was more than a little concerned.

So I went to see a friend and neighbour, a businessman who, like myself, was an amateur farmer. I explained my difficulty.

" Jump into the car," said he, " and we'll soon get ye fixed up."

In a twinkling we were speeding along the roads of Down. Soon we espied a tractor working in a field.

" I think this is our man," said my friend.

" How are ye, Johnny ? " he said as the tractor came to the end of the run.

" Bravely," said Johnny, obviously on the defensive, as though this sort of thing was a daily occurrence, " how's yerself ? "

" Och, I'm rightly; but I'd be a damn sight better if ye'd done the right thing by me friend here. Ye've let us down; what the hell way is that to treat two decent men ? "

The tractor man didn't seem to be in the least put out by this kind of talk; he was used to it.

" Honest to God," said he, " me an' me brother has been workin' day an' night trying to get everybody fixed up, an' we're doin' the best we can. We'll get yer work done in time never you fear; we've never let a man down yet. Honest to God, it's as thrue as yer livin' ! "

" That's all right, Johnny," said my friend, " but we want more than talk. When are ye comin' ? "

" Well, now, let's see," Johnny replied, pushing the cap to the back of his head, and obviously trying to evade the issue of a fixed date. " We might get this field finished a Tuesda, and then there's the four-acre Wensda—say Thursda."

" Right-o ! " my friend said, " an' if ye don't turn up we'll get somebody else."

He didn't turn up until Friday; but when he did how he worked, and how his brother worked ! Night and day, day and night, they ploughed, and harrowed, and cultivated. While one slept in the car the other drove the tractor; they were merciless on themselves, on the tractor and on the soil, until at

last all was ready for the sowing—or at least as nearly ready
as was possible. At the end they said: " Ye'll have to labour it
anyhow," meaning that there was a lot of " scutch " grass
there, which could only be removed by hard manual labour.
And to give our own men their due they, too, worked hard;
and, when it came to the sowing, we all worked whenever
possible. In those less organized days there was an *esprit de corps*
among countrymen of all classes, creeds, and persuasions. Life
was a battle against time and the elements. Relaxation could
come when the storm broke, but when conditions were favourable the battle must go on without counting the cost in time,
or money, or pains and aches.

But another kind of storm was soon to break ! Trouble had
been brewing with the dark woman. Complaint after
complaint had been made; the chief target of her weaponry
was the man across the yard; she could not abide him, nor he
her. Then one day, to facilitate a whitewashing operation at
the back of the house, he had lashed some ladders together with
the bottom one resting on a convenient table. The table
happened to be the property of her ladyship. While our man
was working high up on the roof, she came out of the back
door; seeing the use to which her table had been put by her
arch enemy she furiously whipped it away. Having finished
his job above, our man, also of uncertain temper, with no
thought in mind other than his cup of tea, came hastily down
without looking behind. For a fraction of a minute he was
airborne before hitting the ground much more heavily than
he had anticipated. For most of us a sudden unexpected jolt
is, at least, irritating; but when you have been whitewashing
in a hot sun, when you dislike women in general, and one in
particular who, as you thought, had tried to do you in, you—the
reader—need not be surprised when I say that the imprecations
that followed in the yard, even in these realistic times, would
scarcely bear printing in this book.

That was the end. In the midst of the sowing they left us,
lock, stock, and barrel; so we had to think again. We now
realized that we must put out of our minds any thought of
employing " foreigners." To preserve the peace there was
only one alternative: we must employ the people across the

yard; to do them justice we might have done worse. They threw themselves into the effort whole-heartedly and got us through a difficult period. A daughter was to help in the house; mother would help with the feeding of extra hands when necessary; son was to be a sort of apprentice. Father, a soldier of the first world war who had served in France and North Africa, had some of the worst characteristics of a first world war private soldier. He could work hard at times, and avoid work when he could see some means of getting others to do it. These attributes did not popularize him with local helpers. And he had a rough way with cows; he didn't realize that, when a cow was fractious, it was the milker who was at fault, not the cow.

Eventually all was ready; and the sower went forth with his fiddle to spray his oats, which were then under-sown with small seeds for next year's hay harvest and grazing. And then there were the days of the potato planting when hands appeared from here and there, as though conjured up by some sort of secret agricultural magic. I didn't know the half of the men, or where they came from, but they had come, as they said, " to help us out." There were many head shakings over the state of my seed, and I was, frankly, worried. But we sowed them all, good, bad, and indifferent; then, for a day or two, phosphate dust drifted like slow fires over the fields; finally the drills were closed, and I prayed that nature would in someway or other repair the ravages of delay, ignorance, and perhaps some carelessness.

Was it any wonder that I had now become the lugubrious farmer ? Was it any wonder that I was perpetually worrying about wind and weather; it was too dry: it was too cold; it was too hot; it was too wet; it was never right. When I wasn't worrying about the weather, I was worrying about prices, costs, possible profits, and how to find the money for this or that piece of small equipment. And can you blame me that in that first year, every time I had an opportunity, I was up to the fields watching for the first sign of growth ? Would this or that bare patch never fill up ? There were far too many misses in the drills; and the weeds ! red shank and ragwort, chickweed and charlock, thistle and twitch, they were all there. Though the drills gradually filled up, there were still too many misses; but complacency came with the thought that maybe the good tubers would do better with the extra space. Then I began to worry about mosaic, leaf curl, and all the other uncontrollable factors that might cause a reduced grade on final inspection.

All this time I was learning, not only about the more practical aspects of soil chemistry, and crop treatment, but also that in farming while you do your best with all the knowledge, and skill, and the advice of experts, to load the chances of success in your favour, you must at the same time be prepared to accept calmly the reverses that unkind fate may bring about. The sudden changes of weather, uncontrollable, and sometimes unaccountable, diseases of plant and animal, breakdowns of machinery and man—all these are hazards which may, when seen in their true proportions, inspire in the farmer some of the greatest traits of the human spirit.

How did you find time for all this ? is a question I was often asked. What a silly question when you come to think of it ! You don't find time; you don't make time; you save it; you balance it. Suddenly I found that much that I had regarded as being important before ceased to be of importance. I didn't need to play golf; I did not need to fish; I did not need that extra hour or two in bed of a Sunday morning. The hours and energy I spent on the farm were neither more nor less than the average man might have spent on the golf course. Besides, I was learning much of value to me in my work. I could now look my farmer parents in the face with a ready sympathy; their troubles were more than ever my troubles. We could crack similar jokes about the same things; and we could confide in each other. I came to understand my pupils better, and to spot those who, though they might not be much good at " the book larnin'," would suddenly brighten when you asked them how the cows were doing at present. I was learning more and more about land values, and the correct treatment of land; knowledge which was to prove invaluable when the school came to possess forty acres or so. Though the chemistry, botany, and ecology of the farm came easily to me, I was sometimes surprised at the almost instinctive knowledge of

some of the old farmers around us. For example, there was one
who once said to me: "You mustn't put ammonia on the
ground unless there's plenty o' bone in it." This was his way
of saying that you must not put ammonium sulphate on ground
not previously dressed with the correct balance of phosphate
and lime.

And, of course, I was not the only local professional man to
take up farming. In fact there was a well-known Presbyterian
minister near by who was as good a farmer as an orator. He
tripodded hay, made silage; and used a tractor in the days when
you had to walk in front carrying a red light. I once heard
him make a speech at a farmer's dinner. He spoke for about
an hour; used frequent classical quotations; kept the farmers
interested; and "never had nothin' in his han' the whole time."
I was at the dinner ostensibly to sing; to attempt to sing to a
group of farmers well laced with Guinness is about as easy as
trying to plough clay. Mr. Harry Ferguson, the visionary
millionaire engineer from Dromore, was a guest at the same
dinner; he put before these conservative gentlemen a new vision
of farming which was to be realized within the lifetime of most
of those present. This all happened before the war when
mechanized farming was still in its infancy.

Early in my own farming career, I heard that I might be able
to purchase a good cow from a man I knew in a nearby town.
He was a bank manager. Arrived at the bank I asked if I could
speak to the manager. "Over there," said the clerk. I looked
in the direction to which he pointed, and there I saw a man in an
open-necked shirt; he was on the wrong side of the counter,
obviously striking a bargain with a local farmer; whether the
bargain had to do with a cow or an overdraft I don't know.
Though country banks, especially in Ireland, are different, I had
not previously discovered such a degree of informality.

"You're the manager," I said, "I called to see you about a
cow you have for sale."

"Right," said he, "jump in the car in the yard and we'll
run out to the farm."

On the way out we chatted about our respective professions
in relation to farming.

" Nothin' to beat the farmin'," he said, " grand, open air, active life. When I'm farmin' the days are too short; in the bank they're too long. Besides," he said, " in your job and mine everybody's troubles are yours; at the farmin' you only have your own troubles to worry about."

I did not disagree, though I was not sure of the logic of what he said, especially as I had not yet reached a stage when I could take farming troubles lightly and calmly. He had more than reached this stage; for, when we came into his immense byres, underneath a heap of straw in a " group " there was a dead calf. He just glanced at it and said: " Must have died at the calvin'." For us the death of a calf at this time would have been a tragedy.

But to return to our work and worry. As it happened, our first harvesting season proved to be one of the worst in the history of farming. First we had to save a small field of seed hay; this was early in the season when we got reasonably good weather. We worked in rows gathering the hay together into bundles which we tied with a strap of hay. Then the bundles were collected into " stooks," and later the stooks were made into " shigs " and thatched. Collecting the hay was back-breaking, and it was sore on the hands because of the unavoidable spines of the thistles. This was not the end; later there was the threshing, and then the fanning to blow away the unwanted impurities. When all this had been done the final yield seemed very small; at this time, however, a few bags of good seed would fetch a high price. We could never have carried out all these operations without the generous help and advice, and the equipment of neighbouring farmers.

Then the weather broke ! It rained, and rained, and rained. It rained throughout the remainder of the summer; it rained through the early autumn; and it rained throughout the potato harvest. Our oats grew and grew and grew until they were nearly as tall as myself. With pride I listened to neighbours saying it was the best field of oats they had ever seen. But no oats could stand against those storms; they lodged as if they had been tramped by a herd of elephants.

When the weather cleared for a little the tractor man didn't arrive—of course he didn't, because everybody in the country wanted him at the same time. I tried to get horses and eventually succeeded in getting two on approbation, but they wouldn't work together; when one pulled the other " rusted." In those days one " opened" the field first, by scything a swathe or two all around; when this had been done it looked as though we might have to cut the whole field with a scythe. Then one day I thought of my friend at the local. I telephoned to him. " Aye," said he, " Ah've a field or two o' my own to finish, and then Ah'll be with ye." As good as his word, bless him ! he turned up on the morrow. For a time we made good progress, working day and night, Saturdays, Sundays, every day, as long as the weather held. But it didn't hold. Down came the rain again, soaking the cut sheaves and turning the lower ground into a morass. When we tried again the tractor sank to the axles, so we had no recourse but to finish the job with scythes.

Finish it we did; and in spite of all the difficulties it turned out to be a bumper crop; though time and again we had to rotate the bundles in the stooks to keep them drying. From this experience I learned two lessons: that an oat crop is remarkably resilient, and that, while in a wet year the expense of harvesting may be considerable, this may be more than offset by a good crop. I was to find later that the financial results in a year of drought were much more adverse.

Normally I don't keep a diary; what I have written so far in this book has been almost entirely from memory. As it happened, however, I did make a few notes about those first farming months, possibly with the thought in mind that I might write a book about our experiences. Looking through these notes now I find that in the midst of all this we managed a short holiday that year. I think it must have been between the seed hay harvest and the cutting of the oats. A cousin, mother of Richard Kell, the poet, offered us the use of her flat in Merrion Square, Dublin. We couldn't refuse such an offer. Dublin then was an oasis in a desert of restrictions, controls, and rations.

Besides, I had roots in Dublin. I liked Dublin, and I liked the thought of staying in the heart of this " fair city," surrounded by the aura of the great: Swift and Shaw, Goldsmith

and Yeats, Parnell and Grattan, Wilde and Joyce. What a
strange boiling of poets and patriots, playwrights and writers
of every ilk. Yes, I like Dublin with its lovely Georgian
squares, its decadent Georgian slums, its pubs and parks, its
chapels and chancelleries, brothels and book shops, convents
and colleges. Is there any city that has crowded so much
language and literature, love and licentiousness, humour and
history, into one small area, from Parnell Square to Fitzwilliam
Square, on the one hand; and from Westland Row to Harcourt
Street on the other ? Is there any city where we could have
bathed in the open sea in the morning, watched international
tennis in Fitzwilliam Square in the afternoon, and gone to the
Gaiety, the Gate, or the Abbey in the evening ? Is there, in
fact, any city that can provide such a varied holiday as Dublin ?
You could be in the mountains at six, dining in Jury's at seven,
and in the theatre at eight. At that time there was no place
where you can have done all these things more cheaply; it is
different now.

Soon, all too soon, we were back to horses and harvesting,
poultry and potatoes, and all the sights and sounds of the farm.
The thresher's in the yard. The gang's arrived ! The tractor
wheel's busted ! The hay's heatin' ! The cow's calvin' ! And
sometimes all of them at once. Not a day passed without
accident, disaster or worry. " How did ye stand it, Doctor, an'
you with yer school on yer hands ? " How did I stand it ?
I don't know, save that each acted as a counter-irritant to the
other. Sometimes I think the less we have to do, the more we
tend to worry about what we have to do. Besides I loved the
work. I say this without nostalgia or sentiment. In these days
it is customary to deglamorize and debunk everything, work,
love, religion, even life itself. Maybe much requires debunk-
ing; and most of us feel uncertain at times about some aspects
of our professions; in all there is some measure of the parasitical;
we may have our inward doubts about values: the doctor
about cures, the lawyer about legislation, and the teacher about
his subjects. But there is no such feeling about farming, for
here is the very core of life; without the skills, the ability, and
the work of the farmer, men would cease to exist. I shall never
forget the joy of those days when things were moving, the

tractor throbbing and fussing, the men shouting, the fields clearing, and the cart-loads coming down from the hill to be safely housed. And at the end of each day the thought of a good job well done, and rest for weary horses and weary men.

At the final inspection Grade A for our potatoes ! Now it remained to harvest them. The haulms had previously been burned down with sodium chlorate, when it seemed that the maximum number of tubers were at the seed size. As usual there was the difficulty about getting the digger at the right time. The gangs would be there, but no digger; or the digger might be there, but the weather unsuitable. In potato digging it was essential to have the maximum number of hands at each drill, otherwise the tractor, which waited for no man for time was money, would come bearing down before you could get your patch cleaned. A man's temper would soon become frayed if he didn't have men on either side at a reasonable distance.

But we strove and worked and cursed. Sometimes the Ministry sent good gangs, and sometimes bad ones. Sometimes we had school children who had already learned to be cute about their demands: Mr. McSpud gave us so much, or gave us this or that to eat, they would say, to blackmail us into giving them something more or something better. As for the gangs, most of the men were good workers but they were a motley crew, some veterans of one war, some of two, and some who had been pitch-forked into work for which they had little inclination. And some were born grousers; no matter what you gave them to eat it was wrong. My wife's heart was nearly broken trying to please them.

What shouting and fuss there would be in the yard on the morning of a digging ! " Hi, Paddy, would ye han' me thon collar and hames ! " " Seamus, for jes sake stand clear o' thon pony or she'll kick the arse off ye ! " These and similar remarks seemed a necessary accompaniment to the preparations for going up to the field. And they were right about the pony, for she would have done just this. I bought her from a man for twenty pounds; she certainly did twenty pounds' worth of work for, once in the shafts, she would do the work of two horses without tiring, but she was the devil to get between the shafts.

We had happy days in the fields. One Saturday the Girl Guides, with their Mistress, came out from school to help. The digger didn't turn up but we set to work with as many forks as we could muster; at the end of the day it was surprising the number of drills we had conquered in this way. And then there were Saturdays when one of our masters raised a gang of willing helpers. These were our own people; we knew them; and it was a spontaneous and never-to-be-forgotten, kindly gesture. Nor will we ever forget the parties in our big kitchen; the plates of Irish stew, and the roast apples with syrup in them ! And then back, and backs, to the field; red and black scarves waving in the wind, and the bags and loads piling up. Ah ! tea at last ! A welcome break, thank God ! And at the end of the day the field cleared. Harvest Thanksgivings had always been a great feature of our town and countryside; that year, for most of us, the thanks were more heartfelt than ever.

"The trouble about the spuds is yer never finished with them " said a neighbour man to me; and I was soon to realize the truth of his statement. After the gathering there was the sorting into seed, wares, and chats. Throughout the winter the sorter was going day and night, and we all took our turn at the sorting, bagging, sewing, and labelling; but the bags couldn't be sealed finally until passed by an inspector who, as lief as not, might make you put them through the sorter again. Then there might be a bottle-neck in the shipping. Delay meant that one's badly-needed money was not forthcoming; and there was the added risk of frost damage, which could mean that your potatoes might be returned from the docks for further sorting.

As luck would have it, we had to face one of the worst winters on record. It began to freeze and snow soon after Christmas; it was still freezing at Easter. Day after day the east wind swirled down from the Arctic, forcing its cold breath through every chink and crack. We put up canvas sheets; we burned hurricane lamps all night long in the lofts; anything at all to keep out this devil that seemed determined to destroy our hard-won seed. And, of course, there was no question of getting the bags away: the Ministry did not want them under these conditions.

It was during the frost that I decided never again to be dependent on others for our harvesting operations. Even if the money could have been raised, few tractors were available at the time; besides, most of our neighbours said they wouldn't have a tractor in their fields: " It 'ud pack the groun' ye know, ye'll never grow good crops, if ye have a tractor packin' yer groun' the whole time." Horses it must be; and so I set about looking for suitable animals.

In answer to an advertisement I set off one afternoon after school on the bicycle. Snow piled high to the tops of the hedges billowed out over the fields in white waves. One could scarcely discern the single track of the road through the snow; by dint of riding, walking, and falling off, I eventually reached, what I thought was my destination, away in the wilds of Dechomet. I approached a lonely farmhouse; not a soul in sight—only the east wind rippling over snow-bound hills, and rattling weirdly a tarpaulin hung in front of the potato loft. Then I heard a whinnying; and a lovely white horse, glad of my company, pushed his nose over the half-door of the stable. I hoped he would be my horse, for he and I were soon friends in our loneliness.

But it was not to be; I soon realized I was in the wrong place; so we had to part. Then I saw a large, grey, lonely house, near by. I pulled the wire bell which jangled almost alarmingly in the ghostly darkness somewhere in the depths of the house. There was some movement ! I heard an inhuman pottering ! Suddenly the door was opened; in the half darkness all I could see were a pair of staring eyes, two horns, and a beard. For one awful moment I thought I was seeing some devilish apparition. Then I saw an old woman behind. " What's yer business ? " said she. I explained my mission. " Ah doubt ye're come to the wrong place," she said; and she pointed away across the snow-bound wastes to another hamlet. But I gave up; home, a hot fire, and a meal were all I craved for at this moment. By now, however, the good lady would have prolonged the conversation indefinitely while I, keeping a wary eye on the great white goat in front of her, was seeking an

MOTHER AND DAUGHTER
Castlehaven Verity and Ballievey Verity

opportunity to get away. " Do ye keep a goat ? " was her final gambit. " No," I said, as I backed away. " It's a very useful thing, a goat," said she. I agreed with her and ran.

Though I was disappointed at not getting a horse, or two horses, I shall never forget the journey home. By now the sun, sinking in a rose-red sky, was casting a roseate reflection over the snow-enshrouded land, so that, as I skidded, walked and rode toward the west, I seemed to be encompassed by cold fire.

Later I was to get my two horses. I bought them from a dealer; they say you shouldn't do this, but this was a dealer with a difference: he was honest. If I didn't like them I could bring them back. But I liked them; we all liked them; we even grew to love them. One was a young horse, the other an older one. They worked together as though united by some kind of psychic force. When one went away the other was miserable, and screamed with delight when he heard the clop, clop, clop of his partner's shoes on the high road above the tree-embanked river. The two must long since have gone to the knacker's yard; if there is a valhalla for horses these two deserve to be there.

I have described our first farming year in some detail because it, more than any other, was representative of those difficult times, and of the difficulties of tyros in the business. To go on with such detail would require a book, so from now on I shall merely outline our further ventures and adventures. The next year things were somewhat easier; we had experience behind us and a good deal of equipment. Financially, I found we had more than paid our way; we had done at least as well as if we had let the land, but more important still, we were building up stock and fertility.

We kept on with our potato, oats, and seed hay rotation for another year or two until we realized that the employment and feeding of all these hands was becoming too much for us. Besides, with rising trade and full employment, it became more and more difficult to get good help. And I had read somewhere that the best way to improve your land is to sell from it only that which can walk off on four legs. So once again a decision had to be made. I would sell out everything: horses, harness, and carts, and all the horse-drawn equipment. Perhaps in good

P

time I would buy a tractor; but in the meantime we should try
to build up our live stock, hens and cows, bullocks and heifers.

After many a set-back through loss of chicks, the stock of
laying hens was growing. Herself would often say to me:
" They're looking grand, but I wish they would lay." But they
began to lay in their own good time. When this event
happened the sensation created thereby in the household was
much like the scene in Shaw's *Saint Joan* after the arrival of
the maid at the Castle of Vancouleurs:

Steward : Sir, sir—

Robert : What now ?

Steward : The hens are laying like mad, sir. Five dozen eggs !
Only those who have waited in vain for hens to lay could
appreciate this scene.

Another less dramatic scene sticks in my mind. While we
still had the horse, we needed some feeding for the cows.
Hearing that a local man had a load of turnips for sale I decided
that, as no one else was available, I had no recourse but to go
over for them myself. I harnessed the horse and cart, collected
the turnips, and on my way back perched on my load of red
turnips, I noticed a red and black-capped boy approaching on
a bicycle. He got such a shock when he saw me in this unusual
undignified position that he nearly fell off his bicycle, while I,
in looking down at him, nearly fell off the cart.

Then, as I approached our cross-roads, a man hailed me.
" How are ye, Docthor ? " said he, " Ah believe ye have a cow
due soon. Ah'll give ye five pounds for the calf if she's a
heifer." At this time five pounds was quite a good price for
a scrub calf; I made enquiries and found that the cow had been
with a Friesian bull. Later the cow safely delivered a tiny black
and white heifer; so began a twenty-year interest in this
famous breed.

But that was far from being the end of the beginning, and
further from being the beginning of the end. We must go in
for milk. We must have quantity of milk; therefore we must
have Friesians. Where could we get them ? That was a problem, for at that time the number of herds was limited. There
was to be an auction at Dundonald, near our old home. I remembered a man whom I knew in the old days. I telephoned to

him. " Yes, of course, I'll help you. Come over to see me," he said. Getting to Dundonald in those car-less days was far from easy. After school I had to take a train to Belfast, and then a tram to Dundonald. Alighting at the Dundonald cemetery I walked through the country to the boundary hedge, at a point I judged to be opposite the farm up the hillside on the old Dundonald Road. It was now getting dark and I hadn't reckoned on the hedging efficiency of the North Down farmers. Stumbling through thorn hedges, over ditches, and tearing my clothes to pieces on concealed barb wire, I eventually arrived on the old Dundonald Road, and was soon drinking a welcome cup o' scald with my Friesian-loving friend. Later he stood beside me at the auction, told me what to bid for, and helped me with the bidding for a pure-bred non-pedigree cow with " Royal " blood in it, and a cross-bred Ayrshire Friesian.

Soon I was studying form and yields, and the relationship between rations and yields. I went to auctions; I bought more cows; I bought a pedigree cow for ninety pounds. Our calves began to increase. Hey, presto ! we had a pedigree heifer calf ! I joined the Friesian Society and proudly sent in my sketch-card of the new calf. Our non-pedigree cow did so well that they accepted her for the Supplementary Register. Things were moving on now. We refurbished an old byre to accord with regulations. I began to record and feed according to yield. We electrified the whole place and put in an electric pump.

At about this time our young nephew, Peter, was with us; he had energy enough for three, and he could work in the fields with the men as though he were a man. He accompanied me everywhere; and he was good company. One day we went to an auction. With Peter to support me I made my bids for Castlehaven Verity—a beautiful cow from the Castlehaven herd in County Cork. She fell to me at £140. As the price rose I could feel the colour rising steadily up the back of my neck, especially when I thought of what my bank manager might think or say; but I was banking on the thought that her first heifer calf would offset the original investment. As Joxer Daly might have said, she proved to be " a darlin' cow, a darlin' cow," she was to give many a heifer calf, and a

milk yield far in excess of my highest expectations. On the
way home Peter and the man had to milk her into the
" sheugh "; for she could scarcely carry her heavy bag.

Our newly appointed man proved to be as gentle with the
cows as our previous one had been rough. The first thing he did
was to throw away the stick. I thought this was a good
beginning. Soon the cows were as gentle as he was. He came
from the County Donegal, where they breed good people;
and, although a foreigner, he was soon popular around the
district because of his transparent decency. He rarely let us
down. I remember one " Twelfth " when he, and a cousin
with whose people he lodged, were both working for us. The
milk collector had left a note the evening before stating that he
would be calling for the milk at some extraordinary hour on
the morning of the big day. We wakened at about four
o'clock to hear our two boys bringing in the cows; they were
determined that before leaving for the march all would be in
order. And then there was the night of the motor accident,
when they telephoned to us from the hospital, at two o'clock
in the morning, to tell us what had happened. They rang
again at six because our man was so anxious about the milking.
When I went to see him he was swatched in bandages with
several smashed ribs, teeth knocked in and a variety of other
cuts and abrasions. Still he was worried about the cows !

All that, however, is to anticipate. I bought more pedigree
cows, sometimes paying prices that shocked me let alone my
bank manager. But, as many of these surpassed expectations,
they were a good buy, and a good foundation for the herd.
Some were soon on the Register of Merit, and I was happier to
be able to write R.M. after the name of a cow than to put my
own qualifications after my name.

At this stage there was still much to be done. For a long time
I had to go out every night to give the animals a last feed, and
to water them. Watering entailed carrying two, three or four
bucketfuls to every cow; and as we now had up to twenty cows
this was quite a carry. But I was still young; I was still active;
I enjoyed the exercise as a break in the evening's work. And
then there were calving nights. Sometimes our man was
there; sometimes I was there; sometimes we were both there.

When I was alone on a frosty, moonlight night, listening to the
cows ruminating, I had much time for my own mental
ruminations. Initially, I was unworried by cold, or rats, or
strange noises in the night, my only sensation was one of fear.
Would I be able to cope with the task when the first two tiny
yellow-hoofed, white-socked feet appeared ? But I managed
and soon became something of an expert in animal gynæcology.
When the poor animal stood up for her final effort, the
expulsion of the head, I found the holding of a slippery, hairy
calf to be extremely difficult, especially as I had to get the calf
away immediately, so that the cow would neither see it nor
smell it, and therefore would not fret when it had to be taken
from her. So much effort on the cow's part for so little
satisfaction !

When all was over there would be the excited rush upstairs
to say: " It's a heifer ! " or in more subdued tones: " Another
bull." Soon, however, the prefix Ballievey was to appear
more and more often in the Friesian Society Register: Ballievey
Verity and Venus, Shamrock and Clover, Blackberry and
Snowberry: all these and many more. At first eight hundred
gallons, then a thousand; and before we finished we expected
a cow to be at least a potential two-thousand-galloner at up
to four per cent butter fat.

We had no bull, so at first we had to drive cows here and
there all over the country for services. This could not go on.
Then I read of artificial insemination—surely this was the
answer ! But it was not—at least not a complete answer, for
in those pioneering days there were no local stations; all the
semen had to be transported from Reading, thus we had many
misses. We would rear our own bull. This we did—and what
a bull ! Ballievey Bertus. He sired many a good calf, but
finally became so big and strong that he would walk into a field
and lift the gate away on his head. Once he couldn't be found.
As he could ford the river even in a flood as easily as a hippo-
potamus, I went down the far side. I saw him on the other
side. I removed all the clothing I could and half walked and
half swam across the river. There he was with his chain
wrapped around the branch of a tree. Keeping a wary eye on
him, I unwrapped the chain, expecting a furious lunge at any

moment, but he came home with me as docile as a child. I suppose after about twenty-four hours in this position all the fight had been knocked out of him !

When he made me jump the garden gate, I thought I was now at an age when Olympian feats of this description were no longer for me. We would go back to A.I., especially as we now had our own stations near at hand. Before long we had stock with the blood of all the great herds: Lavenham, Terling, and many others; and one soon learned to spot the progeny of the various breeds of bull.

Of course we now had water in the byres; and long before this we had purchased a tractor and equipment. I doubted the financial wisdom of the venture on such a small acreage, but there seemed no alternative. We experimented with strip grazing, using an electric fence; we grew kale and grazed it by the electric fence method. Then we made silage—at first mainly from oats. Will I ever forget our Herculean labours at our first attempt ? We had no loader, so we had to cut the massive oat crop, fork it into carts, and tip each load into the silo. I usually remained in the silo to get this massive material shaken out and spread before the next load would come in. I quailed before each mountain of this heavy, interwoven, wet cereal crop. But the silage was fairly successful, and in succeeding years grass silage and hay were to be our main standby for bulk feeding, until at the end silage feeding led to tragic results—but more about this later.

The characters and temperaments of our cows were as many and varied as the characters and temperaments of human beings. There were the affectionate ones, the indifferent, the choosey, the leaders, and the bullies. Put the wrong food in the feeding trough of some, and they would scorn it as a caviare eater might scorn a cod steak. Put one in the wrong place and, if you were not careful, she might kill the cow in her stall. We had two who stood beside each other with a partition between; they were always pals. But I had to sell one; the night the farmer came to take her away in the trailer we missed her pal; she had followed the trailer, and we didn't catch her until she reached Magherally Cross-roads. As it happened, the farmer to whom I sold the cow objected to a slight fault—

which, in fact, I had told him about. " Send her back," I said,
nothing loth. That evening when her pal looked over the
partition she almost smiled, and her diminished milk yield
recovered !

There were the breakers. They would always break
at holiday times when our man was away. I remember
once two—presumably Protestant !—heifers celebrated "The
Twelth" by disappearing. They were valuable animals;
I was anxious about them, so my son-in-law-to-be and myself
scoured the country picking up a clue here and there, and
sometimes following their droppings on the hard road. At
length, toward evening, feeling hot and tired, and very cross
at the loss of our day, we espied an old cottager at Magherally
Cross.

I said: " Did you see a couple o' heifers around here ? "

" No," said he, " but Ah'm goin' to tell ye sumpin'. Once
there was a farmer who sent his man to look for a lost cow.
After a while the man came back an' he said, sez he: ' Ah've
looked in ivery possible place, an' there's not a bloody sign of
her anywhere.' Now, sez the farmer: ' Go an' look for her
in all the *im*possible places.' So yer man goes off again, an' after
a wee while, the farmer sees him lookin' up the chimney.
Sez the farmer: ' What in God's name are ye doin' there ? '
' Ah'm lookin' in all the impossible places,' sez yer man."

We looked in all the impossible places and eventually found
our two heifers on the Belfast Road heading for Banbridge
and the Orange procession !

At the end of that holiday new and exciting events began to
happen in that other field of my activities across the Bann.

CHAPTER XI

OAK WOOD

ONE morning I arrived at school as usual; and, as I looked out of the dusty windows of the old staff room, I felt depressed. Nothing was happening, nothing could happen, to change things. Here we were, as it seemed, for all time. Around me now was a good, varied and loyal staff; but for how long ? No teacher, no matter how loyal, would tolerate these conditions for ever. Then something happened that was to change everything. One of my staff came in reading the newspaper. He said: " Did you see that the Castle's for sale ? "

Scarcely stopping to think, or even to look right or left, I was across the road in a thrice, and at my end of the telephone. I rang the Chairman of my Board. He saw the possibilities. I rang the Secretary of the Education Authority; he, too, saw the possibilities. Soon my old friend, the Surveyor, was down; we went over the place and we, too, saw the possibilities—more clearly now on the actual terrain. After that I cannot remember quite what happened. There were meetings; there *must* have been meetings which I had to attend to explain the position; there was some resistance locally by self-interested parties; but the long and the short of it was that the thing was arranged with a speed and rapidity never before known in the annals of local bodies. Even the Ministry was, I think, almost shocked into submission !

The " Castle," Edenderry House, was a fine mansion in forty acres of lovely green, tree-bordered, but for the most part, hilly land. Being within a matter of half a mile or so from the town, it was conveniently situated. From its long windows the view was superb, stretching away through the trees, through the church spires, and over invisible roof-tops, across the Bann, away and away over the foothills of the Mournes to Slieve Donard. All around lay the lands of Bannside, Iveagh, and

THE IRISH FAMILY CROWE—SNAPPED BY THE SWISS FAMILY KUHN

Mourne; all those lands from which our pupils emanated and from which our school houses took their names.

Built of grey Portland stone and Scrabo sandstone, with a columned portico, stately entrance hall, and a big quadrangular yard between the stables on one side, and the house and servants' quarters on the other, the house had a façade of great dignity.

And it had been occupied by a dignified family, the Fergusons who, for many decades, had held positions of great prominence in the town and district. Almost from its inception, Fergusons had taken a lively and active interest in the affairs of Banbridge Academy; it was therefore fitting that, when at last the school found a permanent home, it should have been in this house. It might interest musical readers to know that Howard Ferguson, the distinguished composer and virtuoso, is a member of this family.

In the circumstances in which we were placed at the time I think I would have moved the school, or part of it, almost immediately. But no, the Ministry wisely insisted that we must wait until the building complied with the regulations in every detail. Plans had to be drawn up, specifications agreed, tenders put out. There were delays, and delays, and delays. Once I came down to see how things were going—frosted windows in the Art Room !—good heavens ! if pupils are to be placed in lovely surroundings, they must be allowed to see them. So the frosted glass was removed. Only two laboratories ! We must have at least three ! After further delays and plans a third laboratory was added.

A fine school, in forty acres of green land, a beautiful garden, laboratories, art room, domestic science kitchen, a residential house and two cottages, all for about £50,000 less a considerable sum for the sale of military hutments and equipment; that was the bill; and it was cheap at the price; even then when the most modest school building would have cost at least £100,000. This was not final; additions had to be made: a gymnasium-cum-assembly hall with changing rooms, and a dining hall. Still, it was cheap, especially when one remembers that all schools require additions and extensions from time to time, as numbers increase and horizons enlarge.

R

But in the meantime we had an excellent working unit; though for a while during that summer vacation, it looked as if I might have to say—no building, no school; for we had been somewhat unceremoniously pushed out of the old building before the new one was ready. However, in the end the move was effected. Once again my colleagues rose to the occasion; laboratory equipment was moved; such furniture as we possessed was moved; and all without drawing on the public purse.

And so, at last, after a century or so, Banbridge Academy reopened after the summer vacation in its own building. Elsewhere I have described my feelings on that morning. It is difficult to describe feelings, and even more difficult for others to understand them; but a feeling that has been building up in one's mind and heart for close on two decades is bound to be strong. And so, as I walked up the hill to Edenderry on that September morning, with the first faint smells and colours of the autumn around me; as I watched the red and black-clothed pupils on their way; and as I lifted my eyes to the silent hills above the gracious grey house, I think I said a prayer of thankfulness. Whether our pupils noticed my feelings or not I don't know; but, as I stood on the platform before the assembled school, I found it unusually difficult to speak. Pupils of the school may never again experience what we all felt then: the complete break from a place of which we could not be proud to one of which we might well *be* proud.

Troubles were not yet over, but at least we now had a foundation on which to build. We had visitors from here, there, and everywhere. This seemed to be a time for visitors and visitations, for it was a time of resurgence: business was booming; eagerly new educationists strove toward progressive education; teachers began to travel to see how the business of teaching was carried out in other places. We had teachers from Texas, students from Singapore, French girls and German boys, brown girls and black men; and as each came and went they said: " What lovely premises you have here, Doctor ! " And I was proud. No day was normal; I would say to our Secretary: " When we get a normal day we'll have to get down

to the annual budget," and she would reply: " But what day
is normal?"

And our own pupils began to travel more and more. One
went to Denmark; two to observe in Russia; some travelled
in the U.S.A. and in Canada; they went to conferences in
London; they went in groups to Paris. With our son now
lecturing in Paris, it was natural that we, in spite of the demands
of the farm, should endeavour to broaden our own horizons
by travelling abroad. I can always remember with what joy
one day we went down to the Seine to meet a happy band of
red and black-clothed girls and boys as they stepped off one of
the river boats, accompanied by two or three of our staff
friends. We travelled across Europe to Austria where we joined
in Tyrolean singing in a wine cellar in Klagenfurt; to Yugo-
slavia where, on Easter Day, we watched a communist procession, and went to High Mass in Ljubljana; to Venice where I
remember saying to our son that no city had a right to
monopolize so much beauty. In later trips we saw the Bay of
Naples and didn't die, though we nearly died of depression
when we saw the slums of Naples; we drank wine from the
vats, sitting at wooden tables underneath the stars at Frascati,
and looked down on the Eternal City with its seven hills.
Later we journeyed up the Rhine to Rüdesheim where they
drink wine all day long; we sailed along the Necker at Heidel-
berg and got lost in the Black Forest beyond Freiburg.

All this and Ireland too ! We discovered Ireland, its beautiful
villages and towns: Inistioge and Adare, Killaloe and Kilkenny,
Enniscorthy and Enniskerry, and a host of others that few of
those who so roundly condemn our Irish towns and villages
have ever seen. To weep with joy is one thing, and with
compassion another. We wept with both when we beheld
the lonely cabins among the Connemara hills, but with joy
only when we sucked the Atlantic air from the heights of
Mizzen, or bathed our souls in the coloured air of Corrib, near
Cong. Ah, yes, all this and heaven ! but who would wish for
any heaven other than this ?

These travels were sandwiched between the cultivation of the
soil of Ballievey, the minds of Banbridgeans, and the soil of
Edenderry. The school buildings were well enough. The local

reporter of the *Banbridge Chronicle* at the time described " the
spacious hallway with its parquet flooring and school crest in
rubber, the sixteen class-rooms, many of them large, dignified
and airy; the many modern contrivances: synchronized clocks,
internal broadcasting equipment and all the rest "; and he
ended by describing the garden which, he said, " was in a fine
state of preservation mainly due to the work of the permanent
gardener."

The permanent gardener was also permanent caretaker; he
was not only permanent but conscientious to a fault; he was a
valuable heirloom; his garden was his child to be nursed into
full flowering at the appropriate season. One would think that
a school garden would suffer more from the intrusion of the
school than the weeds; but Andy's garden suffered from
neither, for he respected his beds, and the school respected him.
So his great cherry, his roses, and his apples budded, bloomed,
fruited, and shed their blooms and leaves from year to year,
symbolizing the young fresh lives that came to us like saplings;
matured to young men and women; and then passed on
their way.

Not only did we have a permanent gardener, but also an
impermanent groundsman. He was a character. I met him
first when he came to us as an additional hand at Ballievey.
He could work alone; he could work with others; he could
work alone until sundown; for him working hours were not
established by the clock, but by the sun. He had a feeling for
the land. He was a jobbing peasant who would take a job
wherever he could find it; and if he didn't like you he would
quit and go to someone else. He could—or would—turn his
hand to anything. He made a silo for me, but on the day of
the big wind, when the *Princess Victoria* went down, the roof
lifted and stalled on the county road. He loved making
"shores"; as one of my colleagues remarked, he had made
enough shores to contain the Irish Sea !

He liked big words and deep thoughts. When we were all
having a rest between spells of exhausting work in the fields,
he would say: " Now, Docthor, supposin' a man fired a rifle
in a train travellin' at sixty miles an hour, would the bullet
reach the end o' the train faster or slower than if the train was

standin' still ?" And then, straightening up his head and
drawing in his lips, he would look at me as if he had pro-
pounded a problem as deep as one to do with the moon project.
He told me once that there wasn't "a sensation o' wather in thon
drain "; and another time he said he had lent the motor scythe
to a man who didn't know how to use it; the machine had run
amok cutting through fruit frees, roses and goodness knows
what: " An' man," said George, " if ye'd seen the ciphers of
her ! " " But the flax wather was the cure for the pains," he
told me, " if ye hunker down an' take a good slug o' thon, ye'll
feel it goin' through yer body like oil ! "

He wrought at a great tree in the centre of a field ultimately
to be used as a hockey pitch. In the end we pulled it out, roots
and all, using my tractor and man; before the final pull, however, he had dug a hole around the stump deep enough, as he
said, " to bury the divil himself." Having prepared our pitches
we had to have some way of cutting them; at the time the idea
that we would ultimately possess our own tractor was more a
pipe-dream than reality. Besides, tractors were still in short
supply, so we fell back on the traditional Irish unit of power,
the donkey. He became not only our power unit, but also our
school mascot; on the whole I think he preferred the latter role,
though, once his engine began to tick over, he worked well;
but, like many another engine, he was a doubtful starter.
Shall I ever forget one evening I went down to help with the
first cutting of the lower pitch; we cut and raked, raked and
cut, until the donkey stopped and the moon replaced the sun
in the sky.

In time, however, the fields were professionally laid, drained,
cut, and rolled; and we had two hockey pitches, two rugby
pitches, and two or three hard tennis courts. As the years
moved on, it was with increasing pleasure that I would hear,
through the windows of my room, the sound of bat or foot on
ball, or the cries of " Come on Bann !" and see the red and
black jerseyed figures moving this way and that, to make up
the intricate pattern of a school at play. Maybe the time will
come when all this will disappear to be replaced by great
central comprehensives. But nothing can erase from my
memory, or the memories of those associated with me, the

nobility, patriotism, and loyalty which the local school engenders.

It is the business of a school to teach its pupils to " Render unto Cæsar the things that are Cæsar's "; and not, in my opinion, to teach politics with a political bias; and so, when Lord Brookeborough, as the most important representative of the Government, was invited to open the new school, and later to close my years in office, it was with no political bias, nor in fact did his speech on either occasion emphasize his outlook. But whether you preferred orange or green you could not help liking the man. Not only was he a talented speaker with a strong sense of humour, but he had the common touch: he knew how to speak to each one of us about the things in which we were interested, and on our level. He talked to me about Fermanagh, fishing, and Friesians. He guessed that since my name was Crowe my father's family must have originated in Fermanagh. He was probably right. When we entertained him at Ballievey on his later visit, the cows—as they always did on important occasions—broke out—thus the conversation about Friesians; and I suppose the near proximity of the river led to fishing. Anyhow the talk was so interesting that I thought we would never reach the platform on time. The gist of one of his speeches—I forget which—was never lose your temper or your courage. Did he ever lose either ? I don't think so.

Harry Midgley, former Labour M.P. and later Minister of Education at a time when education was particularly difficult to administer, was also a guest at the opening. Words flowed from him like many waters from the mountains. He distributed the prizes the year we were on the way to Edenderry. Noticing the name Bambrick—the name of a former pupil member of our staff—he quoted the well-known " Slip it to Joe ! "—a reference to the famous Joe Bambrick of Linfield. The remark was particularly apposite as Banbridge Academy F.C. was, I believe, one of the first association clubs to be formed in Ireland. In the " Remarks " column of our Visitors' Book Midgley wrote " Up Linfield ! "

To mention cows and distinguished guests in the same chapter is perhaps a little incongruous, but I'll take the risk. The herd was becoming—if not important—at least well known; buyers appeared from the south, and there was competition for our bulls. It was a great pleasure to me to come home, look at the yields—which we recorded every day—and talk over the feeding and the day's events with our man; and, as my wife had now taken over the feeding of the calves, they, too, were a pleasure to see. Not indeed that we had no troubles—of course we had; no breeder and dairy farmer escapes from the day-to-day difficulties of his difficult business: mastitis and milk fever, calving troubles and calves' troubles. Once I saved two calves that had been given up by our careful vet. They were so weak that they couldn't stand on their feet. I decided to treat them as though they were fresh from their mother's womb. I gave them tiny quantities of milk and watched them, not day by day, but hour by hour. I kept on in this way until they could stand, and then slowly and carefully increased the feed as they gained strength. Both reached maturity—one a fine heifer, but the other had to be sold as a bullock as it was a little under size for breeding purposes.

One of my colleagues lived with us at this time. We usually took an evening walk up the hill before settling down to the evening work. We talked about everything under the sun—or under the stars if you like, for the stars were usually twinkling and sparkling in the great black dome of the sky. We not only talked under the stars, but about the stars, about astronomical distances, the fourth dimension, relativity, poetry and people, language and literature, ornithology and anthropology. He was a good listener and drew from me all I had to give. I hope I was an equally good listener for I had much to learn from him. Anyhow we toyed with ideas up there by Ballievey Fort; and we watched for Sputnik I as it brought its message from the East in its circles around the circling earth. In the light of more recent events Sputnik I is almost mundane; but as we circled Ballievey hills we felt we were on the brink of an era; and we were right.

One snowy night I had business to transact at the home of Dr. Helen Waddell; her people then were great buyers of my bulls. Deep in conversation, we got deeper and deeper into the

snowy hinterland about Magherally. At last we came to a wall
beyond which we could see lights and moving figures, so we
had no recourse but to vault the wall. My friend went over
first, stumbled in the snow and fell; then I went over, caught
my foot in the ivy, and dived head first into the drift on the
other side. The trail of our entry through the back garden was
so well marked that there were scarcely veiled smiles when we
had to repeat the journey a day or two afterwards to collect
my friend's fountain pen, which had dropped in the snow
during the mishap. No doubt they thought we had been
having one over the eight; a supposition that would have been
quite untrue.

Inexorably the years moved on; so many interesting things
happened, however, that the passage of time seemed to gain
in momentum, and I scarcely realized that youth was no longer
on my side. Prizes were presented from the platform of our
new hall in 1957, when our guests were Lord and Lady
Wakehurst. As this was an occasion, and our grounds—and,
in fact, the school—were still far from perfect, a tremendous
effort had to be made, and *was* made, by our staff, our pupils,
and some former pupils. Such a fuss ! The school was like
a beehive. We cut and carted, trimmed and tidied, polished
and prepared, until all the synchronized clocks in the building
had slipped past the midnight hour. It was a heart-warming
experience, and one I have never forgotten. No highly
organized system could ever compare with this spontaneous
voluntary effort !

Maybe due to conditioning, or maybe due to some deep-
seated human need, there is a strange aura about royalty, or
even about their aristocratic representatives. It is not surprising
therefore, that the visit of Lord and Lady Wakehurst excited
more interest than that of any other visitors. As our little
cortège left Ballievey, many were out to salute us on the way;
and for the first and only time in our lives we were humble
participants in this moving acclaim. Lady Wakehurst brought
with her that undeniable charm which endeared her to everybody. His Excellency, however, was a little aloof, and difficult
to talk to, especially as I knew nothing about his pet subject—
photography. Be it said of both that no event was too small

THE OLD NEW SCHOOL
Banbridge Academy as it is

THEIR EXCELLENCIES ARRIVE

for them; they took a profound interest in everybody, and in everything.

The new dining hall was opened at the same time. At tea I pointed out the mural work on the walls. These had been executed mainly by a daughter of the distinguished Ulster poet, W. R. Rodgers, whom I had met on a number of occasions. One night he and his Danish wife came out to see us at Ballievey at a very late hour. Inevitably, the conversation turned on Ireland and I remember how, with poetic imagery, he said that he always thought of Ireland as three old women sitting under a hedge with their shawls happed around them; in their gnarled faces and in their eyes you could see all the joys and sorrows of their country.

There were to be both for us in those last years of our climb up the hill of life, but losses inside the house were our greatest sorrows. One by one, as our boarders moved away from us, I began to miss something; that close intimacy with the life of the school, and the conversations at the end of the day about the daily happenings. I always found it difficult to be impersonal, unsentimental, and objective; for me close personal and emotional ties have always been a necessity. My vocation could never be impersonal, and it never *was*; troubled parents usually favoured me with their most intimate troubles, and I always tried, though often failed, to treat each boy and girl as a separate individual.

I remember one of my distinguished colleagues, a brother headmaster, saying to me that he always distrusted those who had all the answers. I said I thought there was little we could do about the hereditary and environmental traits of our pupils—we could not change characters. He agreed, but said we could only make them conform. I would go further and say that, if we did our job properly, we ought to be able to use their traits to the best advantage. Was I ever able to do this? Once, I think. I had to talk to a somewhat difficult boy who had that mark of intelligence: he knew himself; he knew that to be told to do something was to put him off doing it. I said: " Well, why not try working at times when you are not supposed to work: on Sundays, for example, or very late at night." I asked him about games. No, he didn't like games.

What did he do with his spare time, I asked. He liked to make model aeroplanes. " Right," I said, " I'll allow you the use of the workshop at any time for this purpose; and, what is more, we'll have a model aeroplane section at the school sports." He flew his aeroplanes at the school sports, and he did well in his advanced level subjects. When, as he came out from the chemistry examination, I asked him how he had done, he said: " I think I did well, Sir, and I worked until two o'clock this morning." Later he went into the R.A.F. and then to the university where he took a degree. As to whether all this had any permanent effect I cannot say, but at least it was effective at the time. And what more can we schoolmasters expect ? Would that I could always have been inspired to adopt the right line with our pupils !

My relations with parents were, I hope, good on the whole, though I am quite sure some did not approve of me. In the early days I probably talked too much and wrote too much, forgetting the advice given by my own former headmaster, who is reported to have said to a colleague who had just been appointed to a headship: " When a parent sends a complaining letter, don't reply other than to invite him or her to come down to discuss the matter with you." This, of course, was said at an earlier time when relationships were on a less friendly footing. But there was some sense in it, for when people come together as human beings, how much easier it is to understand each other's problems.

" Never trust an inspector ! " was advice given to me by a principal soon after I began; and a former master of mine said: " Train your inspectors ! " I didn't do either; I tried to treat them cordially as men with a job that they themselves often mistrusted; for I really believe that many of them felt inadequate and frustrated. They knew as often as not that the man or woman behind the desk was more aware of the needs of his or her pupils than they; and they knew also that every experienced and reasonable teacher must, in the end, do the job by the method most suited to his or her personality. No teacher can be adequate under surveillance, especially when he knows that his work is to be recorded in a dossier.

We talk about time moving in full circle—whatever this may mean; and it certainly seemed like circling time when two friends of the "Valley" days, with their ladies, graced our platform. One of these was Sir Ian Fraser, the eminent surgeon, and the other was Air Marshal Sir James Kilpatrick, former Director General of the R.A.F. Medical Services. Sir Ian Fraser's ebullient personality was sufficient to make a successful event, especially when this was coupled with originality of outlook. Though he advised our pupils not to be too hasty about making up their minds about careers, he himself was the antithesis of this advice, for he had geared himself to his future profession from earliest days; at least if I can judge from my earlier talks and walks with him along the Newtownards Road.

The same could not have been said of Sir James. Though he may have intended studying medicine, it was not, I think, his intention to go into the R.A.F. any more than it was mine to become the head of a school, but whatever he did would have been tackled with his characteristic courage, vigour, and ability. This, as I remember it, was the substance of his speech; he advised our boys and girls to compel themselves to bite into a problem no matter how difficult it might be. I said these two, Sir James and Lady Kilpatrick, were friends of the Valley days; I might even have gone as far as to say that Lady Kilpatrick and I had been friends since our pram days.

Though I couldn't claim Professor E. T. S. Walton as an old friend, he hadn't been with us very long before he and his wife seemed to be old friends. But if not an old friend, he was the next-best thing—an old boy of the school; and it is not every school that can claim a Nobel Prizewinner as an old boy. Like most scientists who have gazed into the secrets of the universe, he betrayed an obvious humility in the face of what he had seen. This humility, and yet firmness of purpose, in elucidating the problems of the universe, he managed to convey to all of us when he was our guest speaker in our early days at Edenderry.

We came to our twenty-sixth speech day, in our twenty-fifth year, and on that day the President of the Irish Rugby Football

Union, Ireland's erstwhile wizard full-back, "Ernie" Crawford, opened our new playing fields. The prizes were distributed by Lt.-General Sir Brian Kimmins. At Ballievey the conversation was rich. Sir Clarence Graham, our Chairman at the time, in recounting his many experiences as a young civil engineer, betrayed a love for the whole of Ireland; an unsuspected emotion in one so prominently identified with Unionism. Rugby football, naturally, dominated the conversation, and I remember Sir Brian Kimmins being a little shocked when Ernie Crawford ironically remarked that it was all right to be dirty provided the referee didn't see you. A somewhat ungentle reminder that, no matter what we may teach in school, senior games have in them tougher elements. Was it this year or the year before that after a demonstration rugby match in which a number of the stars of the time played, the staff insisted on a mysterious meeting in the staff room ? It had been called for the purpose of presenting us with two beautiful candlesticks as a memento of our twenty-fifth year. This was no formality; it was both unnecessary and unexpected. It was the last generous gesture and speech of our much-loved young senior master, for he was soon to go from our midst for ever. I had known him since the Leeds days. When, less than a year later and within a couple of hours after my last conversation with him, he collapsed and died, the blow seemed intolerable for all of us.

Twenty-sixth, twenty-seventh, twenty-eights, twenty-ninth ! I would go on no longer. We had climbed to the top of the hill, but instead of pleasant valleys there were more hills; more and more plans of campaign, and more organizing and reorganizing. There had been no sabbatical year—no time to get my breath. I wanted time to think, and leisure to write about what I thought. I needed a change, and the school needed a change. I would retire.

And so for the last time as Headmaster and his wife, we stood on the platform to receive many presentations and eulogies. But what I appreciated more than anything was the surprise meeting with one of my distinguished old boys, Professor W. Mulligan. With great secrecy he had been almost smuggled across from Scotland to make the presentations, not only to

PRIME GRANDCHILD AT A FINAL SPORTS DAY

PRIME MINISTER AT A FINAL SPEECH DAY

us but also to our Secretary, who was retiring after spending a lifetime in the school.

In his fluent, easy speech Mulligan said, in effect, that I had taken them to the top of the hill and shown them what lay beyond. If I had done this for some, then surely my life had not been in vain.

EPILOGUE

THE cutting of the ties that bind one may seem attractive until the cut has been made, then all too often there are so many loose ends that one may feel completely at a loss. Of course I was to miss the school. How could it have been otherwise? The silver chords that tie one to the years are not so easily broken, and in fact never can be broken. Fortunately for us, however, there were compensations.

One day before retirement we had looked across at the blue Ring of Mourne and we thought: " Let's go over the hills to see what lies beyond." And there we found it, a centuries-old Irish cottage, nestling under the pine-laced heights of Slieve Martin and Slieve Dermot. At this stage we might have gone to live anywhere—anywhere in the habitable world—but there are forces that compel one to make certain decisions at certain times. What are these forces? Do they work from outside or from inside ourselves? The question must remain unanswered. But we knew from the moment we saw Canning Cottage in the Kilbroney Valley that no other decision was possible. We must live there; and there we have lived among the hydrangeas and roses ever since.

And what of Ballievey and the farm? Fortunately we had a son-in-law, a daughter, and her family, all happy to return to the old home by the banks of the Bann Water. We tried to keep the farm going for a year after retirement, but it was a disastrous year: one of the coldest winters on record when, for the first time, we had serious losses of stock. At this time our herd was, of course, T.T. and brucellosis free; and though every animal was carefully examined, except for some unknow factor in the silage, there seemed to be no obvious cause for our losses. It remains one of those unsolved problems. Anyhow, at the end of the year we had to make another vital decision: should we continue to farm or give up? We decided to give up, but it was a sad day when we saw our beautiful glossy, black and white animals lumbering up the hill on their way to a new home.

So ended the schoolmastering, singing, and farming years; and so began the writing, lecturing, broadcasting, gardening, walking and travelling years. When people look at me and say: " What do you do with your time now that you are retired ? " I look at them speechless and aghast. As though I had any time to do things with ! As though I had time to do other than what I am doing ! As though I would want to do other than what I am doing ! And if I had time to do no other than look at these immemorial Mourne hills, I would still be happy.

And we have looked at many other hills: the Sierra in Spain; the Portuguese Sera, the Moroccan Mountains, flaming Etna of Sicily, the ephemeral-iris-clad hills of Malta, the eternal snow-clad Alpine peaks, and a host of others. And yet wherever we go we feel drawn back and back to the mist-filled hills of Mourne.

It has been a long haul over the hills from Cherry Valley to Kilbroney Valley, but it has been worth it !

ROSTREVOR–CASCAIS–ROSTREVOR
    May–November, 1970

24.